THE
PARABLES
TO THE
LIVING
AND THE
DEAD

As provided by Jesus Christ using George Sloan

THE WAY TO FORGIVENESS, PEACE, AND LOVE

GEORGE SLOAN

THE PARABLES TO THE LIVING AND THE DEAD
THE WAY TO FORGIVENESS, PEACE, AND LOVE

iUniverse books may be ordered through booksellers or by contacting:

iUniverse
1663 Liberty Drive
Bloomington, IN 47403
www.iuniverse.com
1-800-Authors (1-800-288-4677)

ISBN: 978-1-5320-7857-6 (sc)
ISBN: 978-1-5320-7859-0 (hc)
ISBN: 978-1-5320-7858-3 (e)

Library of Congress Control Number: 2019910528

Print information available on the last page.

iUniverse rev. date: 08/13/2019

INTRODUCTION

Through the Holy Spirit, God has established the holiest of all from the foundation of the world after God finished all His works and rested. In the Bible, the same message is repeated in different ways to communicate the *"only one interpretation"* provided by the indwelled Holy Spirit of God. However, you will take from this exercise exactly what God wants you to know or be denied, just as in any Bible or in any reading; however, when the Lord God chooses to shanghai you to life eternal in Jesus, it is not your choice.

Your eternal salvation is not your choice. You have been predestined before God rested to be eternally with Jesus in heaven or with Satan in the lake of fire. God has determined all since before the foundation of the world when you were mere tiny specks of God's Spirit, or in a wry sense the same spiritual DNA of God, but those who gave the Holy Spirit of God the big middle finger were written "predestined" and written in the big books of the dead that fill the barns of the world. Those God loved were with life eternal and "rested."

❧ GENESIS 2:1-7 ❧

The creation of the host of the heavens and the earth were finished on the seventh day. The Lord God rested and sanctified His creation of the heavens (the priests) and the earth (the tribes) before any plant or herb in the earth had grown nor rain or man to till the ground; then God sent rain to water the whole earth. Then the LORD God formed out of one spirit Adam from the dust and breathed life into Adam.

The Lord God is stuck with you whether you are the elect who will live eternally with Jesus or the elect who will live with Satan in the lake of fire forever.

❧ HEBREWS 4:1–6 ❧

The promise of His rest remains in case any of you fear you have come up short. The gospel has been preached to all; those who could not hear were not called by God because of their unbelief, and without hearing it, they could not profit from it.

We who have been predestined to do so will enter the rest God spoke of concerning the seventh day. Those as spirit of God at the creation of those spirits who gave God the big middle finger, GGTBMF, at the foundations of the world will not enter His rest. (GGTBMF is used in the place of the words *sin*, *sins*, or *sinning*.) In the last forty-five days of Daniel 12:11–13, the elect of God entered His rest while those who GGTBMF did not. God has noted you as dead from the foundations of the world as predestined in the Book of the Dead.

❧ DANIEL 12:7–13 ❧

Daniel heard Jesus above the river; Jesus swore by God, who said it was for a time, times, and half a time, but God changed that to the last four years of the apocalypse to end the seventh day of creation, August 2, 70, with the destruction of Jerusalem and the desolate temple—parable code.

The powers of the holy people had been destroyed by the four Roman legions of General Titus. Daniel did not understand and asked, "My Lord, what shall be the end of these things?" Jesus said, "Go your way, Daniel, for the words are sealed until August 63 (see Revelation 7:1–4) till the time of the end (August 2, 70) with the destruction of the temple in Jerusalem." The elect were made white, purified, and sinless. The wicked Jews marked with death could not understand, but the elect with wisdom understood. (See Josephus, *The New Complete Works of Josephus—The Jewish War*, book 2, chapter 17, section 2, lines 409–10.)

On September 2, 66, Jesus, in the name of the temple governor, Eleazar, brought an end to the daily temple sacrifice and offerings to their Roman god Caesar. Thirty days later, October 2, 66, the abomination of the desolation arrived at the walls of Jerusalem, the Roman Twelfth Legion, with the images of the Roman god Caesar on the standing battle flags.

⊱ HEBREWS 4:7–8 ⊰

God said, "Today, if you hear His voice, do not harden your hearts" (Psalm 95:7–8). If Joshua had given them rest, He would not have spoken of another day for the rest of His people. God entered His rest at the foundation of the world before there was a Garden of Eden.

⊱ HEBREWS 4:11–16 ⊰

Be diligent to enter that rest, for God alone keeps the elect from disobedience. The Word of God alone is the guarantee of the elect; it is sharper than any two-edged sword and is the only power of our life eternal in Jesus. All creatures must be judged by their works. We have in Jesus a great High Priest who keeps the elect eternally. Jesus, our High Priest, sympathizes with our weaknesses; He was tempted but did not sin. The elect should come boldly before the throne of grace to obtain mercy and grace.

Those who GGTBMF fail to live in forgiveness, peace, and love with their family members, neighbors, and all who persecute them are the problem and GGTBMF.

⊱ MATTHEW 27:51–53 ⊰

When Jesus died on April 23, 34, the veil of the temple was torn from top to bottom exposing the holiest of all, the earth quaked, and rocks split.

Three days later, Jesus was resurrected and the dead in Christ at their demise were raised and went into the Holy City and appeared to many.

When Jesus died, the temple and its priests, services, ordinances, doctrines, Commandments, and tithes were nullified. On August 2, AD 70, the temple's destruction was the sign of Jesus's passing into the elect flesh-and-blood images of Jesus Christ. The holiest of all, the 144,000 elect gathered by God, were the bride of Christ married to the Lamb of God.

❧ HEBREWS 9:1–7 ☙

The Law of Moses required temple services, tithes, ordinances, Commandments, and traditions in Jerusalem's temple, heaven on earth. The tabernacle sanctuary with the lampstand, table, and showbread behind the veil was the holiest of all; it held a golden censer, the ark of the covenant overlaid with gold, a golden pot of manna, the budded rod of Aaron, and the tablets of the covenant. Above all were the cherubim of glory over the mercy seat. The priests always went into the first part of the tabernacle to perform services; only once a year could the high priest alone with blood enter the second part behind the veil, the holiest of all, where he offered for himself and the people's sins in ignorance.

God alone was the reason for the salvation of the elect of God.

❧ DANIEL 9:24 ☙

God ended the inequities of His elect and reconciled them to Himself. God called from out of the Jews marked 666 with death in the religions of Judaism to life eternal in Jesus. He brought to the elect of God the gift of everlasting righteousness.

God endowed visions, tongues, and foreign languages on the apostles to facilitate the gospel being preached around the world. By revelation from God to Paul in August 63, Paul declared the gospel preached around the world. The prophecies and the miracles by men facilitated the preaching of the gospel around the world to every last scattered Jew.

God's determined plan was to anoint behind the veil the sign of Jesus in the elect flesh-and-blood images of Jesus Christ.

⊱ Hebrews 9:8–10 ⊰

The Holy Spirit made very clear that the 144,000 elect gathered by God at Pella for the marriage with the Lamb of God could not take place while the first tabernacle in the desolate temple in Jerusalem was still standing; it was destroyed August 2, 70. God alone at that time provided the delusions to the dead men of the religions of Jerusalem then as in the new covenant age to the dead religions since the Greek Orthodox BS narrative and the thousands of copycat popes, priests, and pastors of the extortionist brick-and-mortar churchy services were after the usual wealth, power, and fame (WPF). The dead are never given regard to the Holy Spirit on their consciences. Only the elect called by God to Jesus through the Holy Spirit were given the knowledge of God; salvation is in God's love. Wafers of bread and grape juice at churchy services are the fleshly ordinances of men who lust after the wages of the dead.

⊱ Hebrews 7:14–22 ⊰

Our Lord arose from Judah; the tribes of which Moses never spoke of. It is in the likeness of Melchizedek that Jesus came, not of the fleshly Commandments of the Law of Moses but only to the power of an eternal life. God testified, "You, Jesus, are a priest forever of Melchizedek" (Psalm 100:4).

The Law of Moses was annulled because it made no one perfect, but with Jesus's death came the reformation not of temples and priests, who could not bring salvation, but of the elect called to Jesus by God. The Levitical priests supported by tithes were without oaths, but Jesus was with an oath by God, who said, "You, Jesus, are a priest forever of the order of Melchizedek" (Psalm 110:4). Jesus has been our guarantee of eternal life since September 15, 70.

⊱ Hebrews 9:11–12 ⊰

The coming of the High Priest, Jesus Christ, was the promise of the good things to come with the greater and more perfect kingdom of heaven on earth, which was not made by human hands and certainly was not of this creation. From the foundation of the world, all spirits were the spiritual DNA of God's as determined by God. Those who rejected God at the foundation of the world were predestined to the lake of fire, and those whom God loved were predestined to eternal life in Jesus, not by the blood of bulls and goats but by the blood of Jesus crucified and resurrected; they entered the most holy place (Daniel 7:13–14) in heaven with God.

❧ DANIEL 7:13–14 ❦

On April 25, 34, Jesus was resurrected. Daniel saw Jesus ascending on the clouds and the angels bringing him to God. Jesus was given dominion, glory, and a kingdom that all people would serve his everlasting dominion.

❧ ROMANS 2:11–16 ❦

There is no partiality with God. Those who have sinned without the law will perish without the law, and those who have sinned in the law are judged by the law. The hearers of the law are not justified in the sight of God, but God causes the elect to be the doers of the law who are justified only as are the elect called from out of the Gentiles. The pagans, Christians, Muslims, Protestants, Jews, Buddhists, Roman Catholics, and the Orthodox Greeks or Russians do not have the law, but by their nature, at the indwelling of the Holy Spirit, who accuses or excuses through the conscience is the law written in their hearts, they become fools for Christ with the mind of Jesus. They are doomed to life eternal in Jesus Christ.

❧ HEBREWS 9:13–28 ❦

The blood of bulls and goats and the sprinkling of the ashes of the slain heifer purify and sanctify unclean flesh, but how much more will the blood of Christ cleanse your elect conscience from the dead works to serve the living God? Jesus is the mediator of the new covenant by His death on the cross. God reconciled the predestined elect to receive the promised eternal inheritance. A testament becomes law only after the testator's death. Not even the first covenant was dedicated without blood.

Moses spoke every rule to the people according to the Law, and he took the blood of bulls and goats, water, scarlet wool, and hyssop and sprinkled the book of laws and all the people saying, "This is the blood of the covenant which God has commanded you" (Exodus 24:8). He sprinkled with blood the tabernacle and all the vessels of the ministry of the Law of Moses to purify them. Without the shedding of blood, there is no remission of sin. It was necessary to purify the things in the temple with blood, but the heavenly things were purified with Jesus's blood.

Christ had not entered sham holy places, mere copies of the third heaven, but at the destruction of the desolate temple in Jerusalem came the passing of Jesus into the flesh-and-blood images of Jesus Christ in the temple of God. Jesus put away sin to end the old covenant age; men would die once and not wait in Hades in this new covenant age. At one's demise comes judgment to life eternal with Jesus or to the lake of fire forever. Christ was offered once to bear the sins of the elect. He will appear a second time to save those who wait for Him.

✣ DEUTERONOMY 8:3 ✣

God caused Israel to hunger and to be fed with manna to let them know that man did not live by bread alone but by the Word that proceeds from the mouth of the Lord.

God was not talking about the world but about the elects' hearts, minds, spirits, and souls, the spiritual images of God in a wry sense. Don't argue with churchy men; it will only embarrass them being deluded by God.

The parables were the way Jesus communicated with the multitudes because being God, He knew those predestined to live eternally in Jesus alone would understand them; the others would remain unbelievers until their final judgment.

✣ LIFE IS ETERNAL ✣

All God's spirits were created to receive life eternal, but most GGTBMF. In a sense, God instructed the angel computer to compile two printouts—those who GGTBMF were written in the Book of the Dead that filled the big barns of the world and were predestined to the lake of fire. All the spirits in the old covenant age at their earthly demise waited in Hades. All human life is spiritually eternal; it is either with Jesus or in the lake of fire.

Following His crucifixion, Jesus preached the gospel to those in Hades and prisons where God called the elect to Jesus and life eternal; the predestined dead were thrown into the lake of fire with Satan.

In this new covenant age, the names written in the Book of Life were those God had predestined to eternal life in Jesus Christ. Upon their earthly demise, unbelievers will spend eternity with Satan. All are born dead in Adam's free will and remain dead until the elect are called by God who through parables provides the knowledge of God and thus salvation with life eternal in Jesus.

CHAPTER 1

THE PARABLE CODE IS SPOKEN
IN DEPTH IN MATTHEW 13

The parable code is provided by God to enlighten the elect to salvation and to leave the dead deluded to proceed to their earthly demise in the lake of fire forever.

❧ MATTHEW 13:10 ❧

The disciples asked, "Why do You, Jesus, speak to the multitude in parables?"

❧ MATTHEW 13:11–12 ❧

Jesus said, "Because the mysteries of the kingdom of heaven on earth are for only you disciples and the elect Jews, God's chosen people. Those who GGTBMF in their unbelief cannot know them."

They spitefully crucified their Rock and their Savior, Jesus. They were denied the gospel truth and cut off from Jesus by God forever (see Daniel 9:26). The elect of God were indwelled with the Holy Spirit, who provided through the parables the knowledge of God. Only the elect Jews, the assembly of God (Romans 2:29) were the elect remnant, the 144,000 Jews praised by God. Those of the religion of Judaism were marked with death because of their unbelief and their godless traditions. What the dead have as riches in their unbelief will be taken from them by God.

On earth, there are only the living and the dead from the foundation of the world; all are born dead in Adam and wander on earth dead until the predestined foreordained elect are called and reconciled by God to life eternal in Jesus.

God provided the parables as code to enlighten the elect to salvation and to delude the dead to proceed to their earthly demise in the lake of fire, which is forever.

Do not GGTBMF.

Consider acquiring *The New Complete Works of Josephus—The Jewish War* by William Whiston. And keep a Young's Literal Translation (YLT) Bible for correct use of the words *churches* and *earth*, which are misused hundreds of times in popular Bibles to enhance the God-given, delusional, four-Pinocchio narrative that Jesus is coming back in your future.

Note: this source corrects the dates found in Josephus's works spoken above. It provides the corrected by *Origines Kalendariæ Hellenicæ* or the *History of the Primitive Calendar among the Greeks* before and after the legislation of Solon by Edward Greswell; this clarifies and corrects dates not just of Josephus's *The Jewish War*. These books are for personal knowledge; they are not required for eternal salvation, which is the work of God, but if you have the books, you can check my veracity.

Carry your God-assigned cross—spouse, child, or annoying neighbor—and do not give your annoying neighbor the big middle finger, which is the same as GGTBMF. Carry your God-assigned crosses with forgiveness, peace, and love without sniveling or whining just as Jesus did.

The biblical meaning of the word *folly* is eternal death, while the biblical meaning of the word *wisdom* is life eternal. The elect of God are predestined to life eternal while the foolish are promised the lake of fire.

Do not ever argue your faith in God; few of any religions ever agree, but understand that there are no religions of God; they will hate you and persecute you in the name of their gods' religion. Having been called by God to Jesus means that you commune only with Jesus Christ and fellowship with your spiritual brethren, the elect, flesh-and-blood images of Jesus Christ. There are no religions of God, but no congregation should be judged as dead; judging others is always GGTBMF. Remember that we are not always called to Jesus when we are young and brilliant.

❧ JOHN 6:45 ❧

Scripture tells us that the people of God are taught by God (Isaiah 54:13). Only those who have heard and learned from the Father can come to Jesus.

Free will is a lie, a God-given delusion. God left the world predestined; Jesus Christ is still the stumbling stone as in the latter days. Believers are called to Jesus and separated from the predestined dead.

In *Erasmus and Luther; Discourse of Free Will* by Ernst Winter, Erasmus was the gutless surrogate of the pope, who paid Erasmus to be a lazy, lying snoozer to reject predestination. Martin Luther's *The Bondage of the Will* is very well written and easy to understand unless you are dead. Keep in mind, even in the time of Martin Luther and John Calvin, predestination began to wither and is basically dead in Christianity with very few exceptions.

❧ EPHESIANS 1:1–6 ❧

Paul, an apostle and unpaid servant of Jesus Christ in Ephesus by the will of God preached the gospel to the elect Jews, God's chosen people, by God to be faithful in Christ Jesus: "Grace to you elect Jews, and peace from our God the Father and the Lord Jesus Christ. Blessed be the God and Father of our Lord Jesus Christ who has caused us elect Jews to hear, believe, and have every spiritual blessing in heaven on earth in Jesus Christ. God had chosen us elect in Jesus before the foundation of the world that we elect be holy and without blame in Jesus in love; the chosen elect of God in this last time."

The last forty years of the latter days began in August 30 and were spoken of by Moses in Deuteronomy 31:29. God predestined us elect to adoption in August 63 in Jesus Christ according to the purpose of God's will to the praise of the glory of God's grace wherein God causes the elect to be accepted in the beloved Jesus Christ.

The dead of most religions tout free will. The elect are so few in any congregation that they could not keep the church candles lit. At the hand of God, the dead men and gods cannot know what God does not give them to know. Being denied the knowledge of God, they are stupid eternally.

Most of the religions are taught by the dead to believe in free will.

The only word on the topic is a freewill offering in the Bible spoken of in the time of Leviticus regarding any who chose to give beyond the required tithe when tithing was a requirement of the law, but tithes supported only the Levitical priesthood. Since Jesus's death, the temple, temple services, the priestly system, and tithes are passé.

⊱ 2 CORINTHIANS 3:17–18 ⊰

With the Holy Spirit comes liberty. The elect without the veil are as before a mirror, and they see the glory of the Lord transforming them into the flesh-and-blood glory of Jesus Christ.

There is a great difference between God's Word, Jesus Christ, and the self-serving interpretations, ordinances, traditions, and Commandments of religion aimed at acquiring WPF.

⊱ EPHESIANS 1:7 ⊰

In Jesus, we elect were adopted, redeemed (see Revelation 5:9–10), and sealed (see Revelation 7:1–4) through the blood of Jesus Christ, who was crucified for the forgiveness of sins and the riches of God's grace.

⊱ EPHESIANS 2:7–10 ⊰

In this new covenant age (since September 15, 70), God shows His exceeding riches, grace, and kindness in Christ Jesus. The elect have been saved through God's grace. His blessing, His righteousness, is our faith, the gift of grace, the essential knowledge of God expressed as the elects' faith, not of our works lest anyone boast.

We elect are God's workmanship. We are God's chosen elect who are to walk in the works of God that Jesus Christ does through us.

In the same way, Jesus, in the name of George Sloan and through the fool's mind, spirit, soul, and heart is merely God's workmanship, God's chosen elect from the foundation of the world to walk, talk, and write this parable code that Jesus has done through this fool, George.

⊱ ROMANS 2:25–26 ⊰

Circumcision is indeed profitable if you keep the law; but if you are a breaker of the law, your circumcision has become uncircumcision. Therefore, if an uncircumcised man keeps the righteous requirements of the law, will not his uncircumcision be counted as circumcision?

⊱ ROMANS 8:28–30 ⊰

We disciples know that all things work together for the good of the elect called by God's will and purpose. God foreknew those He loved; they were the elect from the foundation of the world. He predestined the elect to be flesh-and-blood images of Jesus Christ, temples of God. The kingdom of heaven is spiritual, not physical, and Jesus was the firstfruit born among the elect, the ecclesia, the assembly of God, not a brick-and-mortar church. The elect of God are the foreordained of God, and those called by God were justified and thus glorified.

The parable code in the preface to this book is the images of Jesus on my face, which is highlighted here in the parable code as the understanding of the living, but the God-given delusions continue in those predestined to the lake of fire.

God provides the delusions on those who prey on their congregations for tithes-based income. Extortionists deceive Mom and Pop out of their wealth in return for promises of places in heaven. Pastors tell you lies because of their unbelief. Dear friends, buck up. God is always the cause of the message; God even delivers the correct delusions to the most brilliant God deniers. How can religions, none of which are of God, tell you what they cannot know? Men do not have the power to choose between God and the god of Gain. The living elect have but one Communion—with Jesus Christ—since God calls the dead and indwells the Holy Spirit who then through the parable code provides the knowledge of God, salvation. When called, the elect become fools of Christ with the mind of Jesus and are doomed to life eternal.

God easily denies the dead just as He created the hideous high priest Caiaphas, who duped the Romans into crucifying Jesus. God provides the dead pedophiles, popes, priests, pastors, booze, drugs, thugs, diseases, and demons all of who do God's work.

❧ LUKE 9:61–62 ☙

A man said, "Lord, I will follow You, but first let go say my goodbyes at my house." Jesus replied, "No Man having begun to plow then looks back (to extort a congregation for a tithe based income). He is not fit for the kingdom of God."

❧ MATTHEW 8:21–22 ☙

Another asked, "Lord, let me first go and bury my father." Jesus replied, "Follow Me; let the dead bury their own dead."

The sweet atheist Christopher Hitchens laughed in the introduction of his best seller *God Is Not Great*. He recalled the time when a Bible teacher spoke of Matthew 8:22: "Let the dead bury their own dead." Woe to the smartest man on earth overcome by Miss Folly and Mister Stupidity. Please forgive Hitchens; he could not know what he was not given by God to know. He was veiled and denied and could not know. No doubt he is still trying to convince Satan that God does not exist.

Before the promised latter days in the time of Christ and the following thirty-three years were up, the Jews were marked with death from the time of the Babylonian exile. Israel was dead because of its people's unbelief having broken the covenant with God during the forty years of Jeremiah. Those God loved from the foundation of the world were predestined to be called from out of the religions of Judaism marked with death in that last time, the latter days, to life eternal, and even those God called to Jesus from out of Hades.

Forgive the dead; they cannot know why they think or what they think they know. Harlan Ellison said, "The two most common elements in the universe are hydrogen and stupidity."

Being stupid without the Word is a certainty. The ways of stupidity are innumerable, but God is creative. Stupidity in oneself is not even knowable. However, the brilliant stupid often detect stupidity in others' brilliance. The dead are always deluded even in the smartest atheist religions, but still, the most brilliant atheists agree with God in some matters.

❧ ISAIAH 66:4 ❧

The Lord God has chosen the dead delusions, and the dead cannot fear a God they cannot know. When I called, the dead could not answer, and when I spoke, the dead could not hear. However, the dead did evil before my eyes choosing (crucified Jesus) that I do not delight.

The two most brilliant philosophers agree with God even when they are denied knowledge of Him.

The greatest enemy of knowledge is not ignorance; it is the illusion of knowledge. Stephen Hawking agrees with God.

A delusion is something that people believe in despite a total lack of evidence. Richard Dawkins agrees with God.

How will I know I have no choice? —Will Durant, *Story of Philosophy by Spinoza*

Spinoza compared the feeling of "free will" to a stone's thinking as the stone travels through space and the stone determines its own trajectory and the stone selects the place and time of the stones fall (Will Durant, *Story of Philosophy by Spinoza*).

When will I know I have no choice? This quote will immediately blossom in the minds of some. A few … well, very few. When we have the mind of Jesus, which only God gives us, only then can we know through the Holy Spirit, who causes our life on earth a living hell until the elect of God come to know God and fear God, which comes with eternal life.

Spinoza said, "Men think themselves free because they are conscious of their volitions and desires, but they are ignorant of the causes by which they are led to wish and desire" (Will Durant, *Story of Philosophy by Spinoza*).

The Lord God used the atheist Isaac Asimov to shanghai this fool (me) with the mind of Christ. Relax—the destination of our eternal life is not our job or work. Do not worry; think God and thank God.

❧ 1 THESSALONIANS 4:9–12 ❧

You Thessalonians have no reason for I Paul to write you, for you elect are taught by God to love each other; and you elect do so toward the brethren and we encourage you elect to increase in your fellowship; to aspire to lead a quiet life, mind your own business and work with your own hands as we disciples command you elect to walk safely among the dead in the world lacking nothing.

The latter days began with the anointing of Jesus by God in August 30 at the baptism by John and to come with the promised destruction of the temple in Jerusalem on August 2, 70.

At the foundation of the world, God gave of himself as the tiniest spirit. Most of those spirits rejected God, but those who clung to Him were predestined to become His chosen people.

There are two kinds of people on earth—the living and the dead. The living were once born dead in Adam, but God called them to have eternal life in Jesus. The dead rejected God at the foundation of the world by GGTBMF. When God calls even an atheist, he is given the mind of Jesus and is doomed to eternal life in Jesus.

It's always God's will, not ours.

✷ EPHESIANS 4:1–7 ✷

Paul, a prisoner of the Lord Jesus, begs you to walk in your calling with all humility, meekness, gentleness, and forgiveness with your neighbor in God, who keeps you in forgiveness, peace, and love in the elect assembly of God. He gives you His everlasting grace in the same measure given to Jesus Christ at His anointing in August 30.

No one is innocent even when God overlooks the elects' daily failures. Perfection is a self-serving delusion. Only God causes perfection through the elect.

Avoid judging, and do not be a foolish, self-serving busybody or gossip. Don't respond to temptation; doing so is always GGTBMF.

✷ 1 CORINTHIANS 6:1–6 ✷

Why do you, when you're angry, file a lawsuit with unrighteous judges instead of going before the assembly of God of your own fellowship? Will you judge the elect of the world? Will the world be judged by you? You are not worthy to judge even the smallest matters. We elect judge angels and things pertaining to life. If you have judgments about the things in this life, go to the elect ecclesia. Is there not a wise man among you, not even one? Who will be able to judge the elect? A brother who goes to the law of the worldly gods, lawyers, and judges against a brother in the court of unbelievers is dead.

✥ 1 Corinthians 6:7–8 ✥

It is an utter failure for you to go to law—gods, lawyers, and judges against one another. Why do you not let your God cheat you by slapping your face? You do wrong against your brethren, which is against me, your God!

✥ 1 Corinthians 6:9–11 ✥

Fornicators, adulterers, idolaters, homosexuals, sodomites, and temple or church deceivers who extort money can never inherit the kingdom of God. We were all dead, but God called the elect to be indwelt with the Holy Spirit and be sanctified.

✥ Matthew 5:39 ✥

Jesus said do not resist an evil person. Whoever slaps you on your right cheek, turn it so that God can slap you again. God causes the man of God to know He's the one who slaps his face. God causes those to take you to court. God tests you and punishes you because you displease Him. You shall love your neighbor as a service to God. Doing the work of God means loving your annoying neighbor; do not forget that no one of God is perfect or without sin; even the elect fail God daily. Do not resist an evil person; they are sent by God.

Do what is good to those God sends to hate you because you are deserving. Pray for those God causes to spitefully misuse you. You must deserve that or God would not have allowed that. If you love only those who love you, what is your reward?

✥ Matthew 5:43–48 ✥

Leviticus 9:18 tells you to love your neighbor and hate your enemy, but Jesus said, love your enemy. God wants you to bless those who curse you. Do good to those who hate you. Pray for those who persecute you as was Jesus and all honest men such as presidents Lincoln, Reagan, and Trump, who bore their crosses without sniveling and whining. The elect are the sons of the Father in heaven.

God makes the rain fall on the just and the unjust alike. If you love only those who love you, what reward have you from God? Do not even the tax collectors conduct their business in a loving way in the pursuit of their tax extortion? You must be perfect just as your Father in heaven is perfect.

God deludes the dead; they cannot know Him, and being dead, they cannot know they are dead. Until called by God to Jesus, all remain dead. Relax, puppy. It's not your call.

❧ LUKE 23:34 ☙

Jesus said, "Father, forgive them, for they do not know what they do."

True democracies protect their citizens with laws that reflect the will of the people. Secular laws prosecute pedophiles, but many leaders of organizations, governments, and religions protect their precious pedophiles and advance their range and opportunities to engage their attacks on children but always for WPF.

❧ MATTHEW 18:6 ☙

Jesus added, "Whoever (pedophile) causes one of these little ones who believe in Me to sin, it would be better for him (the pedophile) if a millstone were hung around his neck and he was drowned in the sea."

Pedophiles and their supporters alike will share the lake of fire. All brothers and sisters are images of Jesus Christ; whatever anyone does to advance a pedophile is in danger of damnation. Whatever a pedophile does to a child, he is also doing that to Jesus. The men of religion who approve the acts of pedophiles are naming Jesus a pedophile.

❧ DEUTERONOMY 32:39 ☙

Now see that God, even God, is God and that there is no God besides God. I kill. I make alive. I make wise. I make stupid. I wound. I heal. Are there any gods or men who can deliver from God?

❧ LUKE 18:11 ❧

The hypocrite Pharisee stood and prayed by himself, saying, "God, I thank You that I am not like other men—an extortionist, unjust, adulterer—as is that tax collector over there."

❧ 1 CORINTHIANS 5:10–11 ❧

Paul said we were not to fellowship with sexually immoral people, the covetous, the idolaters, the drunkards, or the extortionists. Do not even eat with the dead, who extort tithes from their congregations.

❧ ROMANS 16:17–19 ❧

Those who cause divisions, sects, and religions are offenses to the doctrine you learned. Avoid those who through divisions, religions, sects, and schisms pursue tithes; they do not serve our Lord; they serve their own lusts. Their smooth words are those of the dead. Your obedience to God has become known to all. I am glad on your behalf, but I want you elect to be wise to the evil of those religions.

Who are we to hate, persecute, and kill as did the good Christians of the Reformation error when Martin Luther nailed the ninety-five theses up? For the next hundred years, they persecuted and murdered their perceived heretical good Christian brothers known as Anabaptists until 1618, when began the Thirty Years' War that killed 13 million Germans, half the country's population, and that does not include the good Christians and Roman Catholics of France and the Netherlands.

God used Cardinal Richelieu, who was supported by Pope Urban VIII with trunks of gold, to defeat the Hapsburgs and their domination over Europe and popes of Rome. God installed Cardinal Richelieu, who also hired King Gustavus of Sweden with a million dollars, to attack the Hapsburgs until the Treaty of Westphalia (1848) subjected the religions to the state.

1 Corinthians 6:12

Paul said, "Things are lawful for me, but all things are not helpful. All things are lawful for me, but I Paul will not be brought under the power of any lawful thing."

1 Corinthians 6:15–17

Do I, a member of Christ's body, have sex with someone? Heavens no! Those who do so put Christ's body in the harlot. God long ago said that they shall become one flesh (Genesis 2:24). God's elect are joined to the Lord God as one spirit in the body of Christ. Those who commit sexual immorality with another misuse their bodies, which are the image of Jesus Christ.

1 Corinthians 6:19–20

Your body is the image of Jesus; it is the temple of God as it is indwelled by the Holy Spirit. You, puppy, are not your own. You were purchased by Jesus's death; for that reason, glorify God in your body and in your spirit all of which belong to the Lord God.

Matthew 5:38

You have heard that it was said, "An eye for an eye and a tooth for a tooth" (see Deuteronomy 19:21).

Follow Jesus's example; He carried His cross to His death to make you sinless. Pray that God guides you elect to a lesser cross that you can carry without whining. Jesus was rejected, hated, harangued, persecuted, spat on, whipped, and crucified, but He remained silent knowing and doing God's will.

A cross may also be a cheerful daily work of providing for someone in need; those who do that are doing the will of God.

God does not impute sin to His elect; they have Jesus's mind and have no choice but to walk in God's way. The work they do is the work that Jesus does through them.

Atheists complain that religions are ignorant. Yes, religions have been an incredible embarrassment to God, but there are no religions of God. Those of the religions are dead because of their unbelief unless and until they are called by God to Jesus.

The brilliant dead are the pastors who preach free will but deny the knowledge of God; they have not been given to know. The dead are not allowed to know God; if they knew God existed, they might get silly and fear God.

God causes the elect to live with their consciences sensitized by the Holy Spirit, who excuses or accuses moment by moment to nudge and perfect the elect. They have no choice but to live in the will of God. The carnal dead are predestined to an earthly demise that confirms the lake of fire forever. The gods of religions have no choice but to preach error in the pursuit of tithes.

The ecclesia has always been the image of Jesus, not bricks and mortar.

ACTS 7:48

The most high God does not dwell in buildings made with hands.

ACTS 17:24

God is not worshipped with men's hands as if He needed anything; He gives through predestination all life, breath, and all things.

Useless baptisms are sold by greedy extortionists at the altar of demons, where a piece of bread is traded for 10 percent of a man's income, which goes to pay for the extortionists' new Mercedes-Benz. What you cannot know is not your choice to know. Knowing God is not your choice. Millions of Jews in the latter days were not allowed to know God. Is that surprising? What is the point of enlightening the dead unless God wants that?

MATTHEW 13:34–35

"I will open My mouth in parables; I will utter things kept secret from the foundation of the world" (see Psalm 78:2).

❦ MATTHEW 13:1–9 ❧

A great multitude gathered before Jesus, so that He got into a boat and sat preaching while the multitude listened from the shore. Speaking in the parable code, Jesus began,

A sower went sowing, some seed fell by the wayside and was quickly devoured by the birds. Some seed fell on the stony places, where the seed without much soil sprang up, but with the sun; it withered because it had little root. Some seed fell among thorns (the world of the dead), springing up among the thorns was choked by the works of the dead in the world. Some seed fell on good ground and yielding a great crop: a hundredfold, some sixty, some thirty. God only causes the good seed (the elect of God) to fall on the good ground!

❦ MATTHEW 13:13 ❧

Jesus spoke in parables to the multitude in their unbelief in bondage marked with death in Judaism; they were appointed only to eternal damnation. Those marked with death in Romans 1:28–32 remained veiled by God in their unbelief and debased minds. They could not hear being of the religions of men and cut off from Jesus by God.

❦ LUKE 17:20–21 ❧

Jesus was asked by the Pharisees when the kingdom of God would come. Jesus said, "The kingdom of God does not come with observation. The kingdom of God is in you."

❦ REVELATION 22:18–19 ❧

John declared to all to hear the words of the prophecy of this book. If anyone adds to it, he will be doomed to the plagues mentioned in Revelation.

❧ REVELATION 22:19 ❧

If anyone takes away the words *land* or *Israel* and replaces them with the word *earth* in this prophecy, God will take away his part of the Tree of Life in this book.

❧ MATTHEW 13:14–15 ❧

In those of unbelief in the religions of men, the prophecy of Isaiah 6:9–10 is fulfilled; God would not call those because of their unbelief. Hearing, you will hear but not understand, and seeing, you will see but not perceive; the hearts of this people have grown dull. Their minds are debased by the religions of men; those in the religion of Judaism marked with death are hard of hearing; they have closed their eyes and ears for fear that they will see and hear.

❧ ISAIAH 66:4 ❧

In Isaiah, six hundred years before Jesus's coming, we learn that the last forty years began when God anointed Jesus when He was baptized. God would choose their delusions—their religions marked with death in Judaism—with their coming death by Rome, because when He called them, they did not answer. When He spoke, those Jews marked with death could not hear; but they did evil before God's eyes and spitefully crucified their Rock and Savior.

Mark Twain's *The Innocents Abroad* is a travel book that describes the Holy Land that was the result of the seven years of the apocalypse to end the old covenant age in 70. There was also an earlier period of seventy years of the exile in Babylon, but the prophecy of Isaiah spoke of things to come, and the result was to end the seventh day of creation in August 70.

Twain may not have been called by God. His whole life was a struggle to believe. He might have been the image of the man on the right of Jesus at His crucifixion. A few will come to know if Mark Twain and King Solomon ever made it to heaven. Those who have hearts to perceive and eyes to see and ears to hear are the elect called by God to eternal life.

❧ MATTHEW 13:16–17 ❧

Blessed are you elect for you who see and your ears hear; Truly, I tell you that many prophets and the righteous desired to see what you elect see, but the dead cannot see and cannot hear and what you elect hear the dead cannot hear.

❧ MATTHEW 13:24–29 ❧

Jesus added to the Parable, saying, "The kingdom of heaven is like a man who sowed the good seed in his field; but, while men slept, the enemy Satan came and sowed the tares/weeds the dead among the wheat. When the grain sprouted producing a crop, the tares and weeds also appeared. The servant of the owner asked, 'Sir, did you not sow the good seed in your field? How then does it have weeds and tares?' The farmer (God) continued, 'an enemy; the world has done this.' The servant then asked, 'Do you want us then to go and gather the tares?' No … he replied, lest you gather up the tares/weeds you will uproot the elect wheat of God. Let both the elect wheat and weeds grow together until the harvest August 63. At that time of the harvest, I will say to the angel reapers, "First gather the elect wheat into my barn Revelation 14:1–4 then the angels will gather the tares/weeds Jews marked with death into bundles to burn."

❧ MATTHEW 13:31–32 ❧

Jesus added, "The kingdom of heaven is like a mustard seed which a man took and sowed in his field, the smallest of all seeds; but when grown it as a greater herbs; as a tree with branches with birds nest."

❧ MATTHEW 13:33–35 ❧

He added, "The kingdom of heaven as yeast, which a woman took and hid in three measures of wheat until it was leavened."

Jesus spoke these things to the multitude in parables, and without the parable code, Jesus did not speak to them so that it would be fulfilled spoken by the prophet, "I will open My mouth in parables; I will utter things kept secret from the foundation of the world" (Psalm 78:2).

Jesus sent the multitude away and He went into the house. There His disciples came to Him, asking, "Explain to us the Parable of the tares/weeds of the field." Jesus answered, "He who sows the good seed is the Son of Man. The field is the world, the good seed are the predestined elect sons of the kingdom, but the tares are the sons of the Satan from the time of the seventy years of the Babylonian exile because all had broken the covenant of God and Satan their god converted them to the religions Judaism marked with death."

⊱ MATTHEW 13:39–43 ⊰

The enemy who sowed the tares or weeds was Satan doing God's work. The harvest is to end the old covenant age. The Son of Man sent His angels to bundle those marked with death in the religions of Judaism (see Daniel 9:26). Those God cut off from Jesus were the sons of lawlessness because of their unbelief; they would receive the curses promised in Deuteronomy 28:15–68.

Then as the sign of Jesus, the destruction of the temple occurred in 70. He who has ears to hear, let him hear.

The kingdom of heaven is the treasure hidden in a field, which a man found hidden and for joy he went and sold his part in the world that he had and with the proceeds bought the field "the kingdom of heaven is like a merchant seeking beautiful pearls, who, when he had found one pearl of great price, went and sold his of the world" to buy the pearl.

⊱ MATTHEW 13:47–48 ⊰

The kingdom of heaven was a net thrown into the sea, the world; it was filled and dragged ashore. In 63, the good were gathered and the worldly were thrown back into the sea.

Religions are delusions provided by God to the dead whose purpose in life is the pursuit of WPF.

The elect were born to be called by God alone; God causes them to hear, see, and understand. God gave them in abundance. The religious lived in their God-given delusions and defiled themselves with their man-made Commandments and traditions.

❧ MATTHEW 13:49–50 ☙

The end time came when the temple was destroyed in 70, which ended the old covenant age. The angels separated the wicked from the just and threw the dead into the lake of fire, where there was wailing and gnashing of teeth.

❧ MATTHEW 13:51–52 ☙

Jesus asked, "Have you understood all these things?" They replied said, "Yes, Lord." Jesus said, "Every scribe called to the kingdom of heaven brought out his treasures of Moses, which were the new covenant treasures of God."

❧ MATTHEW 13:53–58 ☙

It came to pass, when Jesus had finished these parables. Jesus went to His own country teaching in the synagogues; marveling they asked, "Where did this Man get this wisdom and these mighty works? Is this not the carpenter's son? Is not His mother called Mary and His brothers; James, Joseph, Simon and Judas and all of his sisters are with us? How does Jesus know these things?" Though they were offended, Jesus replied, "A prophet is not without honor, except in his own country and in his own house." Jesus did not do many great works in His home town of Nazareth because of their unbelief who knew Jesus from His childhood.

CHAPTER 2

Because Israel GGTBMF, it was made to wander in the wilderness for forty years. Do not reject the commands of God as did Israel in Numbers 13–14 when God sent the leaders of the tribes of Israel into the land of milk and honey. They returned with samples of the bounty of the land. They bragged about their adventures until they were told to prepare to go back and take the land by force. They had second thoughts and found it scary to go back to Canaan because the place had many giants who would eat them as if they were bugs, so they rejected God's command and rebelled; they were about to stone Joshua and Caleb.

God came on the scene in voice and condemned those of Israel over twenty years of age to their death over the next forty years to wander in the wilderness until all had died except for Moses, Joshua, Caleb, and the wilderness survivors, the people of Israel. And following are the remarks by Balaam of Beor, yes, the one who conversed with the donkey of Numbers 24, but Balaam saw Jesus.

From the time God called Israel out of Egypt, Israel rebuked Him ten times. Each time, they were forgiven, but He sent unbelieving Israelites as spies to the land of milk and honey.

Genesis speaks of the prophecy of the coming Messiah Jesus in the latter days.

❧ GENESIS 49:1 ❧

Jacob/Israel called his sons saying, "Gather that I tell you what will happen to you in the last forty years to all who have broken the covenant with God." That was August 30, the beginning of Jesus's ministry, until August 63 to end the last seven years with the coming of Jesus on clouds of wrath to kill all Israel who had GGTBMF.

❧ MATTHEW 16:18–19 ❧

"I tell you Peter, on this Rock, I will build My ecclesia, the flesh-and-blood images of Jesus Christ, the assembly of God (not an incorporated brick-and-mortar incorporated church business). The gates of Hades have no effect on the predestined called by God from out of the dead in the religions of Judaism. I have given you elect of God the promised keys of the kingdom of heaven, whom you elect are, and whatever you elect bind on earth, God has already bound in heaven, and whatever you elect loosen on earth, God has already loosened in heaven."

However, when we are deliberately, intentionally, and with forethought GGTBMF, we are in heap big guacamole. Because we are human, most of our days are filled with stupidity. God forgives the elects' stupidity because they also live by every word that proceeds from the mouth of God; even self-serving jackasses can live by the Word. The best example is that of David and Bathsheba. God forgave David's stupidity, and David repented. The moral here is simple—do not judge. David's stupidity began when God lured him to see Bathsheba bathing.

❧ GENESIS 49:7–9 ❧

The Lord cursed the dead in Israel but not the elect of Jacob/Israel, His chosen people. The sword shall not depart Judah/Jesus as a lawgiver until Shiloh comes and the obedience of the people occurs. Jesus in the latter days will bind His donkey to the vine, the elect of Israel. Jesus's garments were washed in the wine and blood of the bitter fruit by the Jews marked with death. The eyes of Jesus are darker than wine and His teeth are whiter than milk.

Numbers 13 contains reminders and warnings to Israel. The first forty years, Israel wandered in the wilderness. The second forty years followed—the time of Jeremiah's tribulations. That was followed with the remnant taken into seventy years of exile in Babylon, where God used Satan to be their god and through God's delusions imposed the religions of Judaism.

The third forty years began in the year AD 30 with the baptism of Jesus.

❧ LUKE 4:5–20 ❧

Satan took Jesus to a high mountain gesturing to Jesus the kingdoms of the world with the wave of his hand. There, Satan said to Jesus, "All this authority I Satan will give You and their glory for this has been delivered to me by God and I Satan give it to whomever I wish. So, if … You will worship me, all will be Yours."

Numbers 14 was veiled to the gods of the religions that prey on their congregations for WPF. It is typical that the dead cannot know God, but yet they populate the earth daily rejecting the Word. Because of their unbelief, they were cursed to wander forty years in the wilderness and die there.

❧ NUMBERS 13:1–3 ❧

The Lord said to Moses, "Send men to spy the land of Canaan the Land I am giving to Israel; from each tribe send the head man." Moses was commanded by God to send Joshua and Caleb and each tribal leader from Paran to Canaan.

❧ NUMBERS 13:17–25 ❧

Moses sent them to spy out the land of Canaan, saying "Go up to the mountains, and check out Canaan and the dwellers as to whether few or many, strong or weak. and the goodness of land where they dwell: good or bad as to the cities, camps or strongholds; the land; rich or poor with forests and the planes. Be courageous and return with the fruit of the land." The ripening season was the time of grapes. They went spying on the land from the Wilderness of Zin as far as Rehob near Hamath. Going South to Hebron, Ahiman, Sheshai, and Talmai, the descendants of Anak the giants. They came to the Valley of Eschol, cutting down a cluster of grapes so large two men were required to carry on a strong pole between them (plus an apple and a pear and a pomegranate … too). From the Valley of Eshcol, they returned after forty days spying Canaan the Land of Milk and Honey.

❧ NUMBERS 13:26–29 ❧

The spy party returned to Moses and Aaron; waiting was the congregation of Israel in the Wilderness of Paran, at Kadesh; where they told of their explorations to the "congregation" showing them the fruit of Canaan. Telling Moses, "We went spying, the land, where you sent us. Canaan truly flows with milk and honey and note its fruit, here on the pole, the size of these giant grapes. However, they continued; the population of Canaan is strong and with large fortified cities where we saw the giants of Anak. The evil Amalekites lived in the South near the Hittites, Jebusites and the Amorites in the mountains and the Canaanites by the sea and also on the banks of the Jordan." Caleb demanded: "Let us go right now into Canaan and take possession; we are strong enough to overcome them." The twelve displayed fear and rejected God, saying, "We 'whining' are not able to go up against those giants 'sniveling' stronger than us." The fearful twelve gave the people of Israel fake news reports of the land of Canaan which the twelve spies "sniveled" lying. The land of Canaan we spied; the giant of Anak eat their inhabitants. "We 'sniveling' were mere bugs to them."

❧ NUMBERS 14:3–4 ❧

The rebellious whimpered, "Why has the Lord brought us to this land to die by the sword and our wives and children become victims?" With a cry in their voice, they sniffled, "Is it not better for us to return to Egypt?"

❧ NUMBERS 14:6–10 ❧

Joshua watched them whine and whimper and tear their clothes. He and Caleb spoke to Israel,

The land we spied out is a good land. God will bring us into that Promised Land, If, the Lord delights in us; He will give us Canaan that flows with milk and honey. Please … do not rebel against the Lord, nor fear those of Canaan, they are our bread and butter; they have no defense, they are dead; the Lord is with us. Do not fear.

Israel was about to stone Joshua and Caleb, but the glory of the Lord appeared in the tabernacle. He asked Moses, "How long will these silly ninnies reject Me? How long can they not believe Me after the ten signs I have performed earlier among them? I will strike Israel with pestilence and disinherit them. I will make from you a greater nation."

Numbers 14:20–25

The Lord said to Moses: "I have pardoned Israel as you have said. The whole earth shall be filled with the glory of the Lord. Israel has seen My glory and the signs ten times; I did in Egypt and in the wilderness, testing Me. Israel is testing Me again; rejecting God."

These ninnies who rejected God would not see the land He promised their fathers. God would bring Caleb into the very land he spied and his descendants inherited. The Lord spoke to Moses and Aaron.

How long will I put up with this evil congregation who complain against Me? I have listened to the complaints of the tribes. The Lord spoke, "just as you have spoken in My hearing, so I declare to you now the dead of Israel will become cadavers having complained against Me; dying in the wilderness over the next forty years until all over twenty years of age are dead."

Numbers 14:30–35

The Lord chose Caleb and Joshua, saying to Moses,

You will not enter Canaan, the land of milk and honey I swore I would cause you to dwell in. Your little ones Israel said would be victims I will bring to Canaan and they shall know the land of milk and honey that the dead of Israel have despised. There in the wilderness your bodies fall dead. Your shepherd sons will bear the brunt of your infidelity for forty years until your carcasses are consumed. For forty days, you spied the land; for forty years, you will know my rejection. This evil congregation gathered against Me will be consumed in the wilderness.

❧ NUMBERS 32:13 ❧

The Lord God made them wander in the wilderness forty years because they had GGTBMF.

Today, the dead gods of the religions pursue a variety of God-provided delusions about the predestined dead with their handed-down traditions and Commandments of the once Greek Orthodox fantasy that first misused the Word. Their business plan was stolen by the Roman Catholic Church and did not become a church until it plagiarized the word *church* used in First Geneva Bible published 1557 by William Wittingham in exile from Bloody Mary's England in 1553.

In this new covenant age, the god of the religions cannot know of their death because of their intrusion in the elects' Communion with Jesus.

❧ BALAAM OF BEOR ❧

Balaam, a sorcerer for hire, was hired by King Balak to curse the Jews that had just arrived in his kingdom. Balaam made it clear that he could not curse those God would not permit Balaam to curse; he needed God's permission to do that. All live by the Word, which proceeds from the mouth of God.

❧ NUMBERS 24:1–9 ❧

Balaam saw that it pleased the Lord to bless Israel. He saw the tribes of Israel and the Spirit of God. His prophecy began,

Balaam hears the words of God, seeing the Almighty vision with his eyes wide open Balaam fell down … How lovely your tents and dwellings, Jacob/Israel! Stretched out are your gardens by the river and your aloes planted by the Lord as cedars beside the waters.

God poured water from his buckets on His elect; His kingdom is naturally higher than Agag's. God brought Jacob/Israel out of Egypt. The Rock with the strength of a wild ox consumed the nations and broke their bones. Who will provoke the Lion, Jesus? Blessed is Jesus in the latter days who blessed the elect and cursed the dead.

❧ NUMBERS 24:12–17 ❧

Balaam said to King Balak, "I told your messengers, if you were to give me your house full of silver and gold, I could not go beyond the Word of the Lord to do good or bad of my own free will. I can speak only what the Lord says. Balaam began the prophecy, 'Balaam the son of Beor, a man whose eyes are opened …' He saw the vision of the almighty and fell with his eyes opened: 'I see Him, but not at this time; I see Him, but not near; I see a star coming out of Jacob/Israel; the sword, Jesus, coming out of Israel battering the brow of Moab destroying the sons of disobedience.'"

CHAPTER 3

The prophecy of the latter days continues with the prophecy of Moses about the Promised Land. In the latter days, however, God renewed the covenant with those who survived the forty years in the desert. Here in Israel, God warned those who rejected God and spoke of His relationship with the elect.

❧ DEUTERONOMY 29 ❧

Moses called all to review their last forty years and in a way spoke as from God to obey His commands and keep those words so they would prosper. The oath God made with Israel was also to those not yet born. God threatened them with the curses of Deuteronomy 28:15–68 if they disobeyed Him and turned to gold and gods. Those whose hearts turned away from Him would suffer the wormwood prophesy.

❧ DEUTERONOMY 30 ❧

God through Moses assured them and the elect that salvation was not in heaven or beyond the sea but in the latter days.

This commandment I command you, Israel, today is not a mystery or far off. It's not in the third heaven that one might ask, "Who will bring it back from heaven that we hear it and do?" Nor beyond the sea, that some ask, "Who will go over the sea for us and bring it to us, that we may hear it and do it?" However, the Word is in your heart to do.

These Old Testament prophecies always point to the events in the latter days ending September 15, 70, thus most in this treatise is in the past tense because all the Bible prophesies are past except in the minds of the dead veiled by the religions of men. There are no religions of God, but yet all religions GGTBMF and don't know they are deluded by God just as the atheists contend.

⊱ Deuteronomy 29:1–7 ⊰

The Lord commanded Moses and warned Israel in the land of Moab with the covenant God made with them earlier on the mountain in Horeb. Moses called all Israel saying,

You have seen all that the Lord did before your eyes in the land of Egypt, to Pharaoh, his servants and all Egypt - You saw with your eyes God's great trials you have lived and seen the Signs and great wonders. Still, Israel, because of your way, the Lord has not given you, Israel, a soul to perceive nor eyes to see or the ears to hear. Moses has led you, Israel, forty years in the wilderness. Your clothes and your sandals did not wear out. Nor have you eaten any bread or wine or anything similar so that you can know that I am the Lord your God. When you came to this place, Sihon king of Heshbon and Og king of Bashan came out to defeat us, but in battle we conquered them.

⊱ Deuteronomy 29:8 ⊰

When at Shiloh, Sihon and Og's land was given as an inheritance to the Reubenites, Gadites, and the half-tribe Manasseh. You, Israel, are to keep the words of this covenant and do them that you may prosper as your leaders, tribes, elders, officers, and the men of Israel today before the Lord your God with your children, wives, and servants who cut your wood and draw your water today.

You, Israel, enter into this covenant with the Lord your God and into His oath that the Lord your God makes with you. Today, God has established you, Israel, and as your God speaks to you just as God had spoken to your fathers, Abraham, Isaac, and Jacob, I make this covenant and oath, but not only with you, Israel, standing with the Lord your God today, but also with him not with us today but in the latter days from the time of the anointing of the Messiah by God at the baptism by John. You do know that we lived in the land of Egypt and that you, Israel, passed by many nations. You, Israel, saw their abominations: idols and gods of wood, stone, silver, and gold. Now there must not be among you, Israel, a man or woman or family or a tribe whose heart turns away from the Lord your God to serve the gods of men, creed, or nations, or Rome not now known to you, but as such they are dead, a root bearing bitterness, wormwood, for GGTBMF. The unbelieving fool hears the words of this curse (Deuteronomy 28:15–68) and blesses himself in his heart saying, "I shall have peace though, I follow the dictates of my heart." Such a fool, a drunkard, could never be included with the sober.

☙ Daniel 9:27 ❧

The prophecy of wormwood (ca. September 67): General Vespasian with the Fifth, Tenth, Twelfth, and Fifteenth Roman Legions arriving at the mountainside city of Taricheae north and west of the Sea of Galilee is a picture of the future Moses mentioned.

☙ Revelation 8:7 ❧

The first angel trumpeted: hail, fire and blood mingled was thrown to the earth from October 2, 66; that began the days of vengeance of four years on the Jews marked with death in the religions of Judaism and ended on the seventh day of creation, August 2, 70. A third of the trees and all green grass were burned.

☙ Revelation 16:1–2 ❧

John heard a loud voice from the temple in the third heaven saying to the seven angels, "Go and pour out God's bowl of the wrath on the earth." The first angel poured out his bowl upon the land/Israel, and foul and loathsome sores came upon the Jews marked with death who worshipped Caesar in the temple in their desire for WPF.

❧ REVELATION 16:3 ❧

The second angel poured out his bowl on the Sea of Galilee; the blood of the rebellious at Taricheae was so much that every creature in the Sea of Galilee died.

❧ REVELATION 16:4–7 ❧

The third angel poured out his bowl on the rivers and springs that became wormwood. I heard the water's angel saying, "You are righteous, O Lord, (Jesus) the One who is and (Jesus) the One who was and (Jesus) the One who now is judging with the sword all things."

The Jews marked with death had shed the blood of the elect and the prophets, and You, Lord, have given those marked with death blood to drink because they GGTBMF. In the third heaven at the altar, one said, "Even so, Lord God almighty, Your judgments are righteous and true."

❧ REVELATION 8:10–12 ❧

The third angel trumpeted, and the great star wormwood fell from heaven as a burning torch on a third of the rivers and the springs of water. Wormwood, the star, poisoned a third of the Sea of Galilee and the rivers and springs, and many died from the poisoned waters.

The fourth angel sounded, and a third of the sun was struck, a third of the moon, and a third of the stars (Jews marked with death) were darkened—killed—and a third of the day, the four years of the great tribulation, day and the night did not shine.

In Josephus's *The Jewish War*, book 3, chapter 10, sections 1, 5, 6, and 9, is a description of the Romans fighting the rebellious on and off the shore in boats shooting arrows at the Romans on the shore. The Romans hastily cobbled together boats and rafts, attacked the rebellious Jews, and killed six thousand of the rebellious for GGTBMF.

Vespasian camped at the city of Tiberias suspecting a long battle because of the number of the rebellious in the city who sat nearby on the shore of the Sea of Galilee with a large number of lake craft Josephus called ships. Seeing the strength and the Romans' preparations, the rebellious went to sea, where they were pursued by the Romans.

Vespasian's son Titus arrived with the four Roman legions. The terrified rebellious defenders on the walls of Taricheae fled in fear to the lake; the Romans killed all attempting to get onboard their ships. The slaughter began in the city; those who had stayed there hoped that by not fighting the Romans, Titus would give them peace and security. The rebels were from all over Galilee. Those of the city of Taricheae had not consented to war, but Titus continued killing until the revolt's leaders were slaughtered.

Titus sent the good news to Vespasian. Titus hoped the greatest part of the war in Galilee was over. Vespasian set a guard over the city Taricheae so that none could escape, and he killed all who tried.

The next day, Vespasian commanded vessels be built to pursue the rebellious offshore. When the vessels were ready, Vespasian manned them. The rebellious in the lake were trapped; the Romans held all the shores. The enemy's small ships fitted for piracy were too weak in a battle with the Romans. The rebel ships were so few and afraid of the Romans, but in desperation, they sailed around the Romans and threw stones at them.

When closer, they fought receiving the greatest harm. They heard their stones hitting Roman armor while the Roman darts reached the Jews marked 666 when they were too close; they suffered the most and did little harm to the Romans, and the rebellious drowned as their ships collided. Those ready to die came close to fight, but the Romans ran them through. Those who jumped overboard drowned or were struck by darts. Those who attempted to board Roman boats or who swam to shore were killed.

The lake was bloodied and full of dead bodies; the lake and shore were putrid with swelling bodies. The Jews' misery was not the only object of their heartbreak; they hated the authors of the rebellion that had caused their misery. The number of the slain in the city of Taricheae, including those earlier killed in the city, was 6,500.

⊱ REVELATION 16:16–18 ⊰

The Lord God gathered the Jews marked with death in the prison of Jerusalem spoken of in Hebrew as the Armageddon. The seventh angel poured out his bowl into the air, and a loud voice from the throne in the third heaven said, "It is done!" On October 2, 66, came the promised great earthquake (see Revelation 6:12–17) with noises, thunder, and lightning which had never occurred since men were on the earth.

❧ REVELATION 8:13 ❧

John saw an eagle flying in the midst of heaven loudly saying, "Woe, woe, woe to those of the Land/Israel because the three angels with trumpets are about to sound!"

❧ DEUTERONOMY 4:30–31 ❧

When you are in distress and all these things come upon you in the latter days, turn to the Lord your God and obey His voice because He is merciful. He will not forsake you or destroy you or let you forget the covenant of your fathers God swore to them and you in these latter days. In the latter days, the anger of the Lord and His jealousy burned against those of unbelief with every curse written in Deuteronomy 28:15–68 settled on those.

Revelation was written as a prophecy; they were the visions Jesus provided John to write while on the Island of Patmos during the thousand years before August 63 that began the apocalypse of the last seven years to end the seventh day of creation, August 2, 70.

❧ DEUTERONOMY 29:21–29 ❧

The Lord separated the dead, the fools, from all the tribes of Israel for adversity with the curses of the covenant written in Deuteronomy 28:15–68. The Beast of Rome brought the plagues on the land. The whole land was burning; it did not bear fruit like Sodom and Gomorrah, Admah, and Zeboim, which the Lord overthrew in His anger and wrath.

The nations all asked, "Why has the Lord done so to Israel? What does the heat of this great anger mean?" They said, "Because of the dead serving other gods forsaking the covenant the Lord made with their fathers and brought them out of Egypt. Israel served and worshipped other gods and the Beast of Rome." They could not know that God had not given them (the dead) to know.

In the latter days, the anger of the Lord brought on Israel every curse in Deuteronomy 28:15–68. The Lord uprooted them from their land in anger and wrath and cast them into another land, Israel as known today. God has revealed secret things to the elect that cause them to be doers of His Word by the Holy Spirit and be doers yesterday, today, and tomorrow.

❧ EZEKIEL 36:27 ☙

God said that in the latter days, He would put His Spirit in the elect, who would walk in His ways and joyfully keep His statutes and judgments.

It is not how or when we kiss up to God; it is how we live in God's forgiveness, peace, and love with eternal life in Jesus.

❧ DEUTERONOMY 30:1–3 ☙

In the latter days, when all these things came upon you, the blessings and the curses set before you, they brought to your mind the blessing and curses on the nations wherever the Lord your God has sent you. Having reconciled you elect to the Lord your God, you elect obey His voice that I command you today. God will bring you and your children with all your heart and with all your soul, Israel, back from Babylonian captivity and gather your elect from out of those nations where the Lord your God has scattered you. But in the latter days in the fullness of the dispensation called and reconciled you elect, God's chosen people, from out of the religions of Judaism.

❧ DEUTERONOMY 30:4–10 ☙

Being driven to distant places under heaven on earth, from Babylon to the latter days, the Lord your God will gather you elect back to Israel, which your fathers had possessed, and then in the latter days, you elect of Israel possessed the land and prospered and increased your numbers greater than your fathers. The Lord your God will circumcise your elect hearts with the Holy Spirit and turn your decadence to love of the Lord your God that you elect will live eternally. In the latter days, the Lord your God will curse the religions of Judaism marked with death, who will hate and persecute you elect.

In the latter days, God will cause His people, the elect, to obey the voice of the Lord and do all His Commandments that I, Moses, command you today. The Lord God as promised causes you elect to prosper in all the work of your hand, the fruit of your body, the increase of your livestock, and the produce of your land. For the Lord in the latter days will again rejoice over you elect for good as He had rejoiced over your fathers, that is, when you obey the voice of the Lord your God and keep His Commandments and His statutes written in this Book of the Law when He causes you elect to turn to the Lord your God with all your heart and soul.

You are not chosen by God because you are a sweetie pie. God called you because God loved you from the foundation of the world, and when God calls the predestined to Jesus Christ somewhere down life's road, the foreordained are transformed by the Holy Spirit to life eternal in Jesus. When God calls you to become a fool of Christ, you, puppy, are doomed to life eternal in Jesus.

❧ DEUTERONOMY 30:11–14 ❧

This commandment which I command you today is not mysterious for you or far away. It is (the Holy Spirit) within you; it is not in the third heaven that you ask, "Who will ascend into the third heaven for us and bring it down to us that we hear it and do it?" Nor is it beyond the sea, that you ask, "Who will go over the sea and bring it to us, that we may hear it and do it?"

Through God's calling in the latter days, the Holy Spirit provided the knowledge of God to those predestined to eternal life. The Word, Jesus Christ, is in your mouth and in your heart, that you live eternally.

CHAPTER 4

In Deuteronomy 31–32, Moses spoke to the promised about the latter days; those of unbelief would be done away with as described in Revelation with Satan over Gog and Magog, a.k.a. the Beast of Rome as prophesied in Ezekiel 38:14–23.

In Deuteronomy 31, God, knowing the coming of the latter days, instructed Moses to speak of the future and the coming of their Rock and Savior whom Israel (Jews marked with death) spitefully crucified. God had Moses prepare the Song of Moses that would haunt Israel in the last seven years.

⊱ DEUTERONOMY 31:1–11 ⊰

The Lord God had spoken to Moses to speak to Israel. Moses said, "I am one hundred and twenty years old today. The Lord has told me, 'You, Moses, cannot cross over the Jordan to Canaan. The Lord your God crosses the Jordon before you, and He will destroy those nations of Canaan, and you, Israel, will take the land as your own. The Lord will do to them as He did to Sihon and Og, the kings of the Amorites and their land when He destroyed them. The Lord will give you their abundance and produce to those who keep My Commandments. Be strong and courageous, and do not fear any, for the Lord your God will not desert you.'"

Moses said to Joshua before all Israel, "Be strong and courageous for you are going with these people to the land of Canaan, which the Lord has sworn to their fathers to inherit the land of Israel. The Lord goes before you and will not abandon you; do not fear or be discouraged."

Moses wrote the law and gave it to the Levitical priests, who carried the ark of the covenant of the Lord and to the elders of Israel. Moses commanded, "At the end of every seven years at the appointed time in the year of release at the Feast of Tabernacles, all Israel must come before the Lord in the place which God chose, and you shall read this law before all Israel in their hearing."

Until Jeremiah, those commands were largely ignored as per Bible history; until Jeremiah, the Laws of Deuteronomy were found and read to the people who were as promised as killed except the remnant of only five thousand taken by God's servant Nebuchadnezzar to seventy years of exile in Babylon.

❧ JEREMIAH 2:6–9 ❧

The Lord continued, "They did not ask, 'Where is the Lord God who brought us from out of the land of Egypt, leading us through the wilderness, deserts and pits, drought and the shadow of death where no one could cross or dwell?' The Lord God brought you into a bountiful land to eat its fruit and its goodness, but when you entered Canaan, you, Israel, defiled My land, Canaan, making My promises an abomination. The priests did not ask, 'Where is the Lord?' Those of the law/religions did not know Me. The temple rulers disobeyed Me, and God deluded the prophecy of Baal, who prophesied walking in ways that did not profit Israel. Thus I will bring charges against you, Israel, and your children in the latter days," said the Lord.

❧ DEUTERONOMY 31:12–16 ❧

Moses commanded all to hear and learn to fear the Lord and follow His Law. The Lord said to Moses, "Know the days approach when you Moses must die; call Joshua and present yourselves in the tabernacle of meeting, that I may install Joshua." So Moses and Joshua went presenting themselves at the tabernacle. There, the Lord appeared in a cloud and said to Moses, "You elect will rest with your fathers, but this people Israel in the latter days will rise and play the harlot with the foreign Roman god Caesar, where they go to be among them, and there Israel will forsake Me and break My covenant."

The followers of Jesus were castigated by the dead Jews as Christians, followers of that Jesus freak who called himself the Messiah, from which the dead religions of Christianity evolved.

There are no religions of God. The elect are called by God to be in Communion only with Jesus and in fellowship only with the assembly of God.

⪛ DEUTERONOMY 31:17–19 ⪚

My anger will be awakened against the dead in the latter days, and I will forsake them because of their unbelief by hiding My face from those marked with death devouring them. Many evils will come on Israel in the latter days and the dead will ask, "Have not these evils come upon us because our God is not among us?" I will hide My face in the latter days because all the evil marked with death have turned to their Roman god Caesar. Moses, write down this song and teach it to the children of Israel; put it in their mouths and hear this Song of Moses as a witness of Me against Israel in the latter days.

Those not called to God with eternal life remained dead awaiting their earthly demise and damnation. The elect are God's chosen people, the 144,000 elect as promised in the latter days.

⪛ DEUTERONOMY 31:20–30 ⪚

God declared, "I have brought them to the land of Canaan flowing with milk and honey, which I promised their fathers, but they have turned to other gods and have broken my covenant. In the latter days when many evils and tribulations come upon them, the Song of Moses will haunt them for it will not be forgotten by their descendants. I know the inclination of their behavior even before I brought them to the land of Canaan."

Moses wrote the Song of Moses and taught it to the children of Israel. Moses installed Joshua: "Be strong and of courage for Joshua brought the children of Israel into the land of Canaan which I swore to them."

When Moses completed writing Deuteronomy, he commanded the Levites, "Take this Book of the Law and put it in the ark beside the covenant of the Lord your God as a witness against you; I know Israel's rebellion and stiff neck. If today while I am alive you have been rebellious against the Lord, how much more will you rebel after my death? Gather the elders and officers of the tribes to teach this law; call the priests of Israel as witnesses against them. I know that after my death, you, Israel, will become utterly corrupt and turn aside from the way I have commanded you. Evil will fall on you in the latter days because you will do evil in the sight of the Lord provoking Him to anger through the work of your hands."

Moses spoke in the hearing of all Israel the words of this Song of Moses until the heaven (desolate temple) and earth (Israel marked with death) were in the lake of fire.

The promise to destroy the old heaven, the temple in Jerusalem, was completed in 70; the temple powers passed to the predestined, the elect.

⋇ HEBREWS 9:9 ⋇

In the latter days, gifts and sacrifices were offered in the temple, but they could not make anyone perfect, but when the elect were indwelled with the Holy Spirit, who through parables taught the knowledge of God, they received eternal life.

⋇ HEBREWS 9:11 ⋇

Christ became the High Priest of the perfect tabernacle, not a church made by hands. The Law of Moses was annulled by Jesus's death. The religions of men then as are the religions today were fully invested in man-made churches. However, the elect, the Jesus freaks of forgiveness, peace, and love, have eternal life guaranteed. The priestly dead in their religions of Judaism continue to crucify Jesus today in the man-made temples at the altar of demons in the usual pursuit of WPF.

In the latter days to come, Israel's rejection of the Lord and Savior in Deuteronomy 32 is a preview of Israel marked with death, which crucified the Messiah. The promised picture of their hell on the land in the seven years of the apocalypse was to enlighten Israel to the things Moses pointed to come in the latter days.

❧ PROVERBS 15:21 ❧

Folly is joy to the fool or the dead who are destitute of discernment, but the elect of God walk uprightly with understanding.

On earth, there are two kinds of people—the dead and the living, but that is not our choice. Stupidity is the sign of the fool, who will end up in the lake of fire. Perfect fools can never discern their predestined damnation sealed by God at the foundation of the world while the wise will have eternal life with Jesus.

If you are not the elect of God, the following may be just another moment of God exercising Isaiah 66:4 delusions and lies to you until your earthly demise. However, the elect of God can be assured of the revelation from God through the Holy Spirit. The dead are already deluded and continue in the ancient language of Babel.

Those who claim to preach God's Word but not in truth are dead, never having been called. God's delusions help fools prey on their congregation in their pursuit of WPF. Being dead, they cannot know they are dead in Adam never having been called. God reconciled the predestined to life eternal with Jesus's baptism.

The Bible clearly distinguishes between the predestined to life eternal in Jesus and the predestined dead in Adam. However, the BS of the seminary narrative spoken by religions is simply the God-given delusions where mere dead gods and men at the altars of demons are in the business of selling salvation.

Jesus died to take away the sins of the elect forever. The religious killed Christ and for the usual WPF protected their Roman god Caesar.

Most religious people attend services where they like their sermonizers and where there are no spoken or distinguishing doctrinal differences between the thousands of religions, sects, and churches. If the donor does not like the pastor, he will cross the street to a man-made church with a more likable, lovable, and darling blabber.

⁄ ISAIAH 14:22 ⁄

"I will rise against them," says the Lord, "and cut off Babylon/Jerusalem from the elect remnant offspring in that last generation the latter days."

This is a prelude to the Song of Moses spoken in Deuteronomy 32 in the land Moses foresaw to come with Israel's rejection of their Lord and Savior. Those who crucified their Messiah will go to hell in the last seven years of the apocalypse.

⁄ DEUTERONOMY 32:1–3 ⁄

"Lend an ear, O heavens you (exalted ones; high priests) of the temple in Jerusalem. I, Moses, will speak; hear, earth (the sons of Israel), the words from my mouth. Let my teaching be as rain drops and my speech as dew on tender herbs and gentle on the grass. I, Moses, proclaim the name of the Lord and all the greatness of our God."

⁄ ISAIAH 1:1–3 ⁄

This is the vision Isaiah saw concerning Judah and Jerusalem in the days of Uzziah, Jotham, Ahaz, and Hezekiah, kings of Judah: "Hear, O heavens, and hear, O earth, the Lord has spoken: 'I have nourished the children who rebelled against Me; the ox knows its owner's crib; but Israel does not know and does not perceive.'"

⁄ DEUTERONOMY 32:4–14 ⁄

Jesus's work is justice, and His ways are perfection; the God of truth is without injustice standing alone in righteousness. Israel had been corrupted; because of their unbelief, they were marked with death as a perverse and crooked generation. Dealing with the Lord, you are a foolish and unwise people. God is your Father, and He purchased you. Has He not established you? Remember, the days passed with many years and generations. Your fathers will tell you; ask your elders when the most high God divided Israel's inheritance as the nations, when God separated the sons of Adam to nations and set the boundaries of the peoples as to the number of the nations of the children of Israel. The Lord's portion was of Jacob and their inheritance of God.

Israel was found in a desert wasteland, a howling wilderness; God gathered and instructed Israel keeping it as the apple of His eye. He is the eagle spreading His wings hovering over Israel as He carries on his wings the young of the nest. The Lord alone led them among no foreign gods.

He rode Israel on the heights of the earth; they were blessed to eat the produce of the fields, draw honey from the rock and oil from the flinty rock, milk from the flocks, fat from the lambs, rams, and goats of Bashan and the grains from the choicest wheat, and you drank the bountiful wine, the blood of grapes.

The ten horns are the ten kings or emperors of the Beast of Rome. The following is pure world history, which cannot be ignored if you want to understand Revelation.

1. Julius Caesar, 45–44 BC
2. Augustus, 31 BC–AD 14
3. Tiberius, 14–37
4. Gaius, 37–41
5. Claudius, 41–54
6. Nero, 54–68 (Rome died for nineteen months in civil war.)
7. Galba, 68–69 (seven months)
8. Otho, 69–69 (three months)
9. Vitellius, 69–69 (nine months)
10. Vespasian, 69–69 (Rome lives.)

❧ JOHN 19:15 ❧

The dead Jews cried out, "Away, crucify Him!" Pilate asked, "Shall I crucify your King?" The dead chief priests answered, "We have no king but Caesar!"

❧ DEUTERONOMY 32:15–16 ❧

In the latter days, Israel, marked with death, grew obese and kicked; they crucified their Messiah, their Rock and Savior. They provoked God to jealousy with their worship of Caesar. They were marked with death in their unbelief.

❧ DEUTERONOMY 32:17–19 ❧

Israel's priests offered sacrifices to Caesar; they remained unmindful and rejected the Lord God, who had purchased them. God spurned Israel because of its injustices.

❧ DEUTERONOMY 32:20–21 ❧

God said that in the last seven years, He would hide His face from those who rejected their Rock. The religious of Judaism were marked with death in that last forty years; they were a perverse generation, dead children without faith.

God would cause them to be jealous of the Gentiles. The elect were called by God to Jesus from out of those marked with death, and God caused the Romans to destroy all the Jews marked with death in the promised seven years of the apocalypse.

❧ DEUTERONOMY 32:22 ❧

My anger began and as a fire. My anger burned to the lowest hell. My everlasting fire consumed the earth. The Lord set on fire the desolate temple, and the temple priests were killed when the Romans destroyed Jerusalem.

❧ DEUTERONOMY 32:23 ❧

The curses of Deuteronomy 28:15–68 as promised were heaped on the Jews because of their unbelief in their Messiah promised by Moses (Deuteronomy 31:29).

❧ DEUTERONOMY 32:24 ❧

Those of Israel who reject me were wasted with hunger in the trap, the pit, the prison of Jerusalem and were devoured by pestilence, famine, the sword, and the destruction of the temple, heaven on earth. God will send against them the teeth of the Beast of Rome (Daniel 7:1–7) in the last four years of the apocalypse.

﹩ DEUTERONOMY 32:25 ﹩

Titus destroyed Jerusalem by 2 August AD 70. From 2 October AD 66, the Lord brought terror into the pit, prison of Jerusalem. The seditious, rebellious Zealots of the Antichrist, John of Gischala, the assassins of the Sicarii, Judas the Galilean, and twenty thousand Idumeans of Simon of Gioras were trapped in the pit, the prison of Jerusalem, for four years of the Great Tribulation until 70 (Deuteronomy 28:15–68). See the index of *The Jewish War* for more on the Antichrist John of Gischala.

﹩ DEUTERONOMY 32:26–28 ﹩

God said, "I will smash them because of their unbelief and make the memory of those who GGTBMF destroyed by killing the number of over three million marked with death from out of the population of Israel." God considered the wrath of the enemy in case their adversaries misunderstand and lest the religious would say, "We of the religions of Judaism (under God's delusion) say our hand is high, that it is not the Lord who has done all this." Those of the religions of Judaism were denied and had no understanding of their unbelief.

﹩ DEUTERONOMY 32:29 ﹩

Be wise and understand; they would better consider the latter days in that last forty years of that last generation chosen by God, the 144,000 elect with eternal life.

﹩ DEUTERONOMY 32:30 ﹩

How could one Roman chase a thousand and two Romans put ten thousand to flight unless the Lord had surrendered them in their unbelief to Caesar?

• DEUTERONOMY 32:31–32 •

Their rock, Caesar, was not like our Rock. Even their enemies judged them to be fools. The vine of Judaism is the vine of Sodom and Gomorrah. Their grapes, the religions of men, are grapes of wrath; they are not fruit but bitter clusters marked with death.

• DEUTERONOMY 32:33 •

Their wine is the poison of serpents and the cruel venom of cobras marked to kill.

• DEUTERONOMY 32:34–35 •

The end of those marked with death has passed and been sealed among My treasures. The days of vengeance are mine, and payment comes with seven years, which began in 63 after the gospel was preached and by revelation from God to Paul. He declared the gospel preached four times. Then came the falling away, the rapture, the adoption, the redemption of the living, and the dead in Jesus Christ. Their foot slipped, and in due time beginning 63, three years of silence commenced (see Revelation 8:1) before the days of vengeance. Their calamities did not wait; Jerusalem was destroyed in 70.

• DEUTERONOMY 32:36 •

The Lord will judge His people and have compassion on His elect 144,000 remnant, but when God saw the high priests putting Jesus to death, from August 63, Jesus began coming on the clouds of wrath using Satan over Gog and Magog, a.k.a. the Beast of Rome. The Jews marked with death were destroyed.

• DEUTERONOMY 32:37–38 •

God asked, "Where is their rock, their Roman god Caesar, idols, and the religions sought as refuge? You marked with death ate the fat of temple sacrifices to Caesar. Let him give you refuge."

DEUTERONOMY 32:39

"I am He, and there is no God besides Me."

DEUTERONOMY 32:40–41

"I rendered judgment as hell on those Jews marked with death because they spitefully crucified their Rock and Savior, Jesus."

DEUTERONOMY 32:42

"I will make My Roman arrows drunk with their blood, and My Roman sword will devour the flesh and blood of the dead captives in the trap when Titus destroys Jerusalem."

DEUTERONOMY: 32:43

Rejoice, you Gentiles of God, for Jesus has avenged the blood of His servants during the days of vengeance on God's adversaries of the religions of Judaism marked with death. God provided atonement for His elect 144,000 remnant.

DEUTERONOMY 32:44–46

Moses spoke all the words of the Song of Moses to Israel and said, "Set your hearts on all the words that I testify to among you today, which you shall command your children to be careful to observe—all the words of this law, the Laws of Moses."

DEUTERONOMY 32:47

"With this word, you will prolong your days in your crossing over the Jordan River to possess the land of Canaan."

≈ DEUTERONOMY 32:48–51 ≈

The Lord told Moses, "Go up this mountain of the Mount Nebo here in the land of Moab near Jericho and view the land of Canaan, which I gave to Israel as a possession. There, You, Moses are to die on that mountain being gathered to your people as Aaron your brother died on Mount Hor gathered to his people because you, Moses, went against Me (GGTBMF) among the children of Israel at the waters of Meribah Kadesh in the wilderness of Zin because you did not respect Me among the people of Israel."

≈ EXODUS 17:7 ≈

He called the place Massah and Meribah because of the contention of the children of Israel; they tempted the Lord, asking, "Is the Lord among us or not?"

≈ NUMBERS 20:1–13 ≈

All Israel came to the wilderness of Zin in that month staying in Kadesh; Miriam died and was buried there. There was no water, so the congregation gathered against Moses and Aaron, whining, "If only we had died as our brethren died before the Lord! Why have you brought Israel into this wilderness to die? Why have you made us come out of Egypt to this evil place? There are no grains, figs, vines, pomegranates, or water."

Moses and Aaron went to the tabernacle and fell on their faces; the glory of the Lord appeared. The Lord told Moses, "Take the rod and gather the congregation. Speak to the rock. Before their eyes, the rock will yield water."

Moses and Aaron gathered the assembly before the rock. Moses said, "Hear now, you rebels! Must we bring water for you out of this rock?" Then Moses struck the rock twice with his rod instead of speaking to it. Water came out abundantly for the congregation and their animals to drink. The Lord told Moses and Aaron, "Because you did not believe Me, you shall not bring Israel into the land of milk and honey I have given them."

Meribah was where Israel contended with the Lord and yet the Lord God was revered among them.

✥ DEUTERONOMY 32:52 ✥

"Yet you, Moses, will see Canaan, though you cannot go into the land that I have promised." Here are two messages. After having renewed His covenant with Israel, God looked ahead to Israel in the latter days and became angry. In Deuteronomy 31, the Lord God was annoyed by His vision of the time after the anointing of the Messiah. He was calling and reconciling His chosen people until 63, the beginning of the last seven years of hell, the apocalypse on Israel ending in 70.

✥ 1 THESSALONIANS 4:7–12 ✥

God did not call the elect to uncleanness but to holiness. He does not reject his elect. "Regarding brotherly love, I, Paul, need not write to you elect. For you elect are taught by God to love each other, and you elect do love your brethren. We disciples urge you to multiply that you elect aspire (YLT, "study") to lead a quiet life. Mind your own business, and work with your own hands as we disciples have commanded that you elect will walk safely among the dead in the world and that you elect have no needs or wants."

The citizens were not required to preach the gospel but to live as instructed.

CHAPTER 5

❧ DANIEL 7 ❧

The Beast of Rome was the fourth most awful beast. The chapter presents the images of the three created Beasts, but the Beast of Rome had several surrogates in that last time—Nero, Galba, Otho, Vitellius, and Vespasian.

❧ DANIEL 7:9–10 ❧

This is the picture of the anointing of Jesus by God at Jesus's baptism. At that moment, the Book of Life was opened and God began calling the elect to Jesus.

❧ DANIEL 7:1–26 ❧

God created the Beasts and the most awful Rome of Daniel 7 and Revelation 17. Daniel 7 was meant to enlighten Israel to the things to come in the latter days on the Jews marked with death because of their unbelief.

Daniel is another prophecy that laid the foundation for the Word to come in the latter days when God was calling and reconciling the elect from out of the Jews marked with death until the rapture, when God sealed the elect (Revelation 7:1–5).

☙ DANIEL 7:1–3 ❧

Daniel wrote, "I saw in my vision the four winds of heaven when the Holy Spirit on earth stirred up the great sea. The four great Beasts came up from the sea each different from the other."

The first three Beasts of Daniel 7:1–7 were to prepare your mind for the fourth, the Beast of Rome, which came in the last seven years to end the seventy weeks of Daniel 9:24 to end the seventh day of creation with the apocalypse of the dead of the old covenant people.

The many faces of the Beasts and the Beast of Rome explored here in Daniel 7:1–7 intrudes on or shares with the false prophets of Revelation 13:2.

☙ REVELATION 13:2 ❧

The Beast of Rome John saw was like a leopard with the feet of a bear and the mouth of a lion. Satan was the dragon over Gog and Magog, the Beast of Rome of his power, his Roman throne, and great authority.

☙ DANIEL 7:4 ❧

The first Beast was a lion—Babylon (Revelation 13:2), with eagle's wings. Daniel watched till its wings were plucked off and it was lifted up from the earth and made to stand on two feet like a man. A heart was given to God's servant, Nebuchadnezzar.

☙ DANIEL 7:5 ❧

The second Beast was a bear—Medes/Persia (Revelation 13:2). It was raised up on one side having three ribs in its teeth and was heard to say, "Arise, devour much flesh!"

✤ DANIEL 7:6 ✤

Daniel saw another Beast (Revelation 13:2), a leopard—Alexander/Greece, with four wings and four heads, the four dominions after Alexander the Great's empire split into four kingdoms.

Daniel 8, 10, and 11 are devoted to the four kings called the Seleucids after the death of Alexander the Great. One of the kingdoms was of the Syrian Seleucid imposter King Antiochus IV Epiphanes (obviously God), who brought about the awakening of the Judas Maccabeus saga 175–172 BC.

✤ DANIEL 7:7 ✤

Daniel saw the dreadful, terrible, and strong Beast of Rome with huge iron teeth. It was devouring, breaking into pieces, and trampling all Israel. The Beast of Rome was different from all the other Beasts in that it had ten horns. The ten horns were the ten emperors mentioned earlier.

✤ REVELATION 13:1 ✤

John saw the Beast of Rome coming from the Mediterranean. Titus and four Roman legions came from north of the Euphrates. After Nero's suicide, the four Roman legions led by General Vespasian stood down in Egypt. Then there began Vespasian's rise as the Beast of Rome with its seven hills. The tenth crown was Vespasian, and on the beast's heads were the blasphemous names of the Roman god Caesar.

John of Revelation fame saw the specter of the Beast of Rome become wounded in civil war but healed when Vespasian became emperor following the murder of Vitellius in 69. The entire world marveled and followed the Beast of Rome, Vespasian.

✤ DANIEL 7:15–17 ✤

Daniel said, "I was grieved in my body and spirit with the visions in my mind troubled me. I asked angel Gabriel, and he made known to me the interpretation of these things: 'Those great Beasts were four, Babylon, Medes/Persia, Greece, and the Beast Rome from out of the earth.'"

⪼ DANIEL 7:19 ⪻

Daniel wished to know the truth about the Beast of Rome, which was different from the others, exceedingly dreadful and teeth of iron and nails of bronze; it devoured, crunched, and trampled Israel.

⪼ DANIEL 7:23 ⪻

Gabriel said, "The fourth Beast on earth was the fourth kingdom and was different from the previous kingdoms; trampling, breaking and devouring the whole earth in pieces."

⪼ DANIEL 7:8 ⪻

Daniel was considering the horns. Nero had a little horn; the first horn came before the three emperors that followed—Galba, Otho, and Vittelius—plucked out by the roots. Nero's horn had the eyes of a man and a mouth speaking pompous words against the most high God.

⪼ DANIEL 7:11–12 ⪻

Daniel watched Nero, the first horn. Nero committed suicide in June 68, and his body was given to the flames of eternal damnation. Galba, Otho, and Vittelius reigned for a time.

⪼ DANIEL 7:20 ⪻

The mouthy horn of Nero had eyes and a mouth; it spoke pompous words against God. Nero's reign was much longer than that of Galba, Otho, and Vittelius.

❧ DANIEL 7:24 ❧

Vespasian was different from the nine emperors who preceded him.

April 25, 34, was the resurrection; Jesus met the disciples and the Marys and later ascended to heaven (see Daniel 7:13–14).

❧ DANIEL 7:18 ❧

The predestined elect received the kingdom forever.

❧ DANIEL 7:22 ❧

Jesus came August 63 with the sword of judgment for seven years, but the elect were sealed to life eternal and gathered by God in the wilderness at Pella for the marriage of the bride of Christ and the Lamb of God.

❧ DANIEL 7:25 ❧

Nero, whose name was 666, spoke haughtily against the Most High and persecuted His elect intending to change times and the law.

The Jews marked with death were given unto Nero's hands for a time and times and half a time; God changed to the three years of silence (see Revelation 8:1).

❧ DANIEL 7:26–27 ❧

The court in the third heaven destroyed Nero's dominion by his suicide. The greatness of the kingdom and dominion under the whole of heaven passed to the elect, those who served and obeyed Jesus.

Revelation was written by John on the Isle of Patmos, during the thousand years from the day of Pentecost, June 14, 34, and ending in August 63. The results of that prophecy were the hideous and terrible horrors and famine that Deuteronomy 28:15–68 promised until Paul declared the gospel preached around the world.

The dead cannot know they are dead; the proof is that they don't know the gospel was preached around the world and declared by Paul four times in the New Testament—Romans 1:8 and 16:25–27, and Colossians 1:4–5 and 1:23. This is ignored by all but a few congregations.

❧ REVELATION 17:1–3 ❧

One angel with seven bowls told John, "Come, I will show you the judgment of the great harlot Jerusalem that sits on many waters with her paramour, Caesar." The Beast of Rome was bribed by the priestly class of Jerusalem for the usual WPF because Jerusalem committed fornication with the kings of Rome and the inhabitants of the world; they were made drunk by the wine of the harlot, Jerusalem. John said, "God carried me away in the Spirit into the wilderness. I saw the woman Jerusalem sitting on the scarlet Beast of Rome; her protector marked all over with the names of the Roman god Caesar; blasphemy; having seven heads (the seven hills of Rome) and ten horns were the specter of the Beast (the first ten emperors of Rome)."

❧ EXODUS 28:4 ❧

Her breastplate, garments, ephod, robe, woven tunic, turban, and sash were holy garments made from the pattern of Aaron, the high priest who ministered to God.

❧ REVELATION 17:4–5 ❧

The woman, Jerusalem, was wrapped in purple and scarlet with gold, precious stones, and pearls. In her hand was a golden cup full of her abominations, the filthiness of Jerusalem's fornication. Written on Jerusalem's forehead was Babylon the great, the mother of harlots and her abominations.

❧ ISAIAH 23:15–18 ❧

It shall come to pass that after the seventy years of Babylonian exile, Tyre will again sing the harlot song: "Take your harp and go about the city and sing your forgotten harlot sweet melody, sing many songs that you will be remembered."

After seventy years, the Lord will visit Tyre, where the harlot will return to her hire and commit fornication with all the kingdoms of the world. Not all of her pay will be banked; some will be set aside by God for the elect who dwell in the Lord to eat abundantly and for fine clothing.

❧ REVELATION 1:19 ❧

The visions Jesus provided John are metaphorical, apocalyptic, and figurative so one could understand the coming seven years of hell on earth to follow. Though much is left out, the idea is that Jesus will come on the clouds of wrath and Satan will be set over Gog and Magog a.k.a. the Beast of Rome, which will destroy Jerusalem.

❧ REVELATION 17:6–8 ❧

John saw the woman Jerusalem drunk with the blood of the elect and the murder of Philip, Stephen, and John the Baptist, the blood of the martyrs of Jesus. When John saw the harlot Jerusalem, he was amazed and marveled greatly. The angel asked John, "Why do you marvel? I will tell you the mystery of the woman Jerusalem and her paramour Rome that carries the harlot Jerusalem. Rome has seven heads and ten horns. The image of the beast you saw was the suicide of Nero."

Rome was dead in civil war for eighteen months until late December 69. Nero ascended from out of Hades to eternal damnation, and those Jews marked with death were not written in the Book of Life.

❧ REVELATION 17:9 ❧

John's visions came from Jesus. Nero was the image of the Beast of Rome. Nero was the mouthy one in Daniel 7 and in a few places in Revelation. All were left nameless in the prophecy by John; Nero was the only one of the beasts at the time in Revelation.

John wrote Revelation on the isle of Patmos under the watchful eye of Roman forces.

Scripture plainly says that the Roman emperors were to destroy Jerusalem. Vespasian, the tenth emperor, sent Titus to destroy Jerusalem.

❧ REVELATION 17:10 ☙

There are also seven kings, and five had fallen. One was Nero; Galba lived for a short time and was murdered in the market; his head was cut off and held for ransom. Five had fallen dead.

❧ REVELATION 17:11–15 ☙

Otho was the eighth going to damnation. These emperors were of one mind, and God gave them power and authority over the Beast of Rome. These emperors made war with the Lamb Jesus and lost because Jesus was the Lord of Lords and King of Kings and the elect were God's chosen people who were foreordained to be faithful. Jesus said, "On the waters, you saw the harlot Jerusalem who sold herself as a prostitute to Rome and to the dead peoples, multitudes, nations and tongues of the world."

❧ REVELATION 18 ☙

The earth's merchants wept and mourned because no one bought Jerusalem's merchandise anymore: gold, silver, pearls and precious stones, fine linens and purples, silk and scarlet, lemon wood, idols of precious wood, bronze, iron, and marble, spices, cinnamon, incense, fragrant oils, the finest wheat, cattle, sheep, horses, chariots, and the bodies and souls of men.

❧ REVELATION 17:16–17 ☙

Jesus told John that the Beast of Rome hated the harlot Jerusalem and made her desolate, naked, ate her flesh, and burned Jerusalem. The Word of God was fulfilled; Jerusalem burned, and that ended the old covenant age and its dead people.

⊱ REVELATION 9:5 ⊰

The apocalyptic demons were not allowed to kill those marked 666 but could torment them for five months from Passover, April 14, 70, to August 2, 70, with the stings of scorpions, their weapons.

⊱ MATTHEW 13:39–42 ⊰

The enemy who sowed them was Satan; the harvest was seven years of judgment. Over three million Jews were marked with death because of their unbelief. Jesus sent His angels to throw all the old covenant people of unbelief into the fire.

Jesus has done well to keep the veil on the incorporated Christianity as expressed. No doubt many in corporate Christianity know all of the above, but in their pursuit of their god of Gain, they receive the wages of the dead.

CHAPTER 6

WHAT GOD DOES!

❧ INTRODUCTION ❧

Daniel 9 is a bigger picture-perfect setting for the latter days of what God has done but to be made knowable to the elect from the Day of Pentecost to end the desolate people, temple, and Jerusalem.

Daniel 9:24 provides the knowledge of God to make the elect of God sinless.

For forty years, God spoke through the mouth of Jeremiah promising the remnant of circa five thousand to be exiled for seventy years in Babylonian. After Babylon, Israel was sent back to rebuild Jerusalem and the temple, heaven on earth, the temple of God over the next seven weeks of forty-nine years.

❧ DANIEL 9:26 ❧

After seven weeks and sixty-two weeks came the sixty-ninth week followed by the seventieth week of seven years of the apocalypse to end the seventh day of creation from August 63, when Paul declared the gospel preached. God cut off Jesus from more than three million Jews in the falling away because of their unbelief with the promised seven years of the curses of Deuteronomy 28:15–68. He then began the promised apocalypse, the destruction of those of unbelief, and by 2 August AD 70 the brick-and-mortar temple of heaven on earth.

What God spoke of in Daniel 9:24–27 were the stepping-stones to understand the true meaning of Daniel's prophecy of what God did in the latter days. Daniel's prayer is an indictment of all who reject God knowingly. God always has the last word, and the predestined dead remain dead and the predestined elect have eternal life in Jesus.

❧ SIMPLE RULES FOR LIFE ETERNAL IN JESUS ❧

The first rule of eternal life in Jesus is that it's not your job to get it. It is how God causes you to live as a doer in forgiveness, peace, and love even with your neighbor about to kill you. He is the work of God; you are deserving because you, puppy, have GGTBMF. The Lord God causes me to know when I am in Samaria and those who needs God's love so I, the elect of God, am there to love them as God loves them.

Salvation is the work of God, and no elect can escape eternal life. God is the cause of our lives to be lived joyously in His peace and love just as the carpenter drives nails, the plumber plumbs, and the painter paints, and then go home as humble servants to love their families. The Lord causes spouse to love each other and their families though they might have crosses to bear. God allows for bad jackasses to be the God-given crosses that good jackasses have to bear. Everyone is to love others as if they were Jesus Christ even though not all on earth have the Spirit of God.

❧ DANIEL 9:1–19 ❧

In year one of the reign of Darius over the Medes, Daniel understood the books and the number of years by the Lord God through Jeremiah. Because of Jerusalem's wretchedness, God sent Israel to the seventy years of Babylonian exile. "I looked to the Lord God begging with prayer, fasting, sackcloth, and ashes. I prayed to the Lord, 'O Lord, great and awesome God who keeps His covenant, mercy and love of those who keep His Commandments, but yes, we Israel have sinned with wicked inequities rejecting your Commandments and judgments. We have ignored your prophets. O Lord God. Righteousness is You, but we are ashamed, the men of Judah and all Israel, the people of Jerusalem and countries near and far, where You have driven them because of their unbelief. O Lord, shamefully, we, our kings, princes, and fathers, have sinned. You are our God of mercy and forgiveness, but we rebelled. We have not obeyed you and have not walked in the Law of Moses and His prophets.

'Israel has rejected You. Your voice curses with oaths written in your prophets and servants of the Law of Moses having been poured out on us because we have sinned against You. God has confirmed His words bringing our judgment; the great disasters under the third heaven never having been done as what is now being done in Jerusalem. It is written in the Law of Moses why all this disaster has come on us; it is because we have not abided before You, our Lord. The dead having turned away through their iniquities and not abiding in Your Word.

'The Lord God sent the curses of Deuteronomy 28:15–68 upon Israel. He is righteous in all He does even though we do not obey His voice. Now, O Lord God, You brought Israel out of Egypt knowing Israel has sinned wickedly! In Your righteousness, Lord God, I pray hoping that Your anger and fury turn away from Jerusalem because of our sins and our father's sins as an indictment of all Israel. Most humbly our God, hear the prayer of this servant begging that you cause your face to shine on Your desolate temple sanctuary. Lord God, incline Your ear and hear; open Your eyes and see our desolations and the city that called by Your name (Salem/Peace), for we do not present our begging before You not because of our unrighteous deeds but because of Your great mercies. O Lord, hear and forgive, listen and act! Please do not delay, my God, for Your city and elect called people by Your name.'"

Daniel was saying that it was not what the people would or could do but what God has already determined, what God has done, and what God causes His people to do as His elect. Daniel was pointing to the people spoken of by Moses because they had broken their covenant with God and did not repent.

❧ HEBREWS 4:1–16 ❧

Since we have God's promise to enter His rest, we elect need not fear if we seem short. God has our back. The gospel was preached to the predestined dead, but that Word they heard through parable code called them to God in faith.

We elect believe and are promised rest. He said, "I swore in My wrath that they shall not enter My rest (Psalm 94:11) though My works were finished from the foundation of the world."

God rested on the seventh day from all His works (Genesis 2:2). Again, in this, the latter days, they shall not enter My rest (Psalm 95:11). The elect 144,000 entered it, but the predestined, because of their disobedience, did not enter it. God told David in Psalm 95:7–8, "Today, if you will hear His voice, Do not harden your hearts." If Joshua had given them rest, why would God have spoken of another day? There remained a rest for God's chosen. At their earthly demise, the elect will enter His rest. Be diligent to enter that rest.

The Word is sharper than any two-edged sword; it pierces the soul and mind of the spiritual DNA of God; He knows the intents of the heart. No man is hidden from His sight; all are naked to Him and must give accounts of themselves to Him. Knowing our great High Priest Jesus, hold fast to your belief. Our High Priest sympathizes with our weaknesses and temptation and failures yet we are without sin but eternal life.

God loved the predestined when they were mere specks of God's Spirit. God is stuck with you, puppy.

✖ DANIEL 9:19–23 ✖

Daniel was praying and confessing his sins and the sins of the Israel of God and begging the Lord God of the holy mountain/temple in Jerusalem. Gabriel told Daniel, "God commanded me to tell you that you are greatly loved. I was sent to you to understand the vision: God's plan to come for the elect."

✖ DANIEL 9:25 ✖

After the ten weeks or seventy years in Babylon came the journey to Jerusalem to restore and rebuild the streets and the walls for seven weeks, forty-nine years, in troublesome times. After that came the sixty-two weeks, 434 years, to the sixty-ninth week when the Lord God through Paul declared the gospel preached around the world. That began the falling away, the Rapture with the adoption and the redemption of the elect.

❧ DANIEL 9:27 ❧

In August 63, God confirmed the covenant and sealed the elect remnant of 144,000 for one week of seven years, but after three years, on September 2, 66 (see *The New Complete Works of Josephus: The Jewish War*, book 2, chapter 17, section 2, lines 409–10), when Jesus, in the name of the temple governor Eleazar, brought an end to the daily temple sacrifice and offerings to the Roman god Caesar. Then thirty days later came October 2, 66, and on the Roman battle flags of Cestius Gallus, the Roman governor of Syria at Jerusalem. On the flags were the images of the Roman god Caesar, the abominations of the promised desolation pointing to the coming destruction of the desolate temple and Jerusalem as determined by God poured out on dead in the religions of Judaism because of their unbelief as determined August 2, 70, at Pella with the marriage of the elect 144,000 bride of Christ with the Lamb of God.

Daniel 5–7 contains the prophecies of the of the last seven years of the apocalypse to end the old covenant age.

CHAPTER 7

Daniel 12 offers stepping-stones and presents one more big-picture prophecy of the latter days, the last four years the days of vengeance the apocalypse referenced in *The Jewish War*, books 3–6.

❧ ISAIAH 66:4 ❧

God chose the dead's delusions and brought on the elects' fear of Him in the latter days because when God called, the dead were veiled and could not hear to fear God. The predestined dead could not hear, and they did evil by crucifying their Messiah.

❧ DANIEL 12 ❧

Jesus came on the clouds of wrath in that last seven years to kill over three million Jews marked 666 with death because of their unbelief and for having crucified their Savior.

❧ REVELATION 1:17–19 ❧

When John saw Jesus, he fell at Jesus's feet as dead, "but with His right hand on me, Jesus said, 'Do not be afraid. I am the First and the Last. I am Jesus, who lives and was dead as you can see, I am alive eternally. I have the keys to Hades and of Death. John, write the visions as you see them take place after this in this prophecy.'"

❧ REVELATION 6:12–17 ❧

John saw Jesus open the sixth seal, the prophecy of a great earthquake when the Romans surrounded Jerusalem, which began the last four years of the days of vengeance of the last seven years of hell on earth when the sun became black as a sackcloth of hair and the moon became like blood. The stars of heaven—Jews marked with death—fell to the earth as if they were figs on a fig tree late in the season that dropped its overripe figs when the mighty wind of God shook them. The sky as a scroll rolled up, and every mountain—old Jerusalem—was moved out of its place. On earth, the dead kings, the great and rich men, mighty men and commanders, and every slave and free man hid in caves and under the rocks pleading to the mountains and rocks, "Fall and hide us from the face of God, who sits on the throne, and the wrath of the Lamb! The promised day of God's wrath has come; but who can stand against God?"

❧ DANIEL 9:27 ❧

Then thirty days later, on 2 October AD 66, came the promised earthquake at the walls of Jerusalem when the Roman governor Gallus arrived to put down the rebellion. But after five days, he abruptly left Jerusalem and retreated nearer the coast to Antipatris though harassed by seditious Jews, criminals, and the rebellious, who killed five thousand Romans. That began the last four years of the apocalypse.

The time of trouble began in August 63, but the elect were sealed (Revelation 7:1–4) to life eternal in Jesus while the dead were cut off from Jesus by God and awarded the promised curses of Deuteronomy 28:15–68. Neither the living elect remnant nor the Jews marked with death could know this was the moment to begin the time of the end.

Revelation 6:1–11 depicts Jesus coming on the clouds of wrath for seven years, but that time was slightly modified by Revelation 6:12–17 but not privy to the dead. However, the prophecy of Daniel 9:27 pointed to September 2, 66, when Jesus took away the daily temple sacrifices to Caesar. However, a few Jews had the knowledge of Daniel 9:27 and shockingly provided the suspected rumors or fake news of the coming horrors promised though as the elect of God, they did know the moment/time was August AD 63.

⊱ LUKE 21:20–22 ⊰

"When the elect see Jerusalem surrounded by the Twelfth Roman Legion, know that these things (parable code for temple buildings destroyed) have come to pass. You elect in Judea flee to Pella in the mountains, and those in Jerusalem, depart. You in Judea do not enter Jerusalem."

The next four years are the days of vengeance that fulfill all prophecies.

⊱ DANIEL 12:1–3 ⊰

From August 63, the Archangel Michael and the name of Jesus began coming on the clouds of wrath. Jesus was the great prince over the sons of the people with the seven years of trouble as never seen since the nation of Israel began.

Jesus commanded, "Daniel, shut up the words and seal the scroll until August 63 to begin the apocalypse, for then the disciples will have preached the gospel around the world." Jesus, who was watching over the elect since there was a nation until August, began the apocalypse, and after three years, He began the days of vengeance, the great tribulation, but the elect were adopted and redeemed to life eternal.

⊱ ROMANS 13:11 ⊰

Do you know the time is high to awake out of your sleep? Our salvation is nearer (August 63) than what we first believed.

⊱ MARK 12:29–31 ⊰

Jesus responded, "The first of all the Commandments is to love the Lord your God with all your heart, with all your soul, all your mind, and all your strength (Deuteronomy 6:4–5). The second is to love your neighbor as yourself (Leviticus 18:19). There are no other Commandments greater than these."

All else is by men of the BS churchy narratives set to acquire a tithe-based income, the wages of sin. The gods of the religions and the hired-hand, blue-fly scholars and theologians with their God-given delusions dwell in their seminary minds with the four-Pinocchio narratives of deceptions and extortions always in their fleshy pursuit of their precious profit, St. Mammon and little sister Greed, in lifestyles that GGTBMF. They infect seminary minds of guacamole with maggot eggs that every four years hatch maggots—more priests and pastors trained to pursue a tithe-based income from their congregations.

August 63 began the half hour of silence of Revelation 8:1 that began hell on earth in Israel instigated by the Beast of Rome and the images of Nero and his evil.

✺ DANIEL 12:5–7 ✺

Daniel saw two in white linen over the river and asked, "How long before the time of the end?" He heard Jesus in white above the river holding up both hands to heaven swearing by God who lives forever saying it was for a time, times, and half a time.

✺ DANIEL 12:8–10 ✺

Daniel asked the Lord what would be the end of these things—the temple. Jesus replied, "Go, Daniel, for the words are sealed up until August 63 to begin the last seven years beginning with the three years of silence of Revelation 8:1." October 2, 66, began the last four years of the days of vengeance.

✺ DANIEL 12:11 ✺

The destruction of the people marked with death came about by their being trapped in the prison of Jerusalem. God's plan was to destroy

Jerusalem at the hands of the coming Roman general Titus along with those marked 666.

❧ DANIEL 12:12 ❧

Blessed (happy) are the elect who lived 1,335 days. God changed to thirty days and four years to August 2, 70, and after the forty-five days of Daniel 12:11–13 came the 1,515 days ending September 15, 70. "At the redemption, you, Daniel, will be called from out of Hades to your eternal inheritance at the end of the days with the elect while the goats will be sent to the lake of fire."

CHAPTER 8

This chapter covers Jesus's works and words from when He was baptized until He ascended to heaven.

MATTHEW 10:23

Jesus said, "When they persecute you in this city, flee to another for I tell you now you will not have gone through all the cities of Israel before the Son of Man comes on the clouds of wrath to kill more than three million Jews marked with death because of their unbelief."

Jesus's ministry will confirm every truth and reveal only the things God wants the elect to know through the parable code. The Word of God is not wasted on the predestined dead.

JOHN 1:29

John the Baptist saw Jesus coming toward him and said, "See! The Lamb of God who takes away sins of the elect called from out of the world!"

The parable code speaks about the heart, soul, and spirit, which contain God's DNA. All earthly beings are the spiritual image of God. The elect called by God to Jesus are the flesh-and-blood images of Jesus Christ.

The kidney, the liver, and the heart are body parts that rot after death. In scripture, the spirit is spoken of as the heart, soul, mind, and spirit of

God. His elect will have life with Him for eternity while the predestined dead, those of Satan, will be in the lake of fire forever.

✢ MATTHEW 12:33–37 ✢

Jesus said, "The good tree bears good fruit and the bad tree bad fruit; the tree is known by its fruit. How can you being evil speak good things? From out of the heart, the mouth speaks. A good person's heart contains treasure, but the heart of the evil person contains evil things. You will give an account at your earthly demise for every stupidity you spoke and be justified or condemned."

✢ MATTHEW 21:33–46 ✢

A parable: a landowner planted a vineyard with a hedge around a winepress and built in a tower. He leased the winepress to those to manage the vineyard while the owner was away in the country. At the vintage time God sent his servants (Prophets) to the managers of the vineyard to collect His share of the fruit. The managers stoned the servant prophets, killing one. The owner (God) again sent more prophets, but the managers of the vinedressers beat and killed the servants (John the Baptist and Stephen). At last … in the latter days (God) sent his son (Jesus) to the managers (those marked with death in the religions of Judaism), God saying, 'surely they are expecting (The Messiah) my son (Jesus the anointed One) from August 30.' When the Managers of the winepress (the temple high priests) saw the son (Jesus) they conspired, 'This is the heir (of the kingdom of God on earth of the temple of God in Jerusalem). Come, said the High Priest Caiaphas, let us kill Him (Jesus) and seize His (kingdom) and His inheritance.' The (Jews marked 666 with death in the Religions of Judaism) took Him (the Son Jesus) and threw the Son, of the owner, out (the kingdom of heaven on earth crucified Jesus outside the city (at Golgotha) Jesus then asked the elders and chief priest, "When (God) the owner of the vineyard comes, what will (God) do to those managers of the winepress?" The elders and chief priests replied, "The King will destroy those wicked men and lease his vineyard (the kingdom of God) to others, to the elect vinedressers (the elect Ecclesia of God) who will render to him (God) their fruit in the season." Jesus then asked the High Priests and the elders of the Religions of Judaism marked 666 with death. "Have you Chief Priests never read in the Scriptures: 'The Rock which the high priests and temple builders (crucified) rejected has become the chief (Rock) cornerstone (Psalm 118:22–23). This was the Lord's doing and marvelous in our eyes.'

I, Jesus, tell you High Priests and elders now, the kingdom of God, the temple in Jerusalem, will be completely destroyed and taken from you High Priest and given to the elect 144,000 Ecclesia as the flesh and blood images of Jesus Christ, the temples of God, the holiest of all, the 144,000 elect remnant gathered by God to Pella as the kingdom of God the Bride of Christ bearing the fruits; the Ecclesia of God. Whoever falls on this Rock Jesus … they will be broken and on whomever the Rock Jesus falls when He comes in wrath, the Rock Jesus will grind to dust because of their unbelief." Then it dawned on the Chief Priests, elders, scribes, and Pharisees having heard this parable, they knew perceiving that Jesus was speaking of them specifically. When the chief priests and elders wanted to grab Jesus; they also feared the multitudes because the multitude knew Jesus was a prophet.

❧ EPHESIANS 1:1–6 ❧

Paul preached the gospel to the elect Jews to be faithful in Christ Jesus. "Grace to you elect Jews, and peace from God our Father and the Lord Jesus Christ. Blessed be the God and Father of our Lord Jesus Christ, who has caused us elect Jews to hear and believe and have every spiritual blessing in heaven on earth in Jesus Christ. God had chosen us elect in Jesus at the foundation of the world that we elect be holy and without blame in Jesus in love; the chosen elect of God in the last time of the last forty years. God has predestined us elect to adoption in Jesus Christ to the purpose of God's will."

❧ JOHN 1:1–3 ❧

The Word, Jesus, was in the beginning. God made all creation through Jesus, and without Jesus Christ, nothing was made. In Jesus Christ was life, and the life of Jesus Christ on earth was the Light of men, the elect.

The Light was Jesus Christ shining in the darkness of Babylon, and the dead could not comprehend Jesus.

❧ JOHN 1:6–10 ❧

John the Baptist was sent to bear witness to Jesus, the promised Light of the latter days spoken of by Moses, to the elect. Jesus was in the world, but the dead cannot know Him.

❧ JOHN 1:11–13 ❧

Jesus came to the elect, but most, being Jews, were marked with death and denied the knowledge of Jesus.

❧ JOHN 1:14–15 ❧

The Word, Jesus, indwelled the elect. John the Baptist cried out, "This is He of whom I speak. He who comes after me is God, because the Lord God was from the beginning long before me."

❧ JOHN 1:16–20 ❧

The anointing of Jesus began the latter days of this last time at the fullness of the dispensation when God called and reconciled the dead in Adam with His grace and faith. The law was given through Moses, but grace and truth came only through Jesus Christ. No one has seen God but Jesus, who is inseparable from Him. When the Jews marked with death sent priests and Levites from Jerusalem to ask John, "Who are you?" John said, "I am not the Christ." John could not know he was the promised Elijah. He could not know what he could not know.

The gods of the dead from the time of the most holy Roman Catholic oppression to further their god of Gain bamboozled all the barbarians to distract them from their pagan god of the winter solstice with the birth of Christ, now known as the happy holidays.

❧ JOHN 2:1–6 ❧

At Cana, Mary told Jesus, "They have no wine."

Jesus replied, "Mother, what has this to do with Me? My hour has not yet come." Mary said to the servants, "Whatever He tells you to do, do it."

There were six stone water pots of twenty or thirty gallons each. Jesus was caught up to speed by the Word from God. Jesus said to the servants, "Fill the pots with water." When filled to the brim, Jesus told a servant, "Draw some and take it to the master of the feast." They did, and when the master of the feast tasted the water that was then a fine, glitzy California Pinot Noir, he told the bridegroom, "Every man at the beginning of the wedding sets out the good wine, and when the guests have drank, the master then sets out the inferior vintage. Holy cow! You've saved the best for last!"

This miracle was Jesus's first; His glory seemed obvious to His believing disciples. Jesus in Capernaum with His mother and her other sons—James, Joseph, Judas, and Simon—and His sisters and the disciples moved the next day.

❧ JOHN 2:13–14 ❧

Passover was near. Jesus found traders who had bribed the high priests so they could sell their animals for sacrifices at steep prices and money changers offering temple money at exorbitant rates for secular money. Jesus made a whip of cords and drove the money changers out of the temple along with their sheep and oxen; He overturned the money changers' tables. Jesus said to those who sold doves, "Take these away! Do not make My Father's house a house of merchandise!" His disciples remembered that it was written, "Zeal for Your house has eaten Me up" (Psalm 69:9).

The Jews marked with death demanded, "What sign do You show to us since You do these things?" Jesus answered, "Destroy (crucify) this temple (Jesus), and it will be raised on the third day." The Jews replied, "It has taken forty-six years to build this temple and You will raise it up in three days?"

❧ HEBREWS 7:16–21 ❧

This speaks of the death of Jesus on the cross (the reformation) when the elect died with Christ and His resurrection, at which the elect were raised from their graves and appeared to many brethren. The man-made temples, the Levitical priesthood, and the temple services, ordinances, Commandments, sacrifices, and tithing became passé.

✣ JOHN 2:21–25 ✣

Of course, Jesus was speaking of His body as the temple of God and the elect, who were indwelled by the Holy Spirit at Pentecost. Jesus had risen from the dead; His disciples remembered what He had said. They believed the scripture and the Word, Jesus. He was in Jerusalem for Passover, and many believed in His name when they saw the signs (miracles) Jesus did. Jesus did not obligate Himself to the dead multitudes because he knew the vagaries of man.

Today's heaven on earth is the elect called by God from out of the dead of the world, the religions of men.

✣ JOHN 3:1–10 ✣

A Pharisee named Nicodemus, a temple ruler of the Jews, came to Jesus at night asking, "Rabbi, we know that You are a teacher from God, for none can do these miracles You do, unless God is with You."

Jesus replied, "Truly, I tell you, in this last time, unless one is called by God from out of the Jews marked with death in the religions of Judaism, he cannot be of the kingdom of God. Unless you are born (again) of water (indwelled with the Holy Spirit), you cannot be of the kingdom of God."

Nicodemus asked, "How can a man be born when he is old? Can he enter a second time into his mother's womb to be born again?"

Jesus replied, "I tell you now, in this the latter days unless one is born of water and indwelled with the Holy Spirit, he cannot be of the kingdom of God. That which is born of the flesh is flesh, but those called by God are the newly born elect. Do not marvel that I say, 'You must be born again.' The wind (Holy Spirit) blows; you hear the sound (of the Holy Spirit), but you know not from where it comes from and goes. Everyone called by God is born by the Holy Spirit."

Nicodemus asked, "How can this be?"

Jesus asked, "Are you Nicodemus; the teacher of Israel and you a priest do not know the calling of the foreordained, the predestined of God?"

Does your pastor preach predestination or the seminary blatherings about free will who cannot believe the gospel?

❦ JOHN 3:11–36 ❧

"Surely, I tell you, Nicodemus, that we speak of what we know and testify to what we have seen, but you do not believe our gospel. I tell you earthly things, and you do not believe; how will you believe when I tell you heavenly things?"

No one had ascended to heaven, but Jesus came down from the third heaven. Moses lifted the serpent in the wilderness to save those bitten by poisonous snakes; even so, the Son of Man must be lifted up (crucified) to save those who believe Jesus was the Messiah. Whoever believes in Jesus will have eternal life.

God gave His only begotten Son that the elect would believe in Jesus and have eternal life. God did not send Jesus into the world to condemn it but to call the elect from out of the dead of the world to life eternal. He who believes in Jesus is not condemned, but he who does not believe is already condemned because he is (predestined) born of Adam and veiled by God and cannot believe in Jesus. This is the condemnation made by evil men who are denied by God the Light—Jesus.

Jesus and His disciples came to the land of Judea, and Jesus remained with them where they were baptizing. John also was baptizing in Aenon near Salim because there was plenty of water there. A dispute began between John's disciples and the Jews about purification. They asked John, "Rabbi, Jesus who was with you beyond the Jordan, whom you have testified; is baptizing all who come!" John replied, "A man can receive nothing unless it has been given to him by God. You yourselves bear witness that I am not the Christ, but I was sent before Him. Jesus, the Bridegroom, has His bride, the elect, and He said, 'My joy is fulfilled.' Jesus must increase, but I must decrease. Jesus is above all, but the dead of the world speak of earthly things (tithes). What He has seen and heard, He testifies to, but the dead cannot receive His testimony."

The elect received Jesus's testimony and believe God is true. Jesus speaks the Word of God because God does not give the Holy Spirit by measure. It is all or nothing. The elect are the brothers and sisters of Jesus with the same Spirit of the Father. The Father loves the Son and has given all things to Jesus. He whom God causes to believe in the Son has eternal life, and he who does not believe in the Son does not have life but death because from their unbelief comes the promised wrath of God.

❧ JOHN 4:20–24 ❧

Jesus having come to Samaria saw a woman at the well who said, "Our fathers worshipped on this mountain, and you Jews say that Jerusalem is the only place to worship." Jesus said, "Woman, believe Me, the hour (of the destruction of the temple) is coming when you will neither on this mountain nor in Jerusalem or at any temple services worship the Father. You worship what you cannot know. We know what we worship. The way of salvation is of the Jews called by God. The elect will worship the Father in spirit and truth, for the Father in this last time is reconciling the foreordained to worship Him. God of the Holy Spirit causes the elect to awaken and worship God in spirit and truth."

❧ JOHN 4:25–26 ❧

The woman said, "At the Messiah's coming, we will know the way of all things."

Jesus replied, "I who speak to you am the Messiah, the Anointed One of God."

❧ JOHN 5:36–47 ❧

I have a greater witness than John; for the works which the Father has given Me to finish—the very works that I do—bear witness of Me that the Father has sent Me. the Father who sent Me has testified of Me. You have neither heard His voice nor seen His form. You do not have His "Word" abiding in you, because whom He sent, Him (Jesus) you (the dead) do not believe. You search the Scriptures for in them you think you have eternal life, but only those called by God testify of Me. You who are not willing to come to Me are dead. I do not receive honor from men. I know you, who do not have in you the love of God. I have come in My Father's name and you cannot receive Me because you are dead, if another comes in his own name, him, you will receive (all the dead popes, priests, and pastors). The dead are deluded by God to receive only dead men. How can you believe, mere men who are honored by other men and yet cannot receive happiness from God? Do not think that I accuse you to the Father; Moses accuses you Jews marked with death and it is Moses who you claim to trust. If you believed Moses, you would believe Me for in Deuteronomy 31:29, Moses spoke of the latter days about Me, thus if you do not believe Moses' how will you believe My words?

The only testament of God is found in the New Testament, the last Word. All Old Testament doctrine must agree with the New Testament. Being deluded by God, the dead continue in the word of Old Testament.

❧ ROMANS 13:1–8 ❧

The elect of God is subject to the Law of the Land for that authority is from God and all authorities are appointed by God. Thus, whoever authorities resists the ordinance of God, and whoever resist are bringing judgment on themselves. The rulers are not a terror to good works, but to evil. Do you want to be unafraid of the authority? Do what is good, (in forgiveness, peace, and love) and you will be praised by God, for presidents, kings, and tyrants over the land are God's minister to you for good. If you do evil, be afraid; for the presidents, kings, and tyrants do not bear the sword in vain; for he is God's minister, an avenger with wrath on all who practices evil. Be subject to the rulers of the land not only because of wrath but by the Indwelled Holy Spirit of God who through the conscience excuses or accuses with the bludgeoning or chastisement to get the elects' attention: for example to cause you to pay taxes for the Rulers are God's ministers who continually pursue that very thing. Render to all their due: taxes are required, customs to whom customs are required, fear to whom fear, honor to whom honor. Owe no one anything except to love one another, for he who loves another has fulfilled the law.

The borders of the United States were designated by God, and the law of the land is to secure the border; that security is not to be violated by the stupidity of the religious based on the usual seminary narrative blabber.

We elect are God's workmanship created in Christ Jesus to do the good works that God had prepared at the foundation of the world that we elect will walk in the works of God that Jesus Christ does through us.

✤ 2 CORINTHIANS 3:14–17 ✤

Until this day, the veil remains in the reading of the Old Testament, but the veil is taken away in Christ. To this day, when Moses is read, the veil remains on their heart. Though when the elect are called by God to Jesus, the veil has been taken away.

The New Testament commands no one to be killed because one is designated a heretic. God has denied to all to kill any man with one exception—His secular laws of Romans 13:1–7 over the presidents, kings, or tyrants commands his army to kill as prescribed by the holy leader under God. Those in war who kill outside the law may be haunted by God for many years with PTSD.

Read Hebrews 7:14–20. If you are of God, He may cause you to understand what has been bastardized by the gods of the religions.

✤ LUKE 3:1 ✤

In the fifteenth year of the reign of Tiberius Caesar, Jesus was baptized. He was crucified by the Jews marked with death. The religions of man are in the business of intruding themselves between you and your Communion with Jesus.

✤ MATTHEW 3:1–11 ✤

John the Baptist preached, "Repent, for the kingdom of heaven is near!" He was spoken of by Isaiah: the voice of one (John the Baptist) crying in the wilderness: "Prepare the way of the Lord; make His paths straight" (Isaiah 40:3). John was clothed in a camel's hair garment with a leather belt; he ate locusts and wild honey. Judeans went to John at the Jordan River and repented their sins as John baptized them. John saw the Pharisees and Sadducees marked with death and ranted, "Brood of vipers! Who warned you (marked with death) to flee from the coming wrath of God to kill more than three million of you Jews marked with death? Bear fruit worthy of repentance. Don't say and think, 'We have Abraham as our father.' God can raise up these stones as children of Abraham."

The ax (sword) in August 63 cut the root of every barren fig tree marked (Jews marked with death) with death.

John said, "I baptize you with water unto repentance, but He who follows after me is mightier, and His sandals I am not worthy to carry." God's judgment is the power to know the heart, mind, and soul of man. God's winnowing fan is judgment; He will thoroughly clean out the temple (commonly known as the threshing floor) and gather his elect.

❧ LUKE 3:21–23 ❧

When Jesus was baptized, heaven opened. The Holy Spirit descended as a dove on Jesus with the voice from heaven saying, "You are My beloved Son; in You, I am well pleased."

God's judgment is perfect. At one's earthly demise in the old covenant, they waited in Hades for the Messiah to redeem them from hell to life eternal. Following was the final judgment of all marked with death.

❧ LUKE 4:1–15 ❧

Jesus was led by the Spirit into the wilderness, where God sent Satan to tempt Jesus. Jesus had fasted forty days and nights and was hungry. Satan said, "If You are the Son of God, command these stones to become bread." Jesus replied, "It is written, 'Man shall not live by bread alone, but by every "Word" that proceeds from the mouth of God'" (Deuteronomy 8:3). Satan took Jesus on the mountain showing Jesus the kingdoms of the world and said, "If You worship me, all this world will be yours." Jesus said, "Satan! It is written, 'You Satan shall worship the Lord your God and Him, only you must serve'" (Deuteronomy 6:3).

Satan brought Jesus to the pinnacle of the temple in Jerusalem and said, "If You are the Son of God, throw Yourself down from here. It is written, 'He shall give His angels charge over you, to keep you, and in their hands, they shall bear you up lest you hurt your foot against a stone'" (Psalm 91:11–12). Jesus answered, "It has been said, 'You shall not tempt the Lord your God.'" Satan departed, and Jesus returned in power of the Spirit to Galilee, where the news of Jesus went throughout the region. Jesus taught in their synagogues and was glorified by all.

The gods of religions cannot deceive the elect of God. God does not impute sin to the elect predestined of God; the elect have no choice but to walk in God's way.

Solomon's folly was incredible. God engaged with him twice, but he continued with his six hundred wives and six hundred concubines and murdered his children by throwing them into the fires of the many idols and gods. What was the fate of such a fool, or was he redeemed because of his repentance? What repentance? The dead in that old covenant age were those God rejected at the foundation of the world.

❧ Genesis 1:27 ☙

God created man in His spiritual image. The elect spirits were loved by God at the foundation of the world; they were the elect to be called in the latter days and from out of Hades to eternal life in Jesus. There never was death of the spirit; the death we have always known is the body's decay. What does a spirit look like? How can a man or woman in an earthly form be the image of God? As in the past, in this new covenant age, all spirits are the images of God; they are His elect and they have God's DNA.

❧ Revelation 20:14 ☙

The dead were thrown into the lake of fire and brimstone with Nero and the false prophet. John saw the dead standing before God in Hades. The barns full of the big books were opened, and the dead were judged according to their works. The sea gave up the dead, and those in Hades were delivered to the final judgment according to their works.

Death and Hades were destroyed in the lake of fire along with those predestined to death at their second demise forever. Death and Hades cannot exist in this new covenant age. Anyone not found in the Book of Life was thrown into the lake of fire.

Hades, not Purgatory, was where the dead waited for the Messiah to come. The final judgment cannot now exist because in this new covenant age, all have been judged from the foundation of the world to eternal life or the lake of fire.

PROVERBS 14:24

The crown is the abundance of the wise, but folly is the foolishness of fools.

HEBREWS 4:7

God said, "Today, if you will hear His voice, do not harden your hearts" (Psalm 95:7–8). Jesus spoke to the dead in the synagogues of Satan; because of their unbelief, they could not know of their being dead just as the gods of the religions of today cannot know.

LUKE 4:16–19

Jesus went to the synagogue and stood to read from Isaiah 61:1: "The Holy Spirit of the Lord is with Me because God alone anointed Me, Jesus, to preach to the poor the gospel. God has sent me to heal the brokenhearted, proclaim liberty to the captives, perform miracles that recovered the sight of the blind, and set man at liberty."

The eyes of the Jews marked with death were fixed on Jesus.

LUKE 4:21–26

Jesus said, "Today, this scripture is fulfilled in your hearing." The dead of the synagogue of Satan witnessed Jesus and marveled at His gracious words. They asked, "Is this not Joseph's son?" Jesus replied, "You will surely mention this proverb to Me, 'Physician, heal yourself!'" The Jews replied, "Whatever we have heard done by you, Jesus, in Capernaum, we command you, Jesus, to do here with us as you did in your country Galilee."

Jesus replied, "Truly, no prophet is accepted in his own country as today I am ignored in Nazareth. Truly, there were many widows in Israel in the days of Elijah, when the heavens were shut for three years and six months without rain and with a great famine in the land. Elijah was not sent to Israel but to the widow Zarephath in Sidon. Lepers plagued Israel in the time of Elisha, and God cleansed no one of Israel except the Syrian General Naaman."

Those God deluded were denied the gospel truths. The Jews in the synagogue were very angry at this fool threatening them. Perhaps many knew about the promised seven years of wrath to come, but there as yet was no specific sign. Surely, some of the dead were familiar with Daniel 9:27. The Jews of the synagogue whose god was Satan tried to kill Jesus because they knew the following two verses and the implications of Isaiah 61:2 though not read: "the days of vengeance," and "to comfort all who mourn." Jesus declared that the verses were fulfilled, and some of those marked with death knew that Jesus was threatening them according to Daniel 7, 9, and 12, as well as Isaiah 61:2.

❧ LUKE 4:28–30 ☙

When those in the synagogue of Satan were reminded about Zarephath and the Syrian General Naaman, they were filled with rage. They took Jesus out of the city to the brow of the hill intending to push Jesus over the cliff. Jesus passed them going away.

Israel lived and died by their actions always, but their judgment awaited the temple destruction.

❧ LUKE 4:31–44 ☙

Jesus was teaching in Capernaum. The people were astonished at Jesus's compelling words. In the synagogue was a man with the spirit of a demon, which cried out, "Is Jesus of Nazareth coming to destroy us? I know who You are—the Holy One of God!" Jesus rebuked the spirit: "Be quiet and come out of the man!" The demon left the man. The people asked, "What is this? Jesus has the power to command unclean demons?" News of His miracles spread to all.

Jesus went to Simon's Peter's house; his mother had a high fever and asked Jesus to help. He rebuked the fever, and it left her. She arose to serve them. Later in the day, Jesus laid hands on the sick, and all were healed.

Early in the day, Jesus went to a deserted place, but the people came trying to keep Jesus from leaving. He said, "I must preach the kingdom of God in all the cities. For this I was sent in this last thirty-three years to preach the coming kingdom of God." He continued preaching in synagogues all over Galilee.

Jesus said, "Believe in God, believe in Me. My Father's house has many rooms. If not, I would tell you. I am going to make a place for you where you can come at the redemption of the dead along with the living elect at the rapture. Where I go, you elect know, and you elect know the way."

Thomas asked, "Lord, we do not know where You are going. How can we know the way?"

Jesus said, "Because you know I am the way, the truth, and the life. No one comes to the Father except through Me. If you know Me, you know My Father, and from now on, you know Him because you, Thomas, have seen Him."

Philip asked, "Lord, show us the Father."

Jesus replied, "Philip, I have been with you a very long time and you do not know Me? He who has seen Me, the Christ, has seen the Father; so how can you ask, 'Show us the Father'? Believe; I am in the Father and the Father is in Me. The Word that I speak to you, I speak not in My power but in the power of the Father, who dwells in Me and wills that I do His works. Believe that I am in the Father and the Father is in Me, or believe Me for the works I do in you. He who believes in Me and the work I do knows that it is God who does God's works through Me and that the great works that I do are the works of My Father that I do through you. Whatever you elect ask in My name, I will do so that the Father will be glorified in the Son. If you elect ask anything in My name, that I will do.

"If you love Me, you elect have no choice but to keep My Commandments. I pray the Father will give you elect another helper (the Holy Spirit) to dwell in You forever. The world cannot receive the Holy Spirit of truth because the world neither sees Him nor can know Him, but you elect know Him because the Holy Spirit dwells in you. I will not leave you as orphans; I will come to you. A while longer, the world (Jews) marked with death will see Me no more, but you elect will see Me because I live in you and you also live in Me.

"In that day of seven years of the coming apocalypse, you will know I'm in My Father and you elect are in Me and I am in you. He who keeps My Commandments loves Me, and he who loves Me is loved by My Father. I love him and make Myself most obvious in the elect."

Judas (not Iscariot) asked, "Lord, how is it that You will manifest Yourself to us and not to the world?"

Jesus replied, "If anyone loves Me, he will keep My word and My Father will love him, and through the Holy Spirit, he has no choice; we make our home in him. He who does not love Me does not keep My Word, and the Word you hear is not Mine but of the Father, who sent Me. While with you, I have spoken these things. The Holy Spirit is in the elect. He will guide you in all things and cause you to know all I have told you. Peace I leave with you elect and not the worldly. Do not let your heart be troubled or afraid. I am going away, but I am coming back to indwell as the Holy Spirit in you because you love Me and you rejoice because I am going to the Father, who is greater than Me.

"Satan is nothing to Me. At My crucifixion, I will no longer talk with you, but I will be with you always even in that last hour of the apocalypse The world cannot know that I am of the Father and that the Father has given Me the gospel to preach."

❧ JOHN 15:1–27 ☙

"I am the true vine, and My Father is the vinedresser. Those who do not bear fruit He takes away, but every vine that bears fruit, He prunes that the elect will bear more fruit. You have been cleansed by the Word I have spoken to you. I abide in you and you in Me. The branch cannot bear fruit unless it abides in the vine; neither can you unless you abide in Me.

"I am the vine of you elect branches. The elect abide in Me, and I in those who bear much fruit. Without Me, you can do nothing. Those God does not call to me cannot abide in Me; that branch withers and is burned. If God causes you to abide in Me, My Word abides in you. What you desire will be done for you.

"In your work, My Father is glorified that you bear much fruit as My disciples. As My Father loved Me, I have loved you. Keep My Commandments, abide in My love just as I have kept My Father's commands, and abide in His love. I have spoken those things to you that My joy remains in you and your joy be full. My commandment is that you love one another as I have loved you. There is no greater love than to lay down one's life for friends. You are My friends if you follow My commands.

"No longer are you servants, for servants do not know what their master does, but I have called you My friends. All that I have heard from My Father I have made known to you. You did not choose Me, but God chose you and appointed you that you will go and bear fruit and your fruit remains and that whatever you ask the Father in My name, He gives to you.

"I command you that you love one another. If the world hates you, know that the world hated Me before hating you. If you are of the world, naturally, the world would love you. Yet because you are not of the world, God has called you from out of the world, so now the world hates you. If the elect keep My word, the elect will keep yours also. What they do to you because of My name is because they cannot know God, who sent Me.

"If I had not preached to them, they would have no sin, but now, they have no excuse for their sins. He who hates Me hates My Father. The Word has been fulfilled: 'They hated Me without a cause' (Psalm 69:4). But at the Day of Pentecost, the Father will send you the Holy Spirit, and He will testify of Me. You will bear witness because you elect have been with Me from the foundation of the world."

❧ JOHN 9:26–29 ☙

The Pharisees asked the man who could now see, "What did Jesus do to you to open your eyes?" He who could then see replied, "I told you already, and you do not listen. Why do you want to hear that again? Do you want to become one of Jesus's disciples?" They reviled him, "You are His disciple, but we are Moses's disciples. We know God spoke to Moses, but we do not know where Jesus is from."

The man replied, "Why, this is a marvelous thing. You do not know where He is from, yet He opened my eyes! God does not hear sinners, only those who do His will. Since the world began, no one has heard of anyone opening the eyes of the blind. If this Man Jesus was not from God, Jesus could do nothing." The Pharisees asked, "You were completely born in sin, but now you are teaching us?" They threw him out of the synagogue of Satan.

Jesus knew the extortionists had thrown the man out; when Jesus found him, Jesus asked, "Do you believe in the Son of God?" He asked, "Who is He, Lord, that I may believe in God?" Jesus said, "You have both seen God; it is God who is talking with you."

While seated on a mountain before multitude and His disciples, Jesus spoke teaching them.

"Blessed (happy) are the poor elect in spirit of the kingdom of heaven.

Blessed (happy) are the elect who mourn; they are comforted.

Blessed (happy) are the elect meek as children who inherit salvation.

Blessed (happy) are the elect who hunger and thirst for righteousness.

Blessed (happy) are the elect who are forgiven.

Blessed (happy) are the elect pure in heart who have seen God.

Blessed (happy) are the elect peacemakers always the sons of God.

Blessed (happy) are the righteous elect who are persecuted for righteous witnesses of Jesus they are the kingdom of heaven.

Blessed (happy) are the elect who are reviled and persecuted as a witness for My name sake, against the false witnesses against Me.

Rejoice and be exceedingly (happy) for you persecuted elect and prophets great is your heavenly reward.

You elect only are the salt of the earth; but the dead without salt have no promised flavor, so how shall the dead be seasoned? The dead as salt are good for nothing but to be thrown out, trampled underfoot by men, and burned. You elect are the light of the world. A city sitting on a hill cannot be hidden. A lamp lit is not put under a bed but on a lampstand giving light to all in the kingdom of God. Let your light shine that others copy your works that glorify your Father in heaven. Please do not think that I came to destroy the Law of Moses or the prophets. I came only to fulfill the Law of Moses ending the old covenant age."

Jesus in every way did fulfill and then annul the Law of Moses (see Hebrews 7:16–20), but the prophecies of Daniel 7, 9, and 12 were yet to be completely fulfilled.

A doer of the Law of God may be an oblivious Gentile who has never heard of God. All the elect are called by God from out of the world of the dead.

✦ MATTHEW 5:18–20 ✦

"Till the old heaven (the temple) and the old earth (the old covenant people marked with death), not one jot or tittle of the Law of Moses will by any means pass until all the Law of Moses is fulfilled. Whoever breaks one of the least of these Commandments such as those who judge, gossip, or are self-serving fools shall be called least in the kingdom of heaven on earth, but whoever follows the law and lives by the law is a doer of the law and is called great in the kingdom of God. Unless your righteousness exceeds the self-serving popes, high priests, pastors, scribes, and Pharisees marked with death, you will by no means enter the kingdom of heaven."

❧ MATTHEW 5:21–30 ❧

"You have heard that it was said in old covenant age, 'You shall not murder' (Deuteronomy 5:17), and whoever murders should expect judgment. I tell you now that whoever is even angry with his brother without a cause is in danger of judgment. Whoever says to his brother, 'You fool!' is in danger of hellfire. If you bring a gift to the altar and there at the altar God causes you to remember that your brother is angry with you, leave your gift there at the altar (before you pray), reconcile with your brother, and then come and offer your gift at the altar as a repentant.

"God wants you to quickly find an agreement with an adversary in case God causes your adversary to deliver you up to a judge and God causes the judge to hand you over to the officers and you are thrown in prison. Truly, you will by no means at the hand of God get out of prison until you have paid the last penny.

"You have heard that it was said to those of old, 'You shall not commit adultery' (Deuteronomy 5:18). Whoever looks at a woman with lust for her has already committed adultery with her in his heart. If your right eye causes you to sin, pluck it out for it is more profitable to be with one eye than to be sent to the lake of fire. If your right hand causes you to sin, cut it off, for it is more profitable than your body sent to the lake of fire."

Clinton said, "I did not have sexual relations with that woman." That depends on what "is" means in the mind of a brilliant, likable ravisher of women. Many cultures promoted an unmarried but betrothed couple to live intimately until the marriage, but they could not have sexual intercourse; the standard "is" is sexual intercourse to have child.

The other is spoken alternately by the great political mind—no sexual intercourse—but sexual pleasure to assure the correct spousal marriage but to have no children until the husband and wife are able to support them.

There are many ways for spouses to sexually pleasure each other without actual intercourse.

⊱ 1 CORINTHIANS 7:2–5 ⊰

Paul said, "Because of sexual immorality, a man must have a wife, and the woman a husband. The husband should render to his wife all affection due her, and she to her husband. She does not have authority over her own body, but is of her husband, and the husband does not have authority over his own body, but she has over her husband's body. Do not deprive one another."

⊱ MATTHEW 5:31–37 ⊰

"It has been said, 'Whoever divorces his wife, let him give her a certificate of divorce.' I am telling you now that whoever divorces his wife for any reason except sexual immorality causes her to commit adultery, and whoever marries that divorced woman also commits adultery. Again, you shall not swear falsely but shall perform your oaths to the Lord. I say do not swear at all neither by heaven, for it is God's throne, nor by the earth, for earth is God's footstool, nor by Jerusalem, for it is the city of our great God. You shall not swear by your head because you cannot or make one hair white or black. Let your yes be yes and your no be no. A no that does not mean no is evil.

"You have heard, 'An eye for an eye and a tooth for a tooth' (Deuteronomy 19:21). Do not resist an evil person. If someone slaps you on your right cheek, turn the other cheek so God can slap you again."

⊱ MATTHEW 5:40–42 ⊰

"Whoever God causes to sue you, God takes away your tunic and causes you to let him have your cloak also. God causes you to go one mile, but God also causes you to go with him two miles. Give to him who asks; God causes him to ask and to borrow from you. God does not want you to turn away from him or God.

"You have heard as it was told, 'You shall love your neighbor and hate your enemy' (Leviticus 9:18). Jesus said, 'Love your enemies.' God wants you to bless those who curse you. Do what is good to the dead of the fake news CNN—Corny Newsy Nonsense—that persecute you as they do daily their Savior Jesus Christ and His images Abraham Lincoln, Ronald Reagan, Donald Trump, Rush Limbaugh, Sean Hannity, Tammy Bruce, Tucker Carlson, Laura Ingram, Candace Owen, Lou Dobbs, and so many more who serve God as doers in their daily works without whining or sniveling.

"You elect are the sons of your Father. God makes the sun rise on the evil and on the good. He distributes rain on the just and the unjust. If you love only those who love you, what reward have you from God? Do not even tax collectors conduct their extortions in a loving way? You must be perfect just as your Father in heaven is perfect.

"God causes those to take you to the law, and their courts condemn you because you GGTBMF when you do evil against your neighbor. God does cause the man of God to know that it is He who causes someone to slap his face. God tests you and punishes you because you displease Him. Pray for those God causes to spitefully use you. You must be deserving of being spitefully used or God would not cause others to spitefully use you."

Perfection is a self-serving delusion at the hand of God. God perfects only through Jesus, who humbles the fool when called by God to life eternal in Jesus.

Jesus's death on the cross has made the elect perfect in the most Holy Communion with Him; there is no other way. The elect are found in Tibet, Russia, and Iran and even in Christian and Catholic communities. God is impartial. Even Christians in the holiest churches are not automatically God's elect. Christians have a long history of murdering other Christians they defined as heretics.

God had Jesus die on the cross for all of the elects' sins. The world is sin; it has no choice being dead in Adam.

⊱ HEBREWS 12:1–13 ⊰

We elect are surrounded by the inequities of the worldly, who want to ensnare us in their folly, so let us run with endurance while on earth as in a race even if we cannot all be US Navy SEALs. Let us look to Jesus, our author and finisher of our faith. The elect are called to be joyous before Jesus, who endured the cross specifically for our forgiveness, peace, and love, which is salvation.

Despising any shame that keeps us away from the right hand of God, Jesus endured the hatred of the religions high priests so that your elect soul would not become weary and discouraged. You elect have not come to bloodshed resisting and striving against sin. Many have forgotten the exhortation that speaks to you as to sons: "My sons, do not despise the chastening of the Lord or be discouraged when you elect are rebuked by Him; those whom the Lord loves He chastens and scourges every son whom He calls" (Proverbs 3:11–12).

If God does not chasten you, you are not a son of God. God causes all human fathers who correct their sons, and God causes the elect to pay their earthly fathers respect. We elect are in subjection to the Father through the Holy Spirit and doomed to life eternal.

Our earthly fathers for a time chastened us as it seemed appropriate to them, but in Jesus, we elect partake of His holiness. Chastening is not joyful, but it yields peaceable fruit of God's righteousness to the elect. So strengthen your hang-down hands and get on your feeble knees so that what is lazy may not turn to dishonor but eternal healing.

For every person young or old, man or woman, consider reading *Make Your Bed* by retired US Navy SEAL Admiral William H. Raven.

❧ LUKE 5:1–11 ❧

Jesus stood at the Lake of Gennesaret, and the multitude pressed about Him to hear the Word of God. Jesus saw two boats at the lake, but the fishermen had gone to clean the nets. He got into one of the boats belonging to Simon and asked Simon to push the boat a little way from the lake. Then Jesus sat in the boat teaching the crowd.

When Jesus finished speaking to the multitude, He said, "Hey Peter, launch out into the deep and let down your nets for a catch."

Simon said, "Master, we have fished all night catching nothing, but I will do as You ask."

They let down the nets, and they netted so many fish that their nets began to break. Simon called to others to help them. The boats were filled and were about to sink. Simon Peter, realizing what had happened fell at Jesus's feet saying, "Depart from me; for I am a sinful man, O Lord!" Jesus said, "Don't be afraid from now on. Come—you will be fishers of men." When the boats landed, they left their parents to follow Jesus.

Please keep in mind that in the time of Jesus Christ, the blind were not blind from birth; they were made blind, denied, or darkened. Today, the foreordained are denied or darkened with the calamities of men who suffer due to their folly. Forgive the dead; it is not their fault—they were predestined to eternal damnation.

❧ Luke 5:27–32 ❧

Jesus saw a tax collector named Matthew/Levi sitting at the tax office, and Jesus said, "Follow Me." Matthew left all and followed Jesus. He gave Jesus a great feast in his house, where there were many tax collectors and other sinners. The self-righteous scribes and Pharisees, gossips, and busybodies complained to Jesus, "Why do You eat and drink with sinner tax collectors (and do not forget our greedy and lazy members of Congress)?"

Jesus said, "Those who are well have no need of a physician, but those who are sick need help. I came to call the sinners to repentance."

Do not pray in public but in private, in a secret place. The substitute for prayer in public is one's daily walk in God that Jesus does in you. Doing your daily work well every day is worshipping God. If you pray for others, do not advertise that. If you blab to others for whom you pray, that blabber is your earthly reward. Those for whom you pray are between you and God. When you elect to feel good telling others that you pray for them, that is gaudy, not godly. God puts on display the dead in the world who persecute you as your cross to carry.

❧ Giving Is Love ❧

Charity is work in the way one expects to receive a tax break for one's donation or a pat on the head by a supreme leader or a memorial plaque on the wall for one's donation; this includes donations to charities, religions, sick and sad dog charities, and other con artist charity corporations thanks to St. Augustine.

❧ Matthew 6:1–5 ❧

When you do a charitable deed, do not sound or trumpet your works as do the hypocrites in the synagogues and churches of the self-serving stupid in the streets. The pompous derive their glory from the approval of men. When you do a charitable deed, do not let your left hand (good friend) know what your right hand (other good friend) has done so your charitable deed will be between you and God.

The dead praying in public is proof that religions are not of God. Even Mahatma Gandhi knew there were no religions of God.

The dead are born dead in this new covenant age; some live their lives in hell on earth till they acquire room temperature, which confirms their eternal damnation. Most of the very rich, extremely wealthy, and the ever-present criminal world were used by God to be the source of the elects' daily testing, blessings, comfort, happiness, subsistence, and crosses.

❧ JEREMIAH 31:31–34 ❧

The day will come in the latter days. Said the Lord, "I will make a new covenant with the elect called from out of Israel. This new covenant will not be as the old covenant I made with their fathers when I took them by the hand from out of Egypt. They broke that old covenant even though I loved them as a husband loves his wife. In this new covenant, I will put my laws in the elects' minds and write it on their hearts. I will be their God, and the elect will be my people. They will not need to teach their neighbors or family. I will forgive the elects' wickedness and never remember their sins."

❧ EZEKIEL 36:23 ❧

"In the latter days, when I am hallowed in you, sanctifying My great name, which has been profaned in Israel and by the Gentiles, the elect will know I am the Lord."

❧ EZEKIEL 36:25–27 ❧

"In the latter days spoken by Moses (Deuteronomy 31:29), I called my elect out of and cleansed them of their religion's filthiness and altar idols. I gave them new hearts through the Holy Spirit. In the latter days, I will send the Holy Spirit to them so they will walk in My two laws, and they will joyfully keep My Commandments."

In this new covenant age, we have no choice. Our calling by God is our guarantee and our anointing as was the anointing of Jesus by God at His baptism. In this new covenant age, God's calling the elect is their guarantee of eternal life. Remember because of God's predestination, God is stuck with you, puppy ... heaven or hell bent.

❧ MATTHEW 6:10–24 ❧

"Our Father in heaven, hallowed be your name. Your kingdom has come on earth as you promised it as it was in the third heaven. Give us this day our daily bread, and forgive us our trespasses as we forgive those who trespass against us. Lead us elect not into temptation, but deliver us elect from evil."

"When you forgive men their trespasses against you, your Father in heaven will forgive you. If you do not, your Father will not forgive you.

"When you fast, do not do as the hypocrites do with a sad face. The hypocrite disfigures his face to appear as fasting for earthly attention. The fool's earthly reward is death. If you fast, comb your hair, wash your face, and do not appear to be fasting because the Father will see you as a hypocrite. Do not lay away treasures on earth where moths and rust can destroy them and thieves can steal them. Set your treasures in heaven. Your heart will be where your treasure is.

"The lamp of the body is the eye, and if your eye is good, your whole body will be the true Light of Jesus If your eye is bad, your whole body will be debased with darkness.

"No one can serve two masters—God and Mammon. Being loyal to one, he will despise the other."

❧ MATTHEW 6:25–34 ❧

"Don't worry about your life or what you will eat or drink or what you will wear. Is not life in Jesus more than food and clothing? The birds do not sow, reap, or gather food, but God feeds them, and aren't you God's elect of more value than a birdy? Your worrying can not add anything to your place in life. Why worry about clothing? See how the lilies of the field grow—they do not toil, but Solomon' glory was not as beautiful as a lily. If

God so clothes the grass of the field, which is today and gone tomorrow, will God not much more fully clothe you of little faith, puppy?

"Don't worry about what you will eat, drink, or wear as the dead do. Your heavenly Father knows what you elect need. Seek the kingdom of God and His righteousness, which is faith, and all those things will come to you. Do not worry about tomorrow because tomorrow has tomorrow to worry about. Today is sufficient with its own trouble."

❧ PSALM 118:8–9 ❧

Trusting in the Lord is better than putting confidence in man. Trusting in the Lord is better than putting confidence in a prince.

❧ ISAIAH 54:13 ❧

The elect were called by God from out of the Jews marked with death. Judging is not seeing a man rob another man at gunpoint; judging is knowing that the thief is going to hell unless he repents.

❧ MATTHEW 7:1–3 ❧

Judge not that you not also be judged. You will be judged by God by the very standard you use to judge others.

There are over ninety thousand charities, each with billions of dollars and billions added each year, but the average yearly giving by charities is less than 10 percent (USGovernment.com). Let God be the cause of your giving. Consider local charities where you may also serve and see how your gifts are used. If God wants you to give to a charity, you will.

Charities spend millions of dollars on commercials showing pictures of mistreated dogs. They beg for money from simpleminded donors many of whom have no negative thoughts about infanticide.

❧ REVELATION 3:20 ❧

Jesus said, "I stand at the door and knock. When the elect hears, he opens the door and I dine with him."

God loved all from the foundation of the world. He had an angel compile a printout of the spirits He loved and those who GGTBMF.

❧ MATTHEW 7:6–14 ❧

"Do not preach God to the dogs. Let Him cause the swine to become pearls in case the swine tear you in pieces as is done among the dead. Seek God and you will find. Knock and God will open the door to you. Who would give his son a stone when he asks for bread? If you know how to give good gifts to your children, how much more will your Father give good things to you? Enter by the narrow gate, for the wide gate leads to the world. The narrow gate is the difficult way to Jesus, but it leads to eternal life."

A very recent pope said that only one in fifty priests (count pastors) are pedophiles, but what religion of God can be of pedophiles? There are no religions of God, only men in the pursuit of WPF (see bishopaccountability.org).

Romans 13 speaks of secular rulers God uses to make laws and war. Please do not expect to see Hitler, Stalin, Pol Pot, or the warring popes in heaven. For a price, the gaudy popes provided their congregations with costly annulments and dispensations and the assurance of heaven. Forgive the popes and the duped; they cannot know what God does not give them to know.

Jesus crucified nullified the elects' sin and reconciled them to God. The high priests could see the miracles, but being denied knowledge or veiled, they were concerned only with their income declining if Jesus were to remain alive. They feared Jesus would be believed and the bribe they paid to Rome to assure their wealth and power and fame would be wasted.

Jesus had to be killed (think President Trump) because with Jesus (Trump) alive, they could see only disaster coming from Rome (Washington, DC). Sorry, you dead congressional puppies! Cheer up—God may still call you to Jesus with eternal life.

❧ MATTHEW 25:41 ❧

Jesus said, "I never knew your lawlessness being dead; depart from Me!"

≽ MATTHEW 7:15–29 ≼

At the final judgment, Jesus will send the goats (congressmen) to the lake of fire. The wise build their houses on the Rock, Jesus, and their houses do not fall. Those who build their houses on sand (religions) will lose them to the floods and wind.

When Jesus ended these sayings, the people were astonished. Jesus taught them to seek only the One having authority—not the scribes, priests, pastors, Pharisees, or pedophile popes seeking tithes.

≽ MATTHEW 8:23–34 ≼

Jesus got in the disciples' boat and slept even during a storm. His fearful disciples awakened Jesus crying, "Lord, save us! We are perishing!" He asked, "Why are you fearful, you of little faith?" Jesus rebuked the winds. The disciples marveled and asked, "Who can this be? Even the wind and the sea obey Him!"

In the country of Gergesenes were two exceedingly fierce and demon-possessed men. The demons cried, "What have we to do with You, Jesus, Son of God? Have You, Jesus, come to torment us in this last hour?" Nearby was a herd of pigs. The demons begged Jesus, "If You cast us out, send us into the piggy herd." Jesus commanded, "Go." They came out and went into the herd of pigs, and the piggy herd ran down the hill into the Sea of Galilee. The piggy herders fled into the city and told of the whole event including what had happened to the demon-possessed men. The whole city came to see Jesus begging Him to leave their region.

The demons knew who Jesus was and what He had come to do. The disciples' knowledge of Jesus was not consistent with prophecies because they were human.

God speaks to whom He speaks specifically. The elect always get a saving message from God. The apparent ignorance of the apostles and the Pharisees were for the benefit of the reader, whom God endows with the sense of understanding and even those without understanding. The Jews marked with death were killed by God in the last seven years of the latter days. Before the temple was burned, the high priests used the temple powers to acquire WPF just as God today provided their most holy delusion to thirty-six thousand five Protestant religions.

❧ ISAIAH 6:9–10 ❧

God said, "Go, Isaiah, and tell this people, 'Keep on hearing, but do not understand; keep on seeing, but do not perceive.' Make the heart of these dead people dull and their ears heavy and shut their eyes lest they see with their eyes and hear with their ears and understand with their heart and return to God to be healed."

❧ ISAIAH 6:11–13 ❧

Isaiah asked, "Lord, how long?" God answered, "Until the cities of Israel are laid waste without inhabitants, the houses without a man, and Israel utterly desolate." The Lord removed men far away in the diaspora and made the land destitute. Yet remaining was the marriage of the Lamb of God with the elect, the bride of Christ, after the temple was destroyed.

Truth comes only to those God causes to know His Word through the Holy Spirit. No religions can be of God. The saving message of God is not academic; it is meant for the elect predestined by God from the foundation of the world.

❧ MATTHEW 26:51–52 ❧

Peter cut off the ear of Malchus, the high priest's servant. Jesus said to Peter, "Put your sword away. All who take to the sword will die by the sword."

Peter came off very human but very slow, but the Bible was not just about Jesus and Peter but how through the will of God, Jesus did God's work and how we do exactly what God wants us to do and to know through the Holy Spirit.

It was God who through the delusions provided the BS that destroyed the temple. Roman Catholicism continues as a knockoff of the three dead religions of Judaism that crucified Jesus and is now under new management of the trumped up Judeo/Christian abomination of the dead and greedy religions.

The religions of Judaism rejected Jesus's Good News, crucified Jesus, and persecuted His followers. His followers were defamed and called followers of that Jesus freak, the Messiah of peace and love.

God knows how to turn events. Those who do not seek God with all their heart, soul, and mind but rely on mere men to guide them carnally will be damned. God has created the gaudy world with its distractions to keep the dead from knowing Jesus.

❧ MARK 2:5–17 ❧

When Jesus saw their faith, He said to the paralytic, "Son, your sins are forgiven." The scribes reasoned in their hearts, *Why does He speak blasphemies? Who can forgive sins but God?* Jesus told them, "Why do you reason such things in your hearts? Which is easier, to say to the paralytic, 'Your sins are forgiven' or 'Arise, take up your bed and walk'? You know that the Son of Man has power on earth to forgive sins." He told the paralytic, "Arise, take up your bed and go home." Immediately, the paralytic arose, gathered his bed, and left the house while all who saw were amazed and glorified God saying, "Never before have I seen anything like this!"

To understand the religions of Judaism and it most obvious folly, read pages 1–109 of Edersheim's *The Life and Time of Jesus, the Messiah*. And consider the destructive ways of education and religion by reading Victor David Hanson's and John Heath's *Who Killed Homer?* They speak about universities rejecting classical education and becoming corrupt. Education in America produces ignorance as proven by our members of Congress purchased by wealthy donors and foreign powers.

❧ MATTHEW 24:36 ❧

Jesus said, "Of that last day, no one knows, not the angels, not the Son, but My Father only."

Jesus in a sense forgave sin by healing all those called by God from out of the religions of Judaism who had been once marked with death. The temple Jews could see only disaster by the Romans taking away their source of wealth power and fame if Jesus lived.

Jesus's sin was that He was perceived a competitor by the three Jewish religions that had a different religious message in the fashion of all religions.

As good Christians pass from one church blathering to another, they rarely discern any doctrinal difference; they like one pastor more than another perhaps due to style or the appearance of likeability, truthfulness, and honesty, but never of God.

The pious charlatan showmen who deceive the multitudes by removing a person's cancer in public are dead. Jesus did not do miracles in public for fame but on God's orders. Jesus always asked the healed to not publicize His works. Keep in mind that all their maladies were awarded by God initially because they were sinners deserving of the horrors of their maladies while they lived and walked and talked in lifestyles that GGTBMF.

<h2>⊱ MATTHEW 9:18–19 ⊰</h2>

A temple ruler came worshipping Jesus and saying, "My daughter has just died. Come that she may live. Lay your hand on her." Jesus and the disciples followed. On the way, a woman who had had no control over her bleeding for twelve years came up behind Jesus and touched His robe thinking, *If I can touch His garment, I can be made well.* Jesus turned to her and said, "Be of good cheer, daughter (of God); your faith has made you well." She was made well that hour.

When Jesus arrived at the temple ruler's house, He saw flute players and a wailing crowd. He said, "Make room for the girl. She is not dead but sleeping." Those gathered mumbled, snickered, and ridiculed Jesus. While the crowd waited outside, Jesus went in and took the girl by the hand, and the girl rose. The report of this went to all the land.

Jesus departed, and two blind men followed Him crying, "Son of David, have mercy on us!" Jesus asked, "Do you believe I am able to do this?" They replied, "Yes, Lord." He touched their eyes, saying, "Your faith lets you see." Their eyes opened, and Jesus sternly said, "Tell no one." They departed and spread the news about Jesus.

The people brought to Jesus a mute, demon-possessed man. When the demon was cast out, the mute spoke, and the multitude said, "This has never been seen in Israel!"

The stuff you hear on radio, TV, or the internet is a prime source from your lying spirits—false prophets and fake news. Relax. God uses the stupid through these modern devices to test the elect. The gossiping, self-serving jackasses are experts in the art of judging, but they do not know and cannot know that they are revealing their predestined demise in the lake of fire. Forgive the Pharisees and the rest of the worldly dead;

they cannot know what they cannot know. The stupid, evil liars are doing God's work to poison the minds of the stupid and the dead. The elect will be called by God to Jesus somewhere down life's road. Until God's calling, all being the born dead remain dead in Adam's free will until the elect are called to life eternal.

⊱ MATTHEW 9:35–38 ⊰

Jesus went among the cities and villages teaching in the synagogues and preaching the gospel of the kingdom of heaven on earth to come. He healed every sickness and disease among the people. Jesus was moved to compassion for the multitudes because they were of the world; they were weary and scattered sheep with no shepherd. Jesus said to the disciples, "The harvest truly is plentiful, but the laborers are few. Pray to the Lord to send laborers to His harvest."

⊱ MATTHEW 10:1–7 ⊰

Jesus called the twelve disciples to have power over the unclean spirits and heal all kinds of sickness and disease. The names of the twelve apostles were Simon called Peter and his brother Andrew and the sons of Zebedee, James and his brother John, Philip, Bartholomew, Thomas, and Matthew the tax collector, James of Alphaeus, and Lebbaeus of Thaddaeus, and the Canaanite Simon and (the dead) Judas of Iscariot, who betrayed Jesus.

Jesus sent out the twelve apostles saying, "Do not go into the way of the Gentiles, and do not enter a city of the Samaritans. Go only to the lost sheep of Israel among the Jews marked with death."

They preached that the kingdom of heaven on earth was at hand.

⊱ TITUS 1:10–16 ⊰

The disobedient are idle gossips and deceivers, those of the circumcision whose mouths ought to be shut but are extorting whole households for gain. A prophet of their own ilk said, "Cretans are always liars; evil beasts, and lazy gluttons. Rebuke them sharply that they may be yet called by God to faith and not continue in Jewish myths and commandments of men far from the truth. Perceiving purity in all things but deluded by God, they are unbelieving and pure in nothing in their mind and conscience. The dead profess to know God, but their own works deny God in every way. They are abominable, disobedient, and dead."

❧ MATTHEW 10:8–23 ❧

Jesus began, "As freely as you disciples have received, give. Heal the sick, cleanse the lepers, raise the dead, and cast out the demons. Take no gold or silver or copper with you. Do not pack a bag for your journey. Take with you only one tunic, a pair of sandals, or a staff, for the doer in this the latter days is worthy of his food. Whatever city or town you enter, find the worthy and stay until you have preached the gospel. When you go to a household, greet it. If the household is worthy, leave your peace upon it. If not, keep your peace. Those who will not receive you or hear your words, leave their houses and shake the dust from your feet."

It was more tolerable for the land of Sodom and Gomorrah than Jerusalem in the coming seven years of the apocalypse.

"I send you out as sheep among the Jews marked with death in the religions of Judaism. I caution you disciples to be wise as serpents and harmless as doves. Beware—the tribulations during the coming thousand years by those Jews marked with death are those who will deliver you to councils and scourge you elect in their synagogues of Satan. You disciples will be brought before governors, kings, and Gentiles for My sake as a testimony to them.

"When they deliver you, do not worry about how or what to speak. In that hour, you will be given what to speak through the Holy Spirit. It will not be you elect who speak but the Holy Spirit. Brother will deliver up brother to death, and children will rise up against their parents causing them to be put to death. You will be hated for My name's sake, but he who God causes to endure will be saved. Flee the Jews marked with death when they persecute you. I tell you now, you disciples will not have gone through all the cities of Israel before the Son of Man comes on the clouds of wrath August AD 63 for seven years of the apocalypse."

The disciples served as unpaid servants of God. That was their earthly task.

❧ LUKE 17:7–10 ❧

"Which of you having a servant plowing or tending sheep would tell him, 'Come at once; sit down and eat'? Instead, he would say, 'Prepare something and serve my supper till I have eaten and drunk; then you can eat and drink.' When you unpaid disciples have done what God has commanded, remind yourself that you are unpaid servants who have done only what God has commanded of you."

❧ LUKE 22:26–27 ❧

"He who is the greatest among you (the pope), let him be as the least in the kingdom and serve as Jesus who served as the least in the kingdom. Who is greater, he who sits at the table or he who serves? I am among you elect as the One who serves."

The elect are not above the pope, nor is the servant pope above men; all the elect are equal in God. They are flesh-and-blood images of His Son. God has deluded the popes, the greatest murderers of all time of Jesus Christ.

Those born in Adam's free will are dead without choice. The gods and the copycats of the dead gods cannot know or be of God without God's calling.

Congregations cannot know or need to know that their leaders are of the gaudy world of gain and lust. Fellowship does not require tithing.

❧ MATTHEW 10:24–25 ❧

A disciple is not above his teacher, nor is a servant above his master. The elect are equal as the brothers of Jesus under their Father. Only religious leaders live by the rules of the dead. It is enough for a disciple that he is like his teacher and a servant like his master all being equal with Jesus Christ under God.

Do not fear them who condemn you elect. All that is hidden in the religions marked with death will be revealed. Whatever you hear in the dark, speak clearly in the light, and what you hear in your ear, preach on the housetops. Do not fear those who kill the body; the dead in the religions of Judaism cannot kill you for the soul is eternal. Fear God, who destroys the souls of the dead with damnation at their second demise.

❧ MATTHEW 10:27–38 ❧

Two sparrows are sold for a copper coin. Unless God wills it, the sparrows cannot fall to the ground. The hairs of your head are numbered. Do not fear; you are more valuable than many sparrows.

Whoever are My elect, I will confess before My Father in heaven. Whoever denies Me before men I will deny from My Father. Do not think that I came to bring peace on earth. I did not come to bring peace but a sword. I have come to set a man against his father, a daughter against her mother, and a daughter-in-law against her mother-in-law. A man's enemies will be those of his own household (Micah 7:6). He who loves a father or a mother more than Me is not worthy of Me. He who loves a son or daughter more than Me is not worthy of Me. He who does not take his God-given earthly cross and follow Me is not worthy of Me.

❧ MATTHEW 10:39–42 ❧

He who finds his life in the world will lose his life, and he who loses his life for My sake as a witness to me will have eternal life. He who receives you elect receives Jesus, and the elect who receive Me also receive God. He who receives a prophet in the name of a prophet shall receive a prophet's reward. He who receives a righteous man in the name of a righteous man receives a righteous man's reward. Whoever gives one of these little ones a cup of water in the name of a disciple, truly I say to you, he shall not lose his reward.

The people of God are the product of God's will. Free will is the mark of death; such is the nonsense of the dead religions and religious doctrines that always stray from the Word of God. No religion can be of God that has one in fifty pastors or priests as pedophiles.

❧ MATTHEW 11:2–19 ❧

While John was in prison hearing about the works of Christ, John the Baptist sent two of his disciples to ask Jesus, "Are You the coming One, or do we look for another?" Jesus replied, "Go, tell John the things which you hear and see. The blind see, the lame walk, the lepers are cleansed, the deaf hear, the dead are raised up, and the poor have the gospel preached to them. Blessed is the man who is not offended because of Me."

When John's men departed, Jesus asked the multitudes about John, "What did you expect to see in the wilderness? A whining, sniveling reed fearful of the scribes and Pharisees marked with death? What did you see? A sissy man clothed in soft garments? Remember those in sissy soft clothes are found only in the palaces of kings.

"What did you go see, a prophet? Elijah is the one of whom it was written, 'Behold, I send My messenger before Your face, who will prepare Your way before You' (Malachi 3:1). I tell you among those born of women, there has not risen one greater than John the Baptist, but John is least in the kingdom of heaven on earth. The elect of God are greater because they are the flesh-and-blood images of Jesus, the temples of the kingdom of God to come.

"Since the days of John the Baptist until now, the temple of God in Jerusalem has suffered violence from temple rulers and the violent high priests. The prophecies and the law were before John. If you are willing to understand and believe, John the Baptist is Elijah, who was promised to come. The elect who God has blessed with ears to hear, let him hear. John came neither eating nor drinking but was accused of having a demon."

Jesus ate and drank, and those marked with death in the religions of Judaism said, "'Look! Jesus is a glutton and a winebibber, a friend of tax collectors and prostitutes!'"

⁓ THE SEED DAVID OF JESUS SAGA ⁓

The Old Testament seed of Christ was David, and after a night of pleasing his many wives, David was exhausted and wandered around the rooftop of his palace. He saw the delightful naked body of Bathsheba bathing and thought, *Holy cow!* Poor David, though fully exhausted from his nightly travails, sent the royal palace guard to fetch the lovely naked woman next door. She arrived, and David shut the door, and at some time during David's infraction (rape) of her body, he discovered her name to be Bathsheba. As most impetuous men do, David began to reflect on his passing fancy and wanted to dump Bathsheba.

Very soon, she told David she was pregnant. David was extremely fearful of retribution; he wanted to avoid being discovered, going to court, and perhaps even being stoned to death. But he could not so easily or quickly dump Bathsheba considering she was pregnant with his child. David was in heap big guacamole and wanted to avoid disaster. Easy! He'd brought her husband, Uriah, a Hittite warrior, from the war to the palace, fed him, and overindulged him with an expensive Chardonnay from the House of David. David tried many ways to get him interested in having sex with Bathsheba so he would think the child must have been his.

But Uriah remained a faithful servant to David and would not leave David unattended even to cross the street to have sexual relations with his wife. The David plan failed, and Uriah was sent back to war.

David was perplexed until he came up with a really cool idea—get Uriah killed in battle. David was not operating well, thank God. Without God, what could that fool do? He could not marry Bathsheba, and his pillow hopping with so many wives was getting boring.

David colluded with his right-hand man, General Joab. In the height of the battle, Joab would send Uriah against the enemy and abandon him. The plan worked!

David was visited by the prophet Nathan and made aware of his advance to death, but David was the elect of God, who forgave all that he had done. But the rest of David's life was daily humiliation, atonement, and repentance. David's daily humiliations were constant reminder to David that he had GGTBMF.

The moral of the story is do not judge. Dead or alive, no one can know tomorrow, even a David, and no one can know why God allowed David's stupidity. Mortals cannot know the ways of God, so they should not judge.

David was a precursor of Jesus. If God calls you to Jesus, you are doomed to life eternal in Jesus, but keep in mind that you are not the cause of your salvation. If that were the case, there would be no limit to the number of self-serving jackasses on earth.

❧ MATTHEW 11:20–30 ☙

Jesus rebuked the cities in which His mighty works had not found repentance. He said, "Woe to you, Chorazin and Bethsaida! If those mighty works were done in you as had been done in Tyre and Sidon, they would have repented in sackcloth and ashes. It would be more tolerable for Tyre and Sidon in the last seven years of your judgment than for you,

Corazon and Bethsaida, with Jesus coming of the clouds of wrath to kill over three million of you Jews marked with death.

"You, Capernaum, exalted to heaven, will be brought down to Hades and damnation at the final judgment. If those works were done in Sodom, Sodom would exist today. I thank You, Lord of heaven and earth, that You have hidden these things from those marked with death in the religions of Judaism and revealed these things only to the elect. No one knows the Son except the Father. All you elect who labor with heavy burdens, come to Me; I give you rest. I am gentle and lowly in heart, and you have peace in your souls. My yoke is easy, and my burden is light."

❧ 1 Corinthians 10:16–17 ❧

The cup of blessing we call the ecclesia is communion with the blood of Christ. The bread we break in fellowship is His body. We elect are many in God but one in Jesus, the Bread of Life.

❧ Luke 6:20–26 ❧

Jesus told His disciples, "Blessed (happy) are you elect whose happiness is the kingdom of God. Blessed are you elect who hunger; you are filled. Blessed are you who wept and now laugh. Blessed are you elect when you are hated, excluded, reviled, and thrown down by the dead as witnesses of Jesus. Rejoice in the rapture! Truly, you elects' reward is heaven as in the way of your fathers and the prophets. Woe to those who seek worldly gain; your earthly demise will confirm your damnation in the lake of fire. Woe to you when you speak well of false prophets as your fathers also spoke well of false prophets."

❧ John 6:4–13 ❧

The Passover feast of the Jews was near. Jesus saw the great multitude. He asked Philip, "Where do we buy bread for these to eat?" Jesus was testing him. "Two hundred denarii worth of bread is not enough to feed all these people." Simon Peter's brother volunteered, "A child here has five barley loaves and two fish."

Jesus told the people to sit. There were five thousand men alone. Jesus took the loaves, gave thanks, and distributed it to the disciples to feed the crowd. After they ate, Jesus had the disciples gather the leftovers, which filled twelve baskets.

The elect saw Jesus's miracle, but the dead could not see or perceive it. The dead continued to pursue Jesus for the bread, but God would not give them to know.

❧ JOHN 6:14 ❧

A few who saw the miracle said, "This Jesus is truly the prophet come to the world."

❧ JOHN 6:22–35 ❧

At Capernaum in the morning, crowds gathered on the shore waiting for Jesus. They knew He and His disciples had come because the disciples had gone off in their boat leaving Jesus behind. When they found Jesus, they asked, "Teacher, how did you get here?" Jesus replied to their unbelief, "The truth is, you want to be with Me because I fed you, not because you saw the miracle. You shouldn't be concerned about perishable things such as food. Spend your energy seeking eternal life that I, the Son of Man, can give you and your eternal life will be assured. God the Father has sent Me for that very purpose."

They asked, "What shall we do that we do the works of God?" Jesus said, "Believe in Jesus, the one God has sent." They said, "You must show us a miraculous sign if You want us to believe in You. What will You do for us? Our ancestors ate manna in the wilderness for forty years! The scriptures say, 'Moses gave them bread from heaven to eat.'"

Jesus replied, "I assure you Moses did not give them bread from heaven. My Father did. Now, God offers you marked with death the true Bread from heaven. The true bread of God is Jesus, who comes down daily from heaven and gives life to the elect of God, not to the dead of the world."

"Sir," they begged, "give us that bread every day of our lives." Jesus replied, "I am the Bread of Life. No one whom God calls to me will ever be hungry or thirsty."

There were three redemptions in the latter days. One, the elect died with Jesus at His crucifixion and arose with Jesus at His resurrection. Two, the elect were called by God at the falling away, and the rapture began with the adoption and redemption of the living and the dead in Christ with life eternal for the elect 144,000. Three, after the temple destruction and in the last forty-five days of Daniel 12:11–13 was the redemption of the elect sheep and the damnation of the goats.

❧ JOHN 3:18 ❧

The man who believes in Jesus is not condemned, but the man who does not believe is already condemned because he has not believed in the name of Jesus. The Holy Spirit gives eternal life.

❧ JOHN 6:36–48 ❧

Jesus said, "You haven't believed in Me even though you have seen Me. Those the Father calls to Me I will never reject. I have come from heaven to do the will of God, who sent Me, not My desires, not My wants, and not my will. It is the will of God that I not lose even one of all those God has given Me. I will raise them to eternal life at the redemption. It is My Father's will that all who believe in Me have eternal life."

The people began to murmur in disagreement because Jesus said, "I am the Bread from heaven." The Jews marked with death murmured, "This is Jesus, the son of Joseph. We know his father and mother. How can Jesus say, 'I came down from heaven'?"

Jesus replied, "Don't complain about what I say. No one can come to Me unless the Father sends them to Me. I will raise them at the final judgment. It is written, 'The elect will be taught by God.' Everyone who hears and learns from the Father comes to Me. Only I, who was sent by Him, have seen Him. I assure you, anyone who believes in Me already has eternal life. I am the Bread of Life."

We elect of God actually do feed on every Word of God; it is not our choice. Jesus does the work of God daily through the elect doers who have eternal life.

☙ JOHN 6:49–59 ❧

Jesus said, "Our ancestors ate manna in the wilderness, but all now are in Hades. I am the living Bread of Life that comes down out of heaven daily. All God causes to eat this Bread from heaven will live forever; this Bread is My flesh offered so the elect will live."

The followers began arguing with each other about Jesus's meaning asking, "How can this man give us his flesh to eat?"

At the hand of God, Jesus right before our eyes was separating the believers from the nonbelievers. Most in the multitudes remained worldly, veiled, and dead. Jesus repeated, "I assure you, unless you eat the flesh of the Son of Man and drink His blood, you will not have eternal life. My flesh is the true food, and My blood is the true drink. I live by the power of the living Father, who sent Me. In the same way, those who partake of Me on earth live eternally because of Me. I am the true Bread from heaven."

☙ ROMANS 4:4 ❧

He who does the works in temple or church services is not counted as grace but as debt for GGTBMF, the wages of the dead.

Remember those two laws of God. The rest of the thousands of the faux laws and commandments of men and gods are meant to deceive congregations to gather a tithe-based income. God calls the elect to live in fellowship with each other. The congregations buy fire insurance policies to keep themselves out of hell.

☙ JOHN 6:60–71 ❧

The dead denied Jesus and murmured, "This is a hard asking; who can understand it?" Jesus asked, "Does this offend you? What then if you saw the Son of Man ascend to the third heaven as before? It is the Holy Spirit who gives life, not fleshly works. The words I speaks in you are spirit and life."

Jesus knew from the beginning those who could not believe and who would betray Him. He said, "That is what I meant when I said that people can't come to Me unless the Father calls them to Me." Many of his disciples marked with death in the religions of Judaism turned away deserting Jesus. Jesus turned to the twelve asking, "Are you going to leave too?" Simon Peter replied, "Lord, to whom would we go? You alone have the Word that gives eternal life. We believe You, Jesus, are the Holy One of God." Jesus replied, "I chose the twelve of you, but Judas is a devil."

Jesus was speaking of Judas, son of Simon Iscariot. Choosing the devil, Judas fulfilled the prophecy. The treasures of the worldly are death. The dead were born dead in this new covenant age and will be cast into the lake of fire. God created the dead to be the elects' daily comfort and subsistence; those blessings come from God (see Isaiah 23:17–18).

☙ Luke 6:27 ❧

"I tell you who are happy being blessed to hear, love your enemies, and do well to those who hate you. Be happy with those who curse you, and pray for those who spitefully misuse you. Give to everyone who asks of you. From him who takes away your goods, do not ask for them back. What you want men to do to you, also do to them. If you do good things only to those who do good things to you, what credit is due you? Even the sinner tax collectors are nice to those they extort. If you lend only to those from whom you expect to receive back, what credit is that to you? Even sinners lend to sinners expecting to receive more back.

"Love your enemies, do well, and lend hoping for nothing in return and your reward will be great. You will be sons of the Most High, who is also kind to the unthankful and evil. Be merciful to all as your Father is also merciful. Judge not and you shall not be judged. Condemn not and you shall not be condemned. Forgive and you will be forgiven. Give, and it will be given to you in good measure pressed down, shaken together, and running over."

☙ 2 Corinthians 1:21–22 ❧

God established and anointed the elect in Christ, and the elect were sealed with life eternal.

❧ ROMANS 11:28–30 ❧

The dead were enemies, but God has called the beloved elect for the sake of their fathers from out of the dead. God's calling makes those gifts irrevocable. You elect were once disobedient, but you have obtained eternal life.

❧ LUKE 6:45–49 ❧

A good man from out of his good treasure of his heart brings forth the good, but from out of the flesh of an evil man comes the evil treasure in his heart.

Jesus said, "Why do you call Me 'Lord' and not do the things I say? Whoever comes to Me and hears My Word and does them are the elect called by God. He is like the one who built a house on a great rock foundation that cannot be shaken by floods. The dead could not hear; they built their houses on sand that the rain washed away."

❧ LUKE 7:36–50 ❧

Simon, a Pharisee, asked Jesus to eat with him at his house. Mary Magdalene, a reformed prostitute, knowing that Jesus was at the Pharisee's house, brought an alabaster flask of fragrant and expensive spikenard. She kneeled at Jesus's feet weeping. She washed His feet with her tears and wiped them with her hair. She kissed His feet and anointed him with spikenard. When the Pharisee saw this, he mumbled to himself, "This man, if He were a prophet, would know what manner of woman she is who is touching Him."

Jesus responded, "Simon, a creditor had two debtors. One owed five hundred denarii and the other fifty denarii. When they had nothing with which to repay, the creditor freely forgave them. Tell Me, which of them would love the creditor more?"

Simon answered, "I suppose the one who was forgiven the five hundred denarii."

Jesus said, "You have rightly judged. Do you see this woman? I entered your house; you gave Me no water for My feet, but she has washed My feet with her tears. You gave Me no kiss, but this woman has not ceased to kiss My feet. You did not anoint My head with oil, but this woman has anointed My feet with fragrant oil. I tell you, her sins, which were many, are forgiven, for she loved much. To whom little is forgiven, that little love is also forgiven little. Mary, your sins are forgiven. Your faith has saved you. Go in peace."

The Pharisees mumbled among themselves, "Who is this who forgives sins?"

⪡ MATTHEW 12:1–12 ⪢

Jesus walked through the grain fields on the Sabbath. His disciples were hungry and plucked grain to eat. The Pharisees seeing this said, "Look! Your disciples are working on the Sabbath!"

Jesus asked, "Have you not read what David did when he was hungry? He entered the house of God and ate the showbread, which was not lawful. Haven't you read in the law that on the Sabbath, the priests in the temple profane the Sabbath by working at the temple services on the Sabbath but they are blameless? On earth, there is only One greater than the temple. If you Pharisees knew what 'I desire mercy and not sacrifice' (Hosea 6:6) meant, you would not have judged and condemned the disciples, who are without guilt. The Son of Man is Lord even of the Sabbath."

Jesus departed entering the synagogue. There was a man with a withered hand. The scribes asked Jesus, "Is it lawful to heal on the Sabbath?" Jesus asked, "Who among you who had a sheep stuck in a pit would not retrieve it on the Sabbath? Is a man not of more value than a sheep? It surely is lawful to do what is good on the Sabbath." Jesus told the man, "Stretch out your hand." The man stretched it out, and his hand was restored.

The Pharisees began plotting to kill Jesus. Jesus knew their objective. Jesus, who had healed many, left the area, and the multitude followed. Jesus warned them not to speak of these miracles knowing they fulfilled Isaiah's prophecy: "My Servant whom I have chosen, My Beloved in whom My soul is well pleased! I will put My Spirit upon Jesus and declare justice to the Gentiles, Jews, Muslims, Christians, and Buddhists. Jesus will not quarrel or cry out. A bruised reed, Jesus will not break until He sends forth justice to victory. In Jesus's name, the Gentiles will trust" (Isaiah 42:1–4).

Herod, the tetrarch, heard about Jesus and told his servants, "This is John the Baptist risen from the dead. Those powers are not his work." The adulterer Herod had imprisoned John because of Herodias, his brother Philip's wife with whom Herod was engaged intimately nightly. John had cautioned Herod, "It is not lawful for you to have Herodias, Philip's wife." Herod wanted to put John to death, but he feared the people because they knew John was a prophet.

When Herod celebrated his birthday, Herodias's daughter Salome danced before all pleasing Herod. Herod had promised to give her whatever she desired. Herodias was told by her mother, "Tell him to give you the head of John the Baptist on a platter." The king was sorry, but because of the oath and fearing the reproach of those nearby, commanded John's head be given to her. John' head was brought on a platter.

His disciples buried John. When Jesus heard about this, He departed from the area by boat to a deserted place alone. The multitude heard and followed Jesus on foot from the cities. Jesus was moved with compassion while continuing to heal the sick.

Later, His disciples said, "This place is deserted, and the hour is late. Send them to the village to buy food." Jesus replied, "Do not send them away. Feed them." They said, "We have only five loaves and two fishes." Jesus said, "Bring them to Me." He commanded the people to sit on the grass. Jesus blessed the loaves and gave them to the disciples to distribute. The people ate and were filled. The leftovers filled twelve baskets.

Jesus had the disciples take a boat to the other side before Him while He remained sending the multitude away. Jesus went up the mountain alone at sundown to pray. The boat in the Sea of Galilee was being tossed by waves and high winds. Later at night, Jesus was walking on the sea to them. The disciples saw Jesus walking on the sea; they feared, "It's a ghost!" Jesus said, "Be of good cheer! It is I, Jesus. Do not fear." Peter asked, "Lord, if it is You, command me to come to You on the water." Jesus said, "Come," and Peter got out of the boat. He walked on the water to Jesus but was distracted by the winds. Peter cried out, "Lord, save me!" Jesus caught Peter by the hand and said, "Peter, you of little faith, why did you doubt?" With Jesus in the boat, the winds ceased. All worshipped Jesus, saying, "Truly You are the Son of God."

They landed on the others side of Gennesaret. The people seeing Jesus went through the region and brought the sick to Jesus and begged just to touch His garment to be made well.

God judges us based on how we interact with our neighbors. The man who acts negatively or unlovingly to his neighbor is GGTBMF. The man who loves his neighbor is loved by Jesus.

✝ ROMANS 9:6–13 ✝

The Word of God has taken effect, but not all Israel is the Israel of God. Most are not of God and not because they are the seed of Abraham but, "In Isaac; your seed (Jacob) you are called" (Genesis 21:12). The children of the flesh are not of God, but the children of Isaac are counted as the promised seed. The word of promise: "At this time, I will come and Sarah shall have a son" (Genesis 18:10, 14). Rebecca conceived by our father Isaac. To Rebecca, it was said, "Esau shall serve Jacob" (Genesis 25:23). "God hated Esau, but God loved Jacob" (Malachi 1:2, 3).

✝ ROMANS 9:14–28 ✝

There is no unrighteousness with God, who told Moses, "I will have mercy on whomever I will have mercy, and I will have compassion on whomever I will have compassion" (Exodus 33:19). It is not free will but God's will to show mercy. "For this very purpose, I have raised you up that I may show My power in you and that My name may be declared in all the earth" (Exodus 9:16). You ask me, "Why does He still find fault or resist God's will?" Oh man! Who are you to reject God? Will the fool ask the Lord, who created him, "Why have you made me like this?" Does God the potter create one bowl for honor and another for dishonor? If God wanted to show His wrath and make His power known, He would do so.

Because of his free will, Adam allowed poor Eve to be duped by Satan, who then lived in the polluted heaven on earth while God lived in the third heaven far above the second heaven, the firmament or cosmos seen in the night sky (Genesis 1:6–9; Revelation 21:1). The third heaven, the sea above the cosmos, has not existed since the advent of the flesh-and-blood images of Jesus Christ, heaven on earth.

God uses determined foolishness of some to improve some men. Even though some will copy your foolishness, some fools will think you are cute. God does not waste a moment of our foolishness on this mortal coil; He sends messages near and far, blessings and fear. God does not cause those smarter than Him to fear Him. The atheists are deluded that they are doing God's work so well. Those with the Holy Spirit cause the elect to fear God because the Holy Spirit makes very clear to the elect that God has their necks clutched in His hand. The logic is not that the dead cannot fear God, but what is the point? They cannot know because they are the dead, so why should they know? God does not exist; ask any atheist.

If the elect are killed by another Las Vegas shooter, they are instantly doomed to life eternal with Jesus. If the dead are killed by another Las Vegas shooter, they are instantly doomed to eternal damnation. But even the wounded elect will struggle to understand and joyfully carry their crosses. Man cannot know God's plan. There are no innocent victims; all of the elect were sinners and at God's Word dwelt in stupidity at various times, but God loved them from the foundations of the world, and they will live eternally.

❧ 2 CHRONICLES 18:18–22 ☙

Micaiah said, "Hear the word of the Lord: I saw the Lord sitting on His throne with the host of heaven at His side. The Lord asked, 'Who will persuade King Ahab of Israel to go to Ramoth Gilead and die by a stray arrow?' No one spoke. A spirit came to the Lord saying, 'I, Lying Spirit, will persuade Ahab.' The Lord asked, 'In what way?' The spirit said, 'I will go and lie as a lying spirit in the mouths of his prophets.' The Lord said by lying to Ahab's prophets, 'You will persuade Ahab and prevail. Go do so.'"

The Lord put a lying spirit in the mouths of Ahab's prophets. The Lord declared disaster against Ahab and the dedicated dead.

❧ 1 CORINTHIANS 2:4–8 ☙

Paul said, "My preaching is not with human wisdom but with the power of the Holy Spirit that your faith is not the wisdom of men but the power of God."

We preach wisdom only to the elect, not to those of the old covenant age or the dead temple rulers. We speak the wisdom of God for the elects' glory that God ordained as the predestined at the foundation of the world.

≈ 1 CORINTHIANS 1:19–20 ≈

Paul said, "I will destroy the wisdom of the wise and bring to nothing the understanding of the prudent" (Isaiah 29:14). Where are the wise, the scribes, and the disputers of this age, the wisdom of this world? God's delusion has made them foolish.

The Jews in their unbelief were attracted to the wisdom of the age, and Satan was their god. Today, the wisdom of the age is in the hand of the gods who hire charismatic pastors to give great sermons and exact tithes.

The wisdom of God can never be passed on by extortionist religions. The power of the Holy Spirit daily nudges the elect to eternal life in Jesus.

≈ 2 TIMOTHY 3:2–7 ≈

Some are self-serving men who deny God though they project godliness. They creep into gullible women's houses and seduce them. The dead cannot have the slightest knowledge of God. They are dead until they are called by God to become fools for Christ.

The dead and the elect live by the Word. Every bit of foolishness we do as the elect of God is the Work of God Jesus does through us.

≈ 1 CORINTHIANS 10:18 ≈

Take notice of Israel in their carnal, fleshly pursuit of mammon in temples who share and eat animal sacrifices at the man-made altars of demons.

≈ LUKE 8:9–10 ≈

Jesus's disciples asked, "What does this parable mean?" Jesus replied, "To you elect, the mysteries of the kingdom of God have been given. Those not of God having heard them do not understand them" (Isaiah 6:9).

⊱ MARK 8:37–38 ⊰

What will a man give in exchange for his soul? Whoever is ashamed of Me and My words in this adulterous and sinful last generation of forty years, the Son of Man is ashamed of, and when Jesus comes August 63 on the clouds of wrath for seven years, He will kill the Jews marked with death until the temple is destroyed.

⊱ MATTHEW 15 ⊰

Jesus died on the cross to take away the sins of the elect. The Holy Spirit excuses or accuses the elect to repent, and God hears what the Holy Spirit hears. Spouses who quarrel offend God. Penance is an unlawful extortion used by the dead churchmen to acquire WPF. Penance is not biblical, nor are purgatory and the popes.

⊱ MATTHEW 15:1–20 ⊰

The scribes and Pharisees from Jerusalem came to Jesus, asking, "Why do Your disciples transgress the traditions of the elders? They do not wash their hands when eating bread." Jesus asked, "Why do you also transgress the commandment of God because of your man-made commandments and traditions? God commanded, 'Honor your father and your mother' and 'He who curses a father or mother, let that man be put to death.' You dead Pharisees say, 'To your father or mother, say, "Whatever support money you might have received from me is a gift to God," thus, you hypocrites avoid honoring your father or mother.' You hypocrites nullify the Commandment to honor thy mother and thy father of God making the commandment to no effect by your Pharisee traditions of greed, the mark of death. Hypocrites! Isaiah did prophesy against you, saying, 'Those hypocrites come near to Me with their mouth and with their lips they honor Me, but because their heart is far from Me; they are dead. In vain, all the religions marked with death worship Me, but being dead, they teach narratives and doctrines and traditions and the commandments of men'" (Isaiah 29:13).

Jesus told the multitude, "Hear and understand: it is not what goes into the mouth that defiles a man but what comes out of the mouth." The disciples asked, "Do You know that the Pharisees were offended when they heard You convict them?" Jesus replied, "Every plant My heavenly Father has not foreordained, He has not planted or called or predestined. Those dead plants are to be pulled as weeds and thrown into the lake of fire. Let them be. They are doing God's work; being veiled leaders of the blind, both are appointed to fall into the ditch."

Peter asked, "Explain this parable to us." Jesus asked, "Are you also still without understanding? Do you not yet understand that whatever enters the mouth goes into the stomach and is eliminated bodily? That which proceeds from out of the mouth comes from the heart, and that defiles a man. From the heart proceed evil thoughts, murder, adultery, extortion, fornication, theft, greed, false witness, and blasphemy. These things defile a man, but a silly religious tradition—to eat with unwashed hands—cannot defile a man."

✸ MATTHEW 15:21–28 ✸

A Canaanite woman cried to Jesus asking, "Have mercy on me, O Lord, Son of David! My daughter is demon possessed." Jesus did not answer. His disciples said, "Send her away for she cries out after us." Jesus replied, "I was sent by God only to the lost sheep of Israel." God caused the woman to persist and worship Jesus, pleading, "Lord, help me!" Jesus replied, "It is not good to take the children's bread and throw it to the little dogs." She responded, "Yes, Lord, but even the little dogs eat the crumbs that fall from their masters' tables." Jesus was shaken, replying, "O woman, great is your faith! Let it be to you as you desire." Her daughter was healed that very hour.

Republicans in Congress likewise live by every crumb that falls from their rich Democrat masters' table in Washington. There are crumbs enough to make the Republican crumbs very happy. Forgive the crumb Republicans for they cannot know their state of deadness. The crumb Republicans that luxuriate are God-sent crumbs doing exactly what dead crumbs are supposed to do—test the Republican electorate to separate the crumbs to the judgment of God.

≈ MATTHEW 16:1–12 ≈

The Pharisees and Sadducees came testing Jesus saying, "Show us a sign from heaven." Jesus replied, "Evening has come and you say, 'Red sky at night, sailors' delight; red sky in the morn, sailors be warned.' Hypocrites, the face of heaven you know, but the signs of the times of this, the latter days promised by Moses (Deuteronomy 31:29), has been veiled to you! This evil last generation seeks a sign, but no sign is given to the dead except the sign of Jonah."

When His disciples arrived at the other side of the lake, they had forgotten to take bread. Jesus said, "Take heed and beware of the leaven, the traditions of these dead religions of the Pharisees and the Sadducees." The disciples misunderstood. "But we have no bread," they said. Jesus said, "You of little faith, did you forget the five loaves that fed thousands? Still, you do not understand that I was not speaking of bread but to beware of the leaven (lies of the dead) of the Pharisees and Sadducees and the gods of the religions none of which are of God." Then they understood that Jesus was saying to beware not of the leaven of bread but of man-made doctrines, ordinances, traditions, and commandments of the Pharisees, Sadducees, and the religions of men.

≈ MATTHEW 16:18–19 ≈

Jesus asked the disciples, "Who do men say I am, the Son of Man?" They said, "Some say John the Baptist, some Elijah, and others, even Jeremiah or one of the prophets." Jesus asked, "But who do you say I am?" Simon Peter replied, "You are the Christ, the Messiah, the Anointed One, the Son of the living God." Jesus replied, "Blessed are you, Simon Bar-Jonah, for flesh and blood has not told that to you, but My Father in heaven.

"Not an incorporated brick-and-mortar business church. The predestined elect called by God from out of the dead in the religions of Judaism on you elect; the gates of Hades have no effect. I have given you elect of God the (promised) keys of the kingdom of heaven and whatever you elect bind on earth, God has already bound in heaven, and whatever you elect loosen on earth, God has already loosened in heaven."

Jesus commanded His disciples to tell no one that He was the Messiah. He began to show to His disciples that He must go to Jerusalem and suffer many things (to carry His God-assigned cross) where the chief priests, the elders, scribes, and Pharisees marked with death crucified Jesus. Peter being Peter, took Jesus aside and rebuked Him, saying, "Far be it from You, Lord; this will not happen to You!" Jesus turned from Peter, saying, "Get behind Me, Satan! You are an offense, for you, Peter, are not mindful of the things of God, only the things of men."

Jesus said to the disciples, "If anyone desires to follow Me, let him deny himself and take up His God-assigned cross and follow Me. Whoever desires to save his life in this world will lose it, but whoever loses his life in the testimony of Jesus will find it. What does it profit a man to gain the fleshly carnality of the world with a dead soul? The Son of Man will come in the glory of His Father with His angels.

"Many shall not taste death till they see the Son of Man coming in His kingdom at the destruction of the temple. Everyone who has left houses, brothers, sisters, fathers, mothers, wives, children, or lands for My name's sake shall receive a hundredfold with the inheritance and the abundance of eternal life. Many now first will be last and the last first."

Even God lives by His Word. There are no accidental deaths, overdoses, shootings, cancer, tyrants, or sad presidents; they are because they were foreordained. Perhaps the doomed mind of the atheist is yet trying to convince Satan that God is not great.

The demons and bad angels all knew who Jesus was and what Jesus had come to do. The disciples' knowledge of Jesus and the prophets and what they spoke was not consistent in the latter days. The things said by the early prophets were for our edification; readers see most obviously what the disciples forgot or failed to recognize. Where was your head, Peter?

God speaks to whom He speaks specifically. The living may receive a message from God different from the one that the dead receive. The apparent ignorance of Peter, the apostles, and the Pharisees were for our benefit, whom God chose to enlighten.

❧ MATTHEW 17:1–4 ☙

Jesus took Peter, James, and John to a mountain, where Jesus was transfigured. Jesus's face shone as the sun, and His clothes were white as light. Moses and Elijah appeared with Jesus. Peter asked Jesus, "Lord, why are we with You? If You, Jesus, wish, we can make three tabernacles, one for each one of You."

Peter's epistle follows as a response of that prophetic voice and vision. As Peter said, there can be no private interpretation of scripture. How many doctrines of God are misused by men in the pursuit of gain? Have you ever heard any sermons that were not biblical?

❧ 2 PETER 1:16–21 ❧

We apostles do not follow deceptive traditions and fables. We made known to you elect the power and the coming prophecy of our Lord Jesus Christ on the clouds of wrath. When Jesus was transfigured, He received from God the Father honor and glory: "This is My beloved Son, in whom I am well pleased." We heard the prophetic Word that has been confirmed and that we should heed. No prophecy of scripture is of any private interpretation of scripture to be misused by the gods of the religions.

❧ MATTHEW 17:5–13 ❧

While Peter was speaking, a bright cloud overshadowed them and a voice said, "This is My beloved Son in whom I am well pleased. Hear Him!" The disciples heard the prophecy and fell on their faces. Jesus touched them, saying, "Arise, and do not be afraid." Opening their eyes, they saw Jesus.

While coming down the mountain, Jesus said, "Tell the vision to no one until the Son of Man is risen from the dead." They asked, "Why do the scribes say Elijah must come first?" Jesus replied, "Truly, Elijah has come first to restore all things. Elijah has already come, and those marked with death could not know him. They beheaded John the Baptist, and the Son of Man is about to suffer at their hands." The disciples did not understand that Jesus was speaking not of John the Baptist but of Jesus's coming crucifixion.

A man kneeled before Jesus and said, "Lord, have mercy on my epileptic son suffering badly falling in the fire and the water. I brought him to Your disciples, but they could not help." Jesus responded, "O faithless and perverse generation, how long shall I be with you? How long shall I bear with you? Bring your son here to Me." Jesus rebuked the demon, which left the child.

The disciples asked, "Why could we not cast out the demon?" Jesus relied, "Because of your unbelief. If you have the faith of a mustard seed, you will tell the mountain, 'Move,' and it will move. Nothing is impossible for you. However, in this, the Spirit responds only to prayer and fasting."

Jesus told the disciples, "The Son of Man is about to be betrayed into the hands of the chief priests marked with death. They will kill Jesus, but He will be resurrected." The disciples were exceedingly sorrowful.

At Capernaum, the temple priests who extorted the temple tax asked Peter, "Doesn't your Teacher pay the temple tax?" "Yes," Peter replied and went to Jesus. Jesus knew of Peter's encounter with the temple taxmen and asked, "What do you think, Peter? From whom do the kings of the earth take customs and taxes, from their sons or from strangers?" Peter replied, "From strangers." Jesus quipped, "Then the sons are free. Let us not offend the priestly temple system. Go to the sea and hook a fish; from its mouth take the coins to the taxmen for you and Me."

Neither Jesus nor Peter went to an ATM as do the gods of the religious. In their pursuit of tithes, they are dead at the hand of God. God appoints gods over their congregations to extort them.

The dead of the world cannot fear a God who does not exist. God created the age of reason to trap the brilliant in their science of the touchy-feely, seemingly tasty, hearing, seeing, and smelly material world in which the empirical essentials are the religion of the dominant science. But many things in the world of science defeat the natural senses such as what happened to Madame Curie, who died from radiation poisoning without seeing, touching, tasting, hearing, or smelling uranium.

⋟ MATTHEW 18:1–11 ⋞

The disciples asked Jesus, "Who is greatest in the kingdom of heaven on earth?" Jesus called over a little child with the innocent mind and said, "Truly, I tell you unless you are as little children, you will by no means enter the kingdom of heaven. Whoever humbles himself as this child does is the greatest in the kingdom of heaven. Whoever receives one little child as this in My name receives Me. It would be better for anyone who causes a little one to sin to have a millstone tied around his neck and be thrown into the sea. Offenses must come, but woe to the men of the world to whom the offense comes.

"Do not despise any of these little ones, for I tell you that in heaven, their angels are always near My Father. The Son of Man has come to call the elect from out of those marked with death. Your Father does not want any of these little ones to perish.

"When your brother sins against you, quietly go to him and tell him his fault. If he hears, you have gained your brother. If he deigns not to hear, go with two more that by three he hears witness to every word. If he refuses to acknowledge, tell it to the assembly. Whatever you elect bind or loose on earth, God has already bound or loosed in heaven. Where two or three are gathered in My name, I am there."

Peter asked Jesus, "Lord, how often shall my brother sin against me and I forgive him? Up to seven times?" Jesus replied, "I do not say seven times but up to seventy times seven if he asks to be forgiven."

Do not even eat with the worldly. Emulate God; love them as you would any atheist, agnostic, or Christian of the gods of the religions and their congregations. Don't hate them or wish their demise or kill them as did the good Christians of the Reformation error. Love them as God wants you to treat and love the dead of the world, who are without God. Just love them as God loves them. They still may be called by God to Jesus. Do not judge.

Suppose a man is accused forty years later of a sinful act after which he became a man of God. Remember that if a man is guilty and does remember, he will be forgiven by God, who knows his heart, soul, mind, and spirit. God makes the honest man admit the act, take the consequences, and repent. Jesus took the consequences of all the elect who had sinned past, present, and future. The predestined dead cannot avoid the lake of fire.

❧ MATTHEW 18:23–35 ❧

The kingdom of heaven is as the king who settled his servant's accounts. The first servant owed the master ten thousand talents. He could pay the master if he sold his wife and children and all possessions. The servant fell on his knees begging, "Master, have patience with me. I will pay you." The master was compassionate and forgave his debt.

The dead servant found a fellow debtor who owed him a hundred denarii and demanded, "Pay now what you owe!" The servant fell at his feet begging, "Have patience with me. I will pay you all." The dead servant did not wait; he had his fellow servant imprisoned until the debt was paid.

The horror saddened his fellow servants, and they told the master all that had transpired. The master called the dead servant and cursed him: "You evil servant! I forgave you your debt because you begged. Where was your compassion for your fellow servant?" The very angry master delivered the dead servant to be tortured until he paid all the debt. Our Father will do to you if you do not forgive your brother his trespasses.

❧ MATTHEW 19:1–9 ❧

Jesus went to Judea, and the multitudes followed; Jesus healed them. Then came the Pharisees to test Jesus: "Is it lawful for a man to divorce his wife?" Jesus replied, "Have you not read that God at the beginning made them male and female and for that reason a man shall leave his father and mother and be joined to his wife becoming one flesh? Whom God joined, no man is to separate." They asked, "Why did Moses command allowing a man to divorce the wife?" Jesus said, "Moses permitted divorce because of the hardness of your hearts from the beginning. Whoever divorces his wife except for sexual immorality and marries another commits adultery, and whoever marries the divorced woman commits adultery."

His disciples asked, "If that is the right way, is it better not to marry?" He replied, "All cannot accept this saying, but only those to whom it has been given by God to remain without a spouse. There are eunuchs who were born such, and others were made eunuchs, and others made themselves eunuchs such as Paul for the kingdom of heaven's sake. He who is able to accept it, let him accept it."

Little children were brought to Jesus to put His hands on them to pray, but the disciples rebuked the parents. Jesus said, "Let the little children come to Me. Do not forbid them because these are the kingdom of heaven." He blessed them by laying His hands on them. One asked, "Good Teacher, what good thing shall I do to gain eternal life?" Jesus asked, "Why do you call Me good? No one is good but One, that is, God. Yet if you want to enter life eternal, keep the Commandments."

The rich man asked Jesus, "Which ones?" Jesus replied, "You shall not murder, you shall not commit adultery, you shall not steal, you shall not bear false witness. Honor your father and your mother, and love your neighbor as yourself."

The rich man said, "I have kept all these things from my youth. What am I lacking?" Jesus said, "If you want to be perfect, sell what you have and give to the poor and you will have treasure in heaven and follow Me."

The young man went away sorrowful because he had great worldly possessions. Jesus said to His disciples, "Truly I tell you, it is hard for a rich man of the world to enter the kingdom of heaven. It's easier for a camel to go through the eye of a needle than for a rich man of the world to enter the kingdom of God."

His disciples were astonished; they asked, "Who then can be saved?" Jesus said, "With and by men, that is impossible, but with God, all things are possible." Peter asked, "Jesus, we have left all and followed You. What do we have?"

In this new covenant age, God causes the elect to have innocent hearts and minds of little children, and after their earthly demise, they become the kingdom of heaven.

Evil of the world is a constant siren song to those who cannot be of God, but the Holy Spirit through the conscience either accuses or excuses as necessary to communicate all that is necessary for the elect to fear God.

Paul was the elect of God, but he was denied the knowledge of God until he was called by God. Poor Paul was helpless; one moment, he was marked with death in a worldly religion of Judaism, and the next moment, he became the image of Jesus Christ free of the worldly passions of the religions of Judaism marked with death. Fools suddenly receiving the mind of Christ are rarely as dramatically transformed as was poor Paul on the Damascus Road; he didn't stand a chance, and he had no choice. Poor Paul became a fool for Christ with the mind of Jesus and was guaranteed eternal life (Romans 2:29).

Many in those thirty-three years responded to Jesus's calling, but only the elect were called by God to Jesus (Daniel 9:26).

❧ ROMANS 6:1–13 ❧

What can we ask? Shall we continue in sin when grace abounds? We elect of God have died to sin to not live in sin any longer. We elect have been anointed as was Jesus by God at His baptism. We were crucified, buried, and resurrected with Him as new creatures.

We elect are the images of Jesus; we are no longer slaves of sin. We died with Jesus, and we live with Jesus. Death no longer has dominion over

Him or us. Jesus died to take away the sins of the elect. We were dead in sin but then called by God to live in Him just as Jesus lives to our Lord God. Do not let sin reign in your earthly body.

Honestly pray to God for strength to live in His way. David and Lot did the most immoral and terrible things to themselves and others, but they were removed from Hades at the hand of God at the redemption.

❧ ROMANS 6:14–23 ❧

Sin has no dominion over the elect; they are not under the Law of Moses but of the Holy Spirit by grace. Shall we sin because we are not under the Law of Moses but under the grace of God? Heavens no! We sinners lust, but the Holy Spirit causes obedience leading to righteousness and eternal life with God. No longer slaves to sin, we are slaves to righteousness.

Paul said, "I speak in human terms because of the weakness of your flesh because you once presented your body parts as slaves of unrighteousness in lustful lawlessness of the worldly, so now you elect present your members as slaves of the Holy Spirit. You elect are holy as God is holy. When you were slaves of sin, you were denied God's righteousness. Reflect on the damned fruit you once were and repent because the end of your sinful fruit was death. Called by God, you elect were set free from sin and became slaves of God; the fruit of the Spirit with eternal life. The wages of sin is death, but the gift of God is eternal life in Christ Jesus our Lord."

To the knowledgeable elect, the gospel was only to be preached in the last time of the latter days as promised to the foreordained elect. Only in the latter days was the gospel to be preached around the Roman world, and from that moment, the gospel was declared preached by Paul four times in the Bible, but the dead of the religions are denied that.

CHAPTER 9

❧ MATTHEW 24 ❧

This is one more big-picture prophecy of the time of the end of the apocalypse as outlined in Daniel 7, 9, and 12, with the ministry of Jesus and here in the famous temple talks, a preview of the time of the end from Pentecost followed by the thousand years, not the half hour of silence of Revelation 8:1 but from October 2, 66. It presents the curses of hell, the great tribulation, the temple destruction, and the end of the old covenant age.

Jesus was asked three questions, the first of which contained three questions, so five in all. The questions addressed the parable code interpreting "these things" as the desolate temple, the fire that was set in it, and its destruction.

Actually, Jesus coming in wrath began August 63, but the sign was of Jesus passing from the destroyed temple to His marriage to the 144,000 remnant elect followed by the redemption at the final judgment out of Hades.

Matthew 24 speaks directly to the Bible setting and in direct opposition to the various religions with their Pinocchio narratives that Jesus is coming back again since the time of the Reformation error. Only the elect can know the truth; all others are doomed to the lake of fire. It is never what one can know or believe but how God causes the doer to live in forgiveness, peace, and love.

In Matthew 24:1–3 are Jesus's answers to these questions. Matthew

24:4–14 speaks of the time from the Pentecost, when the elect were indwelled with the Holy Spirit until Paul declared the gospel had been preached to end the thousand years. Jesus prophesied thirty years before August 63, the time that the gospel would be completely preached around the world. Jesus's prophecy did not provide the actions because He was not privy to the date when the gospel was to be completely preached around the world in advance. August 63 began the first three years of the time of silence (Revelation 8:1) and was the first three years of the apocalypse.

❧ 1 CORINTHIANS 13:8–10 ❧

Love never fails, but when Jesus, who is perfect, comes on the clouds of wrath, the prophecies failed, the knowledge of foreign languages to preach the gospel around the world failed, and the knowledge of God that called the elect vanished. We know only in part and prophesy only in part. Jesus came on the clouds of wrath for seven years of the apocalypse.

❧ MATTHEW 24:1–3 ❧

Jesus departed from the temple, and His disciples pointed to the temple buildings, signs one through three. Jesus said, "Don't you see all these things (parable code for temple buildings)? Surely, not a stone of these temple buildings will be left upon another stone; all will be thrown down when the Romans burn the temple and the melted gold having seeped down thorough temple stones to the foundations. When they retrieve the gold, not one stone will be left upon another stone."

As Jesus sat on Mount of Olives, the disciples came quietly asking, "Tell us, when will these things (parable code for temple buildings) be destroyed? What will be the sign (number 4) of Your coming and the sign (number 5) of the end of the old covenant age?"

❧ MATTHEW 24:32 ❧

"Now learn this parable from the fig tree (the temple buildings): when its branches have become tender (are on fire) and puts forth leaves, you will know that summer (Jesus) is near."

MATTHEW 24:15–16

"When you elect see the prophecy spoken of by Daniel (9:27), the Roman Twelfth Legion with the images of their Roman god Caesar the abomination of the desolation, standing at the walls of Jerusalem, flee to Pella." The battle flags of the Twelfth Legion portended Jerusalem's destruction.

What Jesus will be the sign of your coming?

MATTHEW 24:21

October 2, 66, started the great tribulation—the last four years of the apocalypse, the days of vengeance to end the seventh day of creation.

MATTHEW 24:27–28

"The sign of Jesus coming will be as flashes of lightning from the east and flashes to the west. Jesus will come on the clouds of wrath leaving the dead for the carrion birds."

What Jesus will be the sign of your coming?

MATTHEW 24:39–41

The dead cannot not know the apocalypse when the flood took them all away as it began August 63 at the coming of the Son of Man on the clouds of wrath. The sign of Jesus was when the Roman foragers killed one man and left the other. The sign of Jesus was when the criminals found two women grinding at the mill and killed one and left the other.

MATTHEW 24:33

When you see these things (parable code for temple buildings burned), know that Jesus is at the door.

→ ACTS 7:48–50 ←

"However, the Most High does not dwell in temples made with hands. As the prophet said, 'Heaven is My throne, and earth is My footstool. What house will you build for Me? What is the place of My rest? Has My hand not made all these things?'" (Isaiah 66:1–2).

→ REVELATION 3:20–21 ←

"I stand knocking on the door, and the elect heard My voice, opened the door, and dined with Me. To him, God has caused His elect to overcome. I will grant him to sit with Me as I also had overcome the cross to sit on My throne with My Father on His throne."

→ EPHESIANS 2:19–22 ←

You elect are no longer strangers but are in fellowship as members in the house of God built on the foundation of the apostles and prophets with the Rock, Jesus, in whom grows together as the temples of the Lord indwelled by the Holy Spirit.

→ 1 CORINTHIANS 3:16–17 ←

"Don't you elect know that you are the temples of God and that the Holy Spirit dwells in you? God will destroy anyone who defiles you elect temples of God."

What Jesus will be the sign of the end of the old covenant age?

→ MATTHEW 24:29 ←

Following the great tribulation of the apocalypse, the last four years of the days of vengeance, the sun darkened, and the moon could not give its light. The stars—the Jews—fell from heaven. The temple was destroyed, and the temple powers passed as the sign of Jesus to the elect gathered by God at Pella in the wilderness.

The old covenant ended with the marriage of the Lamb of God with His bride, the redemption of the sheep on the right and the damnation of the goats on the left; it began the new covenant age.

What Jesus will be the sign of the end of the age?

﹩ MATTHEW 24:30 ﹩

Then the sign of the Son of Man will appear in the flesh-and-blood images of Jesus Christ, heaven on earth, and all the tribes of the earth will mourn, and they in Hades will see the Son of Man coming on the clouds of heaven with power and great glory.

﹩ MATTHEW 24:31 ﹩

Following the marriage of the Lamb of God came the redemption of the sheep and the damnation of the goats. In September 70, God sent His angels with a great sound of a trumpet to gather His elect.

﹩ MATTHEW 24:22 ﹩

Unless God shortened those days from three and a half years from March 67 by six months to October 66, no elect could be saved, but for the elects' sake, God shortened those days by six months to three years from March 67 to October 66.

﹩ MATTHEW 24:23–26 ﹩

"Jesus cautioned saying, 'Look, here is the Christ!' or 'There!' Do not believe. God caused the false Christs and false prophets showing great signs and wonders to deceive even the elect. Beware, Jesus is telling you elect to be prepared. When they say, 'Look! Jesus is in the desert!' do not go out. When they say, 'Look! Jesus is in the inner rooms!' do not believe them."

❧ MATTHEW 24:37 ❧

From August 63, as in the day of Noah, the dead were eating, drinking, marrying, and being given in marriage.

❧ MATTHEW 24:42–44 ❧

"You elect cannot know the hour of Jesus's coming. If the master knew when thieves would invade his house, he could have prevented that. Because you are the elect of God, you are doomed to life eternal in Jesus."

Matthew 24 is a prophecy of the coming of Christ in wrath written before Jesus's crucifixion, but keep in mind, all had passed since 15 September 70, so it is only fair to include those conclusions that have already passed and as expressed as prophecies fulfilled of Matthew 24. All that knowledge is passé—after the fact. However, most of the dead religions will disregard Matthew 24.

CHAPTER 10

This chapter deals with the last days of Jesus, including the anointing of Jesus by Mary Magdalene, the Last Supper, the Garden of Gethsemane, the capture of Jesus led by Judas, and His encounter with Pilate.

This is about Jesus's persecution, crucifixion, death, burial, time in Hades, resurrection, and meeting with His followers. He told them to preach the gospel, and He ultimately ascended to heaven. Ten days later came Pentecost.

❧ MATTHEW 27 ❧

As God purposed, the garrison at the praetorium stripped Jesus, robed him in scarlet, twisted a crown of thorns on His head, and put a reed in His hand. They bowed and mocked Him by saying, "Hail, King of the Jews!" They spat on Him and struck His head with the reed. They led him to be crucified.

When Jesus was resurrected, the dead in Christ came out of their graves having fallen asleep (earthly demise); they walked into Jerusalem, where they appeared to many.

After His resurrection, He told His disciples that He would meet them 3 May AD 34 eight days later at the appointed place in Galilee.

The parable code is not limited to the Bible. God alone determines exactly what you will take away from this work or any work whether you are dead or alive.

The prophecy in Isaiah 53:1–12 was written six hundred years before Jesus Christ; it was as though taking place in the first three years of the latter days after Jesus's baptism.

⊱ ISAIAH 53:1–12 ⊰

The elect of the Lord God alone have been called by God to Jesus with eternal life. Jesus grew before God as if a tender plant. It was not Jesus's appearance that caused the elect to follow Him. Jesus was rejected by the dead, but He was acquainted with the sorrow and grief of the blessed poor elect. The predestined dead despised the Jesus they could not know. He bore the elects' grief. He carried our sorrows, and He called us. Jesus was crucified because of our inequities and chastised for the elect to have peace, yet we elect were called by God to eternal life forever in Jesus. We as sheep have gone astray and pursued the dead in Adam's free will having turned to our iniquitous ways. The Lord God had Jesus crucified to heal the elects' iniquities. Jesus was persecuted and afflicted yet never sniveled or whined. He was led as a lamb to the slaughter and sheep before the shearers and remained silent. Jesus was taken by the dead high priests of the religions of Judaism to Pilate and judgment.

Who will declare His generation? Jesus was crucified, cut off from the land of the living, but only for the elects' inequities was Jesus crucified. Jesus was crucified with two felons, but He was put in the tomb of Joseph, a rich man. Jesus did no violence, nor was any deceit in His mouth. Yet the Lord had the high priests of the religions of Judaism crucify Jesus, and it was God who put Jesus to sorrow.

It was the elect being called by God who caused Jesus's death as an offering to God for the sins of the elect. The elect seed of God were called to Jesus, who prolonged their days at the pleasure of the Lord to prosper in Jesus. God saw the trials of Jesus's soul and was satisfied.

Through God's knowledge and His calling, He justified the elect, but because of the elects' inequities, Jesus was crucified. He will divide the living elect from the dead portion in the religions of Judaism. Jesus poured out His soul unto death; burdened with the elects' inequities, Jesus was their intercessor bearing the sins of the elect called by God to Jesus doomed to life eternal with the mind of Jesus.

⊱ MATTHEW 25:12–30 ⊰

The Lord answered, "Surely, I tell you, not being ready; I do not know the predestined dead. Watch is the byword, for you cannot know the day or the hour when you will meet the Son of Man. The kingdom of heaven is like a man (God) traveling in a far country, calling his (elect) servants, and delivering to them his treasures (life eternal with Jesus)."

The first servant was given five talents, the second servant two talents, and the third, the lazy servant, the snoozer, one talent each to his ability. The king went on a journey. He who had received the five talents went trading in the markets and acquired five more talents. He who had received two talents gained two more. The lazy servant with the one talent buried it in the ground and while waiting the king's return, he took long naps mimicking the dead or twiddling his thumbs.

The lord returned to settle accounts with the servants. The servant given the five talents brought five more talents, saying, "Lord, you gave me five talents; look, I gained five more talents." The lord said, "Well done, good and faithful servant; you were faithful over a few things, so I will make you a ruler over many things. Enter the joy of your lord."

The servant given two talents said, "Lord, you gave me two talents; look, I have worked and gained two more talents." The lord said, "Well done, good and faithful servant; you have been faithful over a few things, so I will make you a ruler over many things. Enter the joy of your lord."

The snoozer who had been given one talent came whimpering, "Lord, I know you are a hard man who reaps where you have not sown and gathers where you have not planted. Being afraid, I wisely hid your talent in the ground. Look, here is the talent you gave me, which is yours." The Lord replied, "You wicked, lazy, jackass snoozer! You knew I reap where I have not sown and gather where I have not scattered. You, you lazy, good-for-nothing servant, should have deposited my money in the Bank of Israel where the one talent would have received at least market interest." The lord then said to the servants, "Take the talent from this lazy wimp snoozer and give the talent to the one who earned five talents."

To those who strive for more, more will be given, but even what the snoozers have will be taken away. Watch! The lord commanded the profitable servants to throw the lazy servant to the outer darkness where there was whining, sniveling, weeping, and gnashing of teeth.

❧ EZEKIEL 22:12–13 ❧

The Lord God said, "You extortionists take bribes and shed blood. You increased your extortions, profited from your neighbors, and have forgotten

Me. I will always beat My fists against your dishonest gain you pursue even with bloodshed and by force." Think religions of the world.

Knowing is a source for judging. As spoken by Paul, judging must be based on honest observation, not gossip, speculation, rumor, or fake news. Otherwise, judging is judging God and thus GGTBMF. The living or the dead cannot act without the will of God.

From the day of God's rest at the foundation of the world, all have been predestined. Understand that your daily bread is earned by your honest daily work in the world and that good work is rewarded by Jesus, who comes down daily from heaven as your daily Bread of Life.

❧ 1 CORINTHIANS 5:9 ❧

Paul said, "You elect are not of the world; throughout the day, you honestly work in the world to earn your daily bread. After work, you are to seek fellowship, but avoid fellowship with the sexually immoral, the greedy, the idolatrous, the revilers, the drunks, and the extortionists. Don't even eat with such people because they are the dead of the world."

Whoever abuses you is doing the work of God. The street thug who has hurt you and takes your money is doing the work of God. No one is innocent. What have you done to deserve God's chastising? Remember that giving anyone the big middle finger is giving God the big middle finger.

❧ MATTHEW 5:39–44 ❧

Jesus said to the elect, "Do not resist an evil person. Whoever slaps you on your right cheek, turn the other cheek to that evil person. If someone wants your tunic, give him your cape also. Whoever forces you to go one mile, go with him two miles. Give to him who asks anything of you, and do not turn away whoever wants to borrow from you. You have heard, 'You shall love your neighbor' (Leviticus 19:18), but you must not hate your enemy. Love your enemies, bless those who curse you, do what is good to those who hate you, and be an imitation of Jesus. Your God-assigned daily cross may be an LGBT, and as your neighbor, you are to love them just as God loves you."

Pray for those (LGBT) who spitefully (come for you to bake a cake and serve at their wedding in the world) misuse, persecute, and sue you. If you reject the LGBT, you are rejecting God. You are not of God when you give the LGBT the big middle finger because you are also GGTBMF.

Freedom of religion is a joke; there are no religions of God. We are to love our fellowman in the world; the Lord instructed us to carry the Roman soldiers' load not one mile but two miles. After work, we are to fellowship with the ecclesia, the assembly of God, the elect, who are flesh-and-blood images of Jesus Christ.

It is easy to be of the Christian herd, but being able to follow Jesus with your God-assigned cross is also your daily Bread from heaven. Historically, the Christian herd rarely acts as the body of Jesus the Christ.

When you are in the service to the world, you are to serve the world—liberals, Democrats, Republicans, extortionists, labor unions, and congressional extortionists as if they were the usual street thug who beats you and steals your wallet in the name of their god of Gain. Today, the dead are of the religions of men—evil Democrats and lackey Republicans in the pursuit of WPF and who GGTBMF. The Republicans who live in great wealth from the lucrative crumbs that fall from their Democrat masters' table are the sign that at their earthly demise, they will be cast into the lake of fire.

❧ MATTHEW 5:45–46 ❧

You elect may be sons of your Father in heaven, who makes the sun rise on the evil and the good alike and the rain to fall on the just as well as the unjust. If you love only those who love you, what is your reward? Even tax collectors demonstrate love to those they extort for taxes.

When the Las Vegas shooter killed many good and evil people, those of God went to heaven. The injured elect and their families began to bear their God-appointed crosses. The living dead also acquired their God-given life's burdens.

The essential knowledge of God is salvation. Think about Jesus; the dead could not know the time of their Rock and Savior. Were the dead supposed to know the time of their Savior? What can anyone know when God is the cause of their knowing? Treat your fellowman with forgiveness, peace, and love as if he were Jesus. The dead remain dead until they are called by God to Jesus.

✤ Revelation 20:10 ✤

Satan was thrown into the lake of fire and brimstone to manage the Beast, Nero and the false prophets, where they are tormented eternally. There is no death, only eternal life with Jesus or eternal life in the lake of fire.

You elect are the Spirit of God; Satan is also a spirit of God but in the lake of fire. The flickering fiery message is do not GGTBMF.

Being stupid without the Word is impossible. The ways of stupidity are innumerable, but the Lord God is creative. The stupidity is the biblical folly of the dead, who cannot even begin to know they are the stupid and the dead. Stupid people can detect stupidity in others, but they themselves though brilliant may also be denied knowledge of their own stupidity. As one gets older, one's personal stupidity comes back to haunt one. The problem with folly is that the fool bears his stupidity always at the Word of God.

The elect through the knowledge of God have reason to fear God; those who do not fear Him have been denied or veiled without any reason to even suspect a God; they are awarded God's delusions.

✤ Hebrews 12:5–8 ✤

You have forgotten the exhortation that speaks to you as to sons: "My sons, do not despise the chastening of the Lord, nor be discouraged when you are rebuked by Him, for whom the Lord loves, He chastens and scourges" (Proverbs 3:11–12). If you elect endure chastening, God will deal with you as with sons, for what son is there whom a father (God) has not chastened? If you are without chastening, which all the elect have endured, you are illegitimate and not His son.

When will I know I have no choice? This quote will immediately blossom in the minds of some, a few … well … very few. When we have the mind of Jesus, which only God gives, then we may know by the Holy Spirit, who causes our life on earth to be a living hell until the elect of God are guided by His chastisement, which causes the elect to fear God.

❧ ISAIAH 66:4 ❧

God chose the dead's delusions; when He called, the veiled dead could not answer, and when He spoke, the veiled dead could not hear. The dead did evil before His eyes by choosing to crucify the Lord Jesus, which God did not delight in.

❧ ISAIAH 66:5 ❧

The elect heard the Word of the Lord and feared Him. The dead marked 666 in the religions of Judaism hated the elect, but for His name's sake, the elect glorified the Lord.

❧ LUKE 19:41–44 ❧

Jesus coming near to Jerusalem wept saying, "Jerusalem, if you had known this, the latter days, the love that made for your peace, but God has hidden it from your eyes. The days when Satan over Gog and Magog in the name of the Roman governors from August created hell in Israel for seven years that followed until the Romans destroyed Jerusalem because of your unbelief, leveling Jerusalem to the ground in 70 with your children in you because you Jerusalem could not know the time of your Rock's visitation."

❧ MATTHEW 26:1–5 ❧

Jesus finished speaking of the coming final judgment in the last forty-five days of Daniel 12:11–13. He told His disciples, "Two days from today is Passover, when the Lamb of God will be delivered up to sacrifice and be crucified."

The chief priests, scribes, and the elders of the religions of Judaism marked with death assembled at the palace of the high priest Caiaphas; they plotted to take Jesus by trickery and kill Him. "To avoid the people rioting, we can do nothing during the Passover feast," they said.

❧ MATTHEW 26:6–13 ❧

Jesus was invited to the house of Simon the leper. Mary Magdalene, a reformed prostitute, anointed Jesus with an alabaster flask of spikenard, a very costly oil. When the disciples caught the scent of the spikenard, they griped, "Why this waste? This spikenard could be sold for a pretty penny and the money could be given the poor." Jesus asked, "Why trouble this woman? She is doing God's work anointing Me for My coming crucifixion. You will always have the dead and the poor, but you will soon not have Me. Mary through the Holy Spirit is anointing My body with this fragrant oil for My burial. Truly, wherever this gospel is preached in the world, Mary Magdalene's anointing Me will be spoken as a memorial to her."

❧ MATTHEW 26:14–19 ❧

Judas Iscariot, one of the twelve spoken about in Isaiah, asked the dead priests, "What will you give me to deliver Jesus to you?" They counted out thirty pieces of silver. That moment was when Judas betrayed Jesus to the dead religions of Judaism.

On the first day of the celebration of the unleavened bread, the disciples asked Jesus, "Where do You want us to prepare for You the Passover?" Jesus said, "Go into the city to a man with a water pitcher and tell him, 'The Teacher says, "My time has come, I will keep the Passover at your house with My disciples in the upper room."'"

The disciples did as Jesus directed preparing for Passover.

❧ MATTHEW 26:20–25 ❧

That evening while eating, Jesus said to the twelve, "Actually, one of you will betray Me." Sorrowfully, all asked, "Lord, is it I?" He replied, "He who dips with Me in this dish will betray Me. Woe to that man who betrays the Son of Man. It would have been better if he had never been born." Judas, the betrayer, asked, "Rabbi, is it I?" Jesus replied, "You have said it."

⊱ JOHN 6:33–35 ⊰

Jesus, who comes down daily from heaven, is our daily bread who gives life to the elect. They asked, "Lord, give us this bread." Jesus replied, "I am the Bread of Life. Those whom God calls to me will never hunger or thirst again."

⊱ MATTHEW 26:26–27 ⊰

Jesus took bread, blessed it, broke it, and gave it to the disciples, saying, "Take, eat. This is My (our spiritual DNA) body." Jesus then took the cup and giving thanks passed it around, saying, "Drink from it. You elect are My flesh-and-blood images."

⊱ JOHN 6:53–58 ⊰

Jesus said, "I assure you, unless you eat the flesh of the Son of Man and drink his blood, you will not have eternal life. Those who eat His flesh and drink His blood will be raised by God on the last day. My flesh is the true food, and my blood is the true drink. All who eat my flesh and drink my blood remain in Me and I in them. I live by the power of the living Father, who sent Me in the same way those who partake of Me on earth will live eternally because of Me. I am the true Bread from heaven. Those God causes to eat this Bread will live forever and not die as your ancestors did even though they ate the manna from God."

Do you in your unbelief turn away from drinking Jesus's blood and eating Jesus's flesh? High-class Christians in man-made churches forbid explorations of Jesus, our daily Bread, because they are not doers of God but are of seminary BS narrative bound religions and their god of Gain.

⊱ MATTHEW 26:28 ⊰

This is My blood of the new covenant for the elect for the remission of their sins whom God in the fullness of the dispensation in the first thirty-three years of the latter days reconciled the elect to Jesus with life eternal.

❧ JOHN 6:47–48 ❧

"I assure you; anyone who believes in Me already has eternal life. Yes, I, Jesus, am the Bread of Life."

❧ LUKE 10:27 ❧

The rich man replied, "You shall love the Lord your God with all your heart, with all your soul, with all your strength, and with your entire mind, and your neighbor as yourself" (Leviticus 19:18).

❧ MATTHEW 26:29 ❧

"I will not drink of this wine with you until after the temple destruction, and at Pella, I will marry you elect 144,000 remnant."

❧ MATTHEW 26:31–38 ❧

Jesus warned, "All of you disciples will stumble because of Me this night, as written, 'I will strike the Shepherd (Jesus) and the sheep (disciples) will be scattered' (Zechariah 13:7). After I am crucified and resurrected, I will ascend to the third heaven, and eight days later, I will meet you disciples in Galilee at the appointed place."

Peter said, "Even if we are made to stumble because of You, I will never stumble." Jesus replied, "Surely, Peter, this very night, before the rooster crows, you will have denied Me three times." Peter replied, "Even if I have to die with You, I will not deny You!" All the apostles mumbled as much.

They came to a place called Gethsemane, a garden, and Jesus said to the disciples, "Sit here while I go and pray." Jesus took Peter, John, and James of Zebedee. Jesus said, "My soul is exceedingly sorrowful even to death. Stay here and watch with Me."

The will is not of Jesus or of man because all live by the will of God. The elect live in the liberty of God. The elect are guided and governed by the Holy Spirit. The dead are from the foundation of the world predestined to live the natural spirit in the life of the dead but always doing the work of God, and this includes Stalin, Hitler, and Mao.

God causes the wealthy to provide for the poor knowingly or unknowingly. The predestined world killers merely help burn the dead weeds, the dead street thugs, drug dealers, the dead druggies, and the dead who hate their neighbor while on earth GGTBMF.

The men of religions preach free will, but the dead cannot know they are dead. Being dead, they cannot know that God denies them the knowledge of God. The religions' leaders are most often self-serving extortionists and liars. The elects' salvation is always and only at the will and calling by God, who draws the elect from out of the dead of the world to life eternal.

ROMANS 2:11–16

There is no partiality with God. Those who have sinned without law will also perish without law, and those who have sinned in the law will be judged by the law. The hearers of the law are not justified in the sight of God, but the doers of the law are justified. Gentiles, Pagans, Christians, Muslims, Protestants, Jews, Buddhists, Roman Catholics, and Russians do not have the law, but by their nature with the indwelled Holy Spirit, they are doomed to eternal life in Jesus. When God shanghaies fools from out of the world, He replaces their debased minds with the mind of Jesus and they are then assured eternal life.

MATTHEW 26:39

Jesus went a little farther away in the garden and fell on His face, praying, "O My Father, if it is possible, let this cup pass from Me. Still, not as I will, but only, Father, as You will."

MATTHEW 26:40–50

Jesus came to the disciples and found them asleep. He asked Peter, "What? Could you not watch with Me one hour? Watch and pray to avoid temptation. The spirit is willing, but the flesh is weak."

Jesus prayed, "O My Father, if this cup (of crucifixion) cannot pass away from Me unless I drink it, Your will be done." Jesus found them asleep again; their eyes were heavy. Jesus left again praying a third time the same words. He came to His disciples asking, "Still sleeping and resting? See. The hour is at hand. The Son of Man is being betrayed into the hands of sinners. Let us be going. Rise. My betrayer (Judas) is at hand."

Jesus was still speaking as Judas arrived with a multitude armed with swords and clubs from the chief priests and elders. Judas told them, "Whomever I kiss, He is the One. Seize Him." Judas boldly went up to Jesus saying, "Greetings, Rabbi!" and kissed Jesus. Jesus said, "Friend, why have you come?" Then the mob arrested Jesus and took Him.

No man can kill another man for any reason, not even self-defense, except by the will of God through secular rulers. No man of any religion can be a secular ruler and be of God (Romans 13:1–14), not even the most holy Roman Catholic pope, who once had oppressed all secular rulers.

Only secular rulers can command you under God as soldiers of the country to kill others as prescribed by the laws of the rulers. Even in war zones, no proscribed killing of another is allowed, but if it is done, it is murder. It may appear you have succeeded, but keep in mind that after battle, many suffer from PTSD.

≽ MATTHEW 26:54 ≼

Jesus inquired, "How can the scriptures be fulfilled unless I am crucified?"

The Jews marked with death for hundreds of years were the power behind the religions of Judaism; they politicized the religion to acquire WPF just as any branch of government, religions, business, and corporations when they become corrupt, but this is noticed by only a few.

≽ MATTHEW 26:55–61 ≼

Jesus asked the multitudes, "Have you come against robbers with swords and clubs to take Me? While I sat daily in the temple teaching, you did not arrest Me. This was done that the scriptures of the prophets be fulfilled."

Then as foretold, the disciples scattered from Jesus. Those who arrested Jesus led him to Caiaphas, the high priest, where the scribes and elders were gathered. Peter followed Jesus at a distance to the high priest's courtyard and went in with the servants. The chief priests, elders, and the council sought testimony to put Jesus to death. They found none even though much fake news and many false witnesses came forward, but at last, two false witnesses said, "This man said, 'I am able to destroy the temple of God and rebuild it in three days.'"

The high priest was doing God's work by convicting Jesus of blasphemy as written in the scripture. There is no reason to deny God. Jesus remained silent in the presence of God, the high priest, Governor Pilate, and the Roman soldiers, who spat at, whipped, beat, lashed, cursed, crowned with thorns, and crucified Jesus.

See Romans 13 to understand that your tribulations always come from God because you GGTBMF. Remember that the crazies of the Democrats and the Republicans are always doing God's work when they extort taxes from you for their own WPF.

There are no innocent people; not all who die horrible deaths are steeped in the commandments of men. Only Jesus was sinless, but Jesus was killed by God as atonement for the sins of the elect of yesterday, today, and tomorrow. The Old Testament has made very clear that in bad times, God has called His elect to heaven to escape the daily tribulations of life on earth.

No one is innocent except children, but they are also born dead in Adam, and no traditional water baptism can change that. The Lord protects the elect because He loved them from the foundation of the world as the brethren of Jesus.

❧ MATTHEW 26:62–64 ❧

The high priest asked Jesus, "Do You answer? Nothing! These men testify against You?" Jesus remained silent. The high priest cried, "I put You under oath by the living God: Tell us if You are the Christ, the Son of God!" Jesus replied, "As you say. However, at the final judgment, you will see the Son of Man sitting at the right hand of power coming on the clouds of heaven."

❧ MATTHEW 26:65–75 ❧

The self-serving high priest tore his clothes saying, "Jesus blasphemed! What further need do we have of more witnesses? Look, now you have heard His blasphemy! What do you think?" They responded, "He deserves death." As required by God, they spat in His face and beat Him, and others slapped Jesus asking, "Prophesy to us, Christ! Who slapped you?"

In the courtyard, a servant girl said to Peter, "You are with Jesus of Galilee." Peter said, "I do not know what you are talking about." A little later, a young woman said, "This man was with Jesus of Nazareth." Peter again denied Jesus with an oath: "I do not know the Man!" Others said to Peter, "Truly, you are of Jesus from Galilee; your accent betrays you." Peter cursed and swore; for a third time, he denied Christ by saying, "I do not know the Man!" A rooster crowed. Peter remembered what Jesus had said: "Before the rooster crows, you will have denied Me three times." Peter was crushed and went away weeping bitterly.

MATTHEW 27:1–23

That morning, the chief priests and elders plotted to kill Jesus. Jesus was bound and led to the Roman governor Pontius Pilate. In remorse, Judas returned the thirty pieces of silver to the chief priests and elders saying, "I have sinned by betraying innocent blood." The dead of the religions asked, "What's that to us?" Judas threw down the silver and departed. He hanged himself. The chief priests took the silver saying, "It is not lawful to put the silver back in the treasury because it was the price of blood." They consulted agreeing to buy the potter's field to bury strangers. From that day forward, it was called the Field of Blood. Jeremiah's prophecy (32:6–9) was fulfilled.

Pilate asked Jesus, "Are You the King of the Jews?" Jesus replied, "As you say." While being accused by the chief priests and elders, Jesus made no reply as required by God. Pilate asked, "Do You not hear how many things the religious leaders charged You with?" Jesus again remained quiet, and Pilate marveled at him.

At Passover, the custom was to release any prisoner the multitude wished. Barabbas was a notorious and seditious murderer. Pilate asked, "Whom do you want me to release to you, Barabbas or Jesus?" Pilate knew the religious were envious of Jesus. While he was in the judgment seat, he received a message from his wife that read, "Have nothing to do with that just Man. I have suffered many things today in my conscience because of Him."

The chief priests and elders persuaded the multitude to ask for

Barabbas's release and Jesus's crucifixion. Governor Pilate asked, "Which of the two do you want me to release to you?" They cried, "Barabbas!" Pilate asked, "What shall I do with Jesus, who is called the Messiah?" All cried, "Let Him be crucified!" The governor asked, "Why? What evil has He done?" They cried louder, "Let Him be crucified!"

❧ JOHN 19:15 ❧

They cried, "Away with Jesus! Crucify Him!" Pilate asked, "Shall I crucify your King?" The dead chief priests cried, "We have no king but Caesar!"

❧ MATTHEW 27:24–34 ❧

When Pilate realized that he could not prevail, he washed his hands before the multitude and said, "I am innocent of the blood of this Jesus. Do as you wish." The multitude replied, "His blood is on us and on our children."

Pilate released Barabbas and sent Jesus to be scourged and crucified. The Roman soldiers took Jesus to the praetorium, where the whole garrison was gathered. Stripping Jesus, they put a scarlet robe on Him. They put a crown of thorns on His head and put a reed in His hand. Then bowing before Jesus and mocking Him, they said, "Hail, King of the Jews!" They struck His head all as required by God. They removed His robe, put on His clothes, and led Him to be crucified. The Roman commanded Simon of Cyrene to carry Jesus's cross. Coming to Golgotha, the Place of a Skull, they gave Jesus some sour, salty wine. Tasting, Jesus did not drink.

❧ MATTHEW 27:35–44 ❧

They crucified Jesus and cast lots for His garments in fulfillment of the prophecy (Psalm 22:18). The Roman soldiers watched over Jesus. Over Jesus's head was written, This Is Jesus, the King of the Jews. Crucified on both sides of Jesus were robbers. Passers-by cursed and taunted Jesus saying, "You who can destroy the temple and in three days rebuild it again, save Yourself. If You are the Son of God, come down from the cross."

The chief priests, scribes, and elders mocked Jesus saying as required by God, "He saved others but cannot save Himself. If He is the King of Israel, let Him now come down from the cross so that we can believe Him. He trusted in God; let God save Him if God will save Him." Jesus replied, "I am the Son of God." The robbers on each side reviled Jesus as required by God.

❧ MATTHEW 27:45–46 ☙

From six to the ninth hour, darkness came over the land. Jesus cried with a loud voice at the ninth hour, "Eli, Eli, lama sabachthani?" that is, "My God, My God, why have You forsaken Me?"

❧ MATTHEW 27:47–49 ☙

Some heard Him and said, "This Man is calling for Elijah!" One took a sponge with sour wine on a reed and offered it to Jesus to drink. Others countered, "Let Him alone; let's see if Elijah will come save Him."

❧ MATTHEW 27:50–51 ☙

Jesus cried out, yielding up the ghost. The temple veil was torn in two from top to bottom exposing the holiest of all. An earthquake spat rocks.

The dead priests of all religions are always killing Jesus; all that happened to Jesus was the work of God spoken in Old Testament prophecies that pointed to Jesus as the loving Messiah. What the men of the religions did to kill Jesus was the Word that proceeded from the mouth of God.

The high priests had witnessed Jesus's miracles, but being dead, they had not been called by God to the Light, Jesus. We as people of God still fail bigly. Some dead shall remain dead until their earthly demise, which will confirm their eternal damnation.

❧ 1 PETER 4:6 ☙

While Jesus was in the ground three days following the crucifixion, He preached the gospel to the dead in Hades and those in prisons while God continued to call the elect from out of the dead of the nations of Israel to life eternal in Jesus.

✦ Ephesians 4:8–10 ✦

Paul said, "When Jesus ascended on high, He led captivity captive giving gifts to men" (Psalm 68:18). Jesus first descended to Hades to preach the gospel and ascended three days later to fulfill all things (see Daniel 7:13–14).

Jesus's death for the sins of the elect was the reformation; at the resurrection with Jesus were the dead in Christ through Jesus. That first day, Jesus met with the women and the disciples, and later in the day, He ascended to the third heaven.

✦ Matthew 27:52–53 ✦

At Jesus's resurrection, the graves were opened and the dead in Christ who had been killed for the witness of Jesus were raised; they came out of their graves and went to the Holy City, where they appeared to many.

The same day, Jesus met with Mary Magdalene, Mary, His mother, the other Marys, other women, the disciples, and the two men who had encountered Him on the road to Emmaus. The Emmaus two returned that very first day telling the apostles of their meeting with Jesus, but the apostles did not believe them. Jesus ascended to heaven later on the first day of His resurrection.

✦ Daniel 7:13–14 ✦

Daniel saw Jesus ascending on the clouds to the third heaven. The angels brought Jesus before God, and Jesus was given dominion and glory and a kingdom of all peoples, nations, and languages that serve Jesus forever.

Eight days later, Jesus met with the disciples in Galilee.

Hades was where David, Moses, Isaiah, and Jeremiah were held along with Lazarus in the bosom of Abraham until the redemption and final judgment to end the old covenant people and age. Hades was a holding tank where all the souls from the foundation of the world were held in waiting for judgment by the Messiah.

The worldly before being called by God are human with every human frailty and fault but also goodness. Once called by God to Jesus, they are doomed to life eternal as the flesh-and-blood images of Jesus. How can the elect fail when they absolutely live by every Word that proceeds from the mouth of God and yet are free from sin?

In the old covenant age, tithes took the form of farm produce or sacrificial animals to support the Levitical priesthood. The crucifixion annulled the Law of Moses and this extortionist tithing system. But in this new covenant age, the extorted congregations take out fire insurance policies to be safe from the fires of hell.

❧ EPHESIANS 2:9–10 ☙

In this new covenant age, we elect have been saved by God's calling. Our faith is the gift of God's grace, the righteousness of God and not of our doing lest we want to boast. We elect are God's workmanship created in Christ Jesus to do those good works God has prepared at the foundation of the world that we elect would walk in the works of God that Jesus Christ does through us.

It is not what a man blabbers or what the fool knows or thinks he knows. God alone causes the doer of God to live in forgiveness, peace, and love with his neighbor. The elect of God have no choice because God causes the doer to be doomed with the mind of Jesus with eternal life in Him.

In time, people, religions, countries, and governments fail as God plans. Some of the most glaring failures are seen in the worldly religions; that mindlessness is always at the hand of God. Stupidity dominates the churchy bodies just as it does corporations, universities, businesses, governments, charities, and countries. However, God can never be corrupted because He calls only the elect out of the world; He baptizes the fools with the mind of Christ and guarantees them life eternal.

❧ MATTHEW 27:54–63 ☙

The Roman centurion guarding Jesus felt the earthquake that had happened. He was fearful and said, "Truly this was the Son of God!" The servant women could see Jesus of Galilee on the cross from a distance as could Mary Magdalene, the others Marys, Jesus's mother, His brothers James and Joseph, and the mother of the Zebedees, John and James.

Joseph of Arimathea asked Pilate for the body of Jesus. Joseph swaddled the body of Jesus in clean linen and put it in his tomb. Mary Magdalene and Jesus's mother were there.

The next day, the chief priests and Pharisees told Pilate, "Sir, we remember that after three days, He would rise. Please command the tomb to be made secure until the third day in case Jesus's disciples come by night and steal the body of Jesus and tell the people, 'Jesus has risen from the dead.' That deception of Jesus would be worse than the first." Pilate replied, "Make your guard as secure as you know how." They went and made the tomb secure, sealing the stone and setting the guard.

❧ MATTHEW 28:1–10 ☙

The first day after the Sabbath, Mary Magdalene and the other Marys came to the tomb. An angel rolled back the stone with an earthquake. The angel's face was as lightning, and his robe was white as snow. The guards in fear became as dead. "Do not be afraid," said the angel. "I know you are seeking the crucified Jesus. He is risen. Come see the place where the Lord lay, and go tell His disciples that Jesus is risen and will meet you in Galilee in eight days."

The women in fear but also in great joy ran from the tomb to tell His disciples. The women on the run met Jesus and said, "Rejoice!" The women worshipped Jesus. Jesus said, "Do not be afraid. Go and tell My brethren I will meet you as appointed in Galilee."

❧ MATTHEW 28:11–15 ☙

The guards came into the city reporting to the chief priests what had happened. The assembled elders gave the soldiers a large sum of money telling them to say that the disciples had taken Jesus's body at night. "If Pilate hears, we will appease him with the usual bribe making you secure." They took the money, and as instructed, they spread the report among the Jews until this day.

✥ CORINTHIANS 15:3–6 ✥

"I, Paul, delivered to you ecclesia what I received from God to preach that Christ died for the sins of the predestined elect ecclesia of the scriptures."

Jesus was buried and rose again on the third day as per the scriptures. He was seen by Peter and then by the eleven. In the following days, more than five hundred saw Him. Some of them have fallen to their earthly demise and were waiting in Hades.

✥ LUKE 24:33–45 ✥

The Emmaus two told the disciples what had taken place with Jesus on the road to Emmaus and breaking bread with Jesus. While speaking, Jesus stood among them saying, "Peace to you." All were terrified and frightened supposing Jesus was a spirit. He asked, "Why are you troubled? Have doubts in your heart? See My hands and feet. Touch Me and see Me; a spirit does not have flesh and bones as you can see."

Jesus showed His hands and feet. They remained frightened but marveled believing with joy. Jesus asked, "Have you any food here?" They gave Jesus a piece of a broiled fish and a honeycomb. He stood before them eating. He said, "Here are the words I have spoken while with you—all things written in the Law of Moses must be fulfilled and the prophecies and psalms concerning Me." Jesus then opened their understanding to comprehend the imminence of the scriptures.

Mark's version is the simplest with the most direct and honest version eight days later in Galilee.

✥ MARK 16:14–16 ✥

Jesus appeared eight days later with the eleven in Galilee and rebuked them because of their unbelief and hardness of their hearts because they had not believed the Emmaus two, who had seen Jesus the very day He had risen. He said, "Go into the world and preach the gospel to every creature. He who believes is baptized and saved, but the nonbeliever is already condemned."

❧ JOHN 20:18–23 ❧

On the day of the resurrection, Mary Magdalene told the disciples that she had seen the Lord and that He had spoken many things to her. That same day when the disciples were assembled, Jesus appeared in their midst saying, "Peace to you." He showed them His hands and the wound in His side. The disciples were happy to see the Lord. Again, Jesus said, "Peace to you! And as the Father has sent Me, I also send you."

He then breathed on them saying, "Receive the Holy Spirit. If you forgive sins, they are forgiven. If you don't forgive sins, they are not forgiven."

❧ JOHN 20:26 ❧

In Galilee eight days later, Jesus appeared to His disciples and with Thomas where they were gathered saying, "Peace to you!"

❧ MATTHEW 28:16–18 ❧

The eleven met at the appointed place in Galilee and worshipped Jesus, yet one (Thomas) doubted. Jesus said. "All authority has been given to Me in heaven and on earth."

The Greek word *disciple* means to preach or teach. Just remember that these mistakes made by the gods of the religions may not be mistakes but by design; they are GGTBMF by extorting tithes.

❧ MATTHEW 28:16–20 CORRECTED VERSION ❧

The eleven disciples went to Galilee eight days later and gathered at the appointed place. Seeing Jesus, they bowed to Him, but some doubted. Having come near, Jesus said, "It has been given to me all authority in heaven and on earth. Go and preach to all the nations baptizing them in My name and that of the Father and the Holy Spirit. Teach them to observe all I have commanded you. I will be with you elect to the end of the old covenant age."

The only William Tyndale error was corrected in most Bibles. The

King James Version copied the Tyndale error as expected, but see how many religions copy such nonsense still looking to the end of the world; it is as bad as the global warming hoax.

Tyndale's first English language version of Matthew 28:20 is corrected here: "Jesus came and speaking to them, saying, all power is given unto me in heaven and earth. Go preach all the nations, baptizing them in the My ~~name of the Father, and of the Son, and of the Holy Ghost~~: Teaching them to observe all things I have commanded you and know I am with you always unto the end of the end of the world." Only the Lord knows why He allowed the Tyndale Bible to be marred by this most glaring error.

The elect were baptized, and remember in this new covenant age that the elect called by God are baptized as was Jesus with the Holy Spirit.

ACTS 1:1–5

This account Luke made to Theophilus from the time Jesus began to do and teach until He ascended to heaven. He had given the Commandments to the chosen apostles. He appeared after the resurrection alive after suffering and with many infallible proofs. He was seen for forty days until June 4, 34, and that included their reunion in Galilee eight days after His resurrection. Jesus commanded the disciples not to leave Jerusalem but to wait for the promised Holy Spirit.

ACTS 1:5–8

The disciples asked, "Lord, will You at this time restore the kingdom to Israel?" Jesus replied, "It is not for you elect to know the times or the season of the Father's authority. The Holy Spirit will give you the power to be My witnesses in Jerusalem, Judea, and Samaria to the end of this old covenant age."

ACTS 1:9–11

While the disciples looked steadfastly toward the heavens, Jesus was taken up out of their sight in a cloud to heaven. Angels asked, "Men of Galilee, why are you gazing into the heavens? Jesus was taken up from you in a cloud to heaven, and when he returns, He will come in like manner to earth on the clouds of wrath."

❧ ACTS 1:12–16 ❧

The apostles returned to Jerusalem from Mount Olivet. They went to the upper room where they were staying: Peter, James, John, Andrew, Philip, Thomas, Bartholomew, Matthew; James of Alphaeus, Simon the Zealot, and James, the son of Judas. They along with Mary, the mother of Jesus, and with His brothers continued in prayer as one. Peter was with about a hundred and twenty disciples saying, "This scripture had to be fulfilled, which the Holy Spirit spoke by the mouth of David concerning Judas, who became a guide to those who arrested Jesus."

❧ ACTS 1:17–26 ❧

"Judas was one of us as a part in this ministry." By his deceit, Judas had purchased a field with the wages of his iniquity. When he fell headlong, his stomach burst open and his entrails gushed out. All dwelling in Jerusalem came to know the field as Akel Dama, the Field of Blood.

"Let his dwelling place be desolate and let no one live in it" (Psalm 69:25), and "Let another take his office" (Psalm 108:9). Two names were offered to replace Judas—Joseph called Barsabas who was surnamed Justus, and Matthias. They prayed, "You, O Lord, who knows the hearts of all men, show us of the two; the one You have chosen as apostles in this ministry from which Judas fell." The lots cast were to Matthias, who became the twelfth apostle.

❧ GOSPEL PREACHED ❧

However, the gospel had to be completely preached around the world by August AD 63 on revelation from God to Paul; he declared the gospel preached around the world to every Jew scattered by God.

The gospel was preached; the Bible tells me so: Romans 1:8, 16:25–27, Colossians 1:4–5, 1:23.

⪧ MATTHEW 26:13 ⪦

Jesus said, "Truly, I tell you, wherever this gospel is preached in the whole world, what Mary Magdalene, this former prostitute, has done will also be told as a memorial to her."

⪧ ROMANS 1:8 ⪦

First, I Paul thank my God through Jesus Christ for you elect Jews of the Ecclesia called as "God's Chosen People" that your faith in Jesus are spoken of in the rest of the entire world.

⪧ ROMANS 16:25–27 ⪦

To the Lord God who has established you according to my gospel and the preaching of Jesus Christ the revelation of the mystery kept secret since the foundations of the world but now made manifest by the prophetic scriptures now known to all nations through the commandment of the everlasting God, for obedience to the faith—to God be glory through Jesus Christ forever.

⪧ COLOSSIANS 1:3–6 ⪦

We disciples give thanks to the God and Father of our Lord Jesus Christ praying always for you Jews, God's chosen people, since we disciples heard of your faith in Christ Jesus and brotherly love because of the promise to you elect Jews praised by God in heaven and on earth of which you Jews, God's chosen people, heard the gospel truth, which has come to you elect Jews as the gospel of truth has in the world to the elect 144,000 remnant bringing forth fruit among you since the day you elect Jews heard and knew the grace of God in truth.

If you elect Jews continue in the faith and grounded and steadfast in the gospel you elect Jews heard preached to every creature under heaven of which I (Paul) became a minister.

The dead in the world or the gods and men of the religions in their carnal pursuit of their precious profit, St. Mammon and big sister Greed, for a tithe-based income for the usual WPF are denied that. They know only how to GGTBMF, but at their earthly demise, they will only confirm their predestined eternal damnation in the lake of fire forever.

CHAPTER 11

The thousand years began with the Day of Pentecost and ended thirty years later, when Paul declared the gospel preached in August 63, which began the rapture.

On the fortieth day after the resurrection, Jesus ascended to heaven, and ten days later, on the day of Pentecost the Holy Spirit began to indwell the elect. Then chosen disciples were provided the many gifts of knowledge to facilitate their preaching the gospel around the world for the next thirty years to end the thousand years with gospel preached.

The Beast in the form of Emperor Nero was to come to create hell on earth that extended through the first three years of silence (see *The Jewish War*, book 2, chapters 13–19). After October 2, 66, Revelation defined the last four years at the great tribulation ending in 70.

In Matthew 24:4–14 were prophesies of what would happen in the thirty years ending in 63 to begin the seven years of the apocalypse ending in 70 with the destruction of the temple in Jerusalem (*The Jewish War*, book 6, chapter 5, section 3).

ACTS 2:1–4

Pentecost had come with the disciples in one place. The sound of a mighty wind from heaven filled the house. Over each disciple was a tongue of fire, and they began speaking in foreign languages by which the Holy Spirit allowed them to preach the gospel around the world.

✺ 1 CORINTHIANS 13:8–10 ✺

Love never fails, but from August 63 at the coming of Jesus Christ regardless of the prophecies, the prophecies failed, and tongues and the knowledge that facilitated the preaching of the gospel around the known Roman world ceased. We know in part and prophesy in part, though when Jesus came in 63 on the clouds of wrath, preaching the gospel ended.

✺ ACTS 2:5–11 ✺

From every nation, the devout Jews flocked to Jerusalem and gathered at the sound. They were confused because they heard the Jews speaking in their own tongues. The foreigners marveled asking, "Look at all these speaking in my language, and they are Galileans! How can it be that we hear and understand the language from wherever we were born? We are from Mesopotamia, Parthia Cappadocia, Pontus, Phrygia, Pamphylia, Egypt, Libya, and Rome, but we hear them speaking in our languages! Is this wonderful work of God?"

Speaking in tongues is man scam BS promoted by the dead religions of men of glossolalia fame; speaking in tongues is not godly but gaudy.

✺ ACTS 2:12–17 ✺

"What is happening? What can this mean?" The dead Jews scorned them as if they were drunk on wine before nine. Peter said, "Men of Judea who live in Jerusalem and in Judea, this is being made known to you by the Holy Spirit. We are not drunk. The prophet Joel said, 'It shall come to pass in the latter days says the Lord God, I will pour out My Spirit on all flesh; your sons and your daughters prophesying, your young men seeing visions and old men dreaming dreams'" (Joel 2:28–32).

✺ ACTS 2:18–28 ✺

"I will pour out My Spirit on My elect menservants and maidservants in the latter days, and they will prophesy and show wonders in heaven of the signs on the earth, blood and fire and smoke. The sun will turn to darkness and the moon to blood beginning the seven years of Jesus coming on the clouds of wrath on that great and awesome day (of the seven years of the apocalypse) of the Lord. Those called by God to Jesus are saved (Joel 2:28–32).

"Men of Israel, hear these words of Jesus of Nazareth, a Man confirmed by God to you by miracles, signs, and wonders through God, which Jesus did among you as you elect know. Jesus with God's foreknowledge delivered the predestined as God purposed from out of you Jews marked with death who lawlessly crucified your Rock and Savior. God raised Jesus from death to take away the sins of the elect and give them life eternal.

"David said concerning Him, 'I foresaw the Lord always before my face He is at my right hand, that I may not be moved' (Psalm 16:8–11). 'My heart rejoiced, my tongue was glad, and my flesh rested in your promise. God will not leave my soul. You have made me to know the ways of life; you will make me full of joy in your presence'" (Psalm 16:8–11).

❧ ACTS 2:29–33 ☙

Peter said that David had spoken about the resurrection of the Christ—His soul was not left in Hades nor was His body corruptible; He was in heaven, and the elect received the Holy Spirit. David did not ascend into the third heaven, but he said, "The Lord said to my Lord Jesus, 'Sit at My right hand, till I make Your enemies (those Jews of unbelief) Your footstool'" (Psalm 110:1). "Let the Israel of God know Jesus, who you Jews marked with death crucified your Savior, Lord, Christ the Messiah."

When the elect of God heard this, they were heartbroken, and they asked Peter and the apostles, "What shall we do?" Peter responded, "You elect repent, be heartily sorry, and be baptized in the name of Jesus Christ for the remission of sins. Receive the gift that is the Holy Spirit promised to you elect and those in faraway places that the Lord God has called you elect to Jesus."

Penance is works; a traditional construct of extortionists suffering from God's delusion.

❧ ACTS 2:40–42 ☙

Peter exhorted them, "Be saved from the Jews marked with death in this perverse generation." Three thousand were baptized by the end of that first day. The called elect of God continued in the doctrine of God and in fellowship as flesh-and-blood images of Jesus who broke bread.

⊱ ACTS 2:43–47 ⊰

Fear came upon every elect soul and the apostles with many signs and wonders. The elect sold their possessions and distributed them as needed. The images of Jesus continued daily with one accord from house to house breaking bread and eating with gladness and the simplicity of their hearts. They praised God, who had called them to life eternal in Jesus.

⊱ ACTS 3:19–24 ⊰

"Repent and convert that your sins are blotted out. This time of refreshing comes from the Lord, who sent Jesus Christ to preach to you what God has spoken through His holy prophets. Moses said to the fathers, 'The Lord your God will raise up for you a prophet like me from your brethren. Him you shall hear in all things whatever He says to you. It shall be that every soul who will not hear the prophet will be destroyed'" (see Deuteronomy 28:15, 18–19). The prophets from Samuel spoke of the latter days.

⊱ DEUTERONOMY 28:15, 18–19 ⊰

"In the latter days it shall come to pass, if you do not obey the Lord your God, His Commandments and statutes that I, Moses, command you today, that all these curses of Deuteronomy 28:15–68 will come over you: the cursed the fruit of your body, the produce of your land, the increase of your cattle and flocks offspring. Cursed when you come and when you go."

⊱ ACTS 3:25–26 ⊰

"You are sons of the prophets and the covenant God made with our fathers saying to Abraham, 'In your seed, families of the earth are blessed'" (Genesis 28:14; Deuteronomy 29:14–15). "You elect are called by God to life as Jesus's death took away your iniquities. If you do not believe, you are not the body of Jesus Christ."

❧ Genesis 5:1–2 ❧

God created male and female. All born on earth in the spirit of Adam continue in this new covenant age predestined at the foundation of the world as were all the spirits of God. The image of God is spiritual; we have His spiritual DNA. Until they are called by God to Jesus, the dead traverse this mortal coil in carnal, fleshly spirits of the dead in Adam, and at their earthly demise, they are judged to the lake of fire forever.

❧ Psalm 110:4 ❧

God said, "You, Jesus, are a priest forever according to the order of Melchizedek." Jesus's crucifixion annulled the Law of Moses because it could save no man from eternal damnation. Jesus brought the perfect way of life through the calling of God. We elect are called by God to life eternal in Jesus. Jesus is the elects' guarantee of life in the new covenant age. Jesus's gospel was intended for the new covenant age, which began with His anointing. We now live from the time of Jesus, but Jesus is not coming back again in this new covenant age. He came back only to destroy the temple, heaven on earth. In this new covenant age, heaven and earth are the flesh-and-blood images of Jesus Christ all one in God.

The Old Testament's only purpose then as today was to point to the coming of the Messiah (Deuteronomy 31:29).

Pentecost began the tribulation, which ended in 66, when the Great Tribulation of the last four years of the days of vengeance ended in 70 with the temple's destruction. The thousand years began on Pentecost to complete the gospel preached around the world.

❧ Revelation 20:1–3 ❧

While Jesus was in the ground for three days, John saw Him come down from the third heaven with the key to the bottomless pit. Jesus bound Satan in the abyss for the thousand years until August 63 so Satan could not deceive the nations of Israel while the gospel was being preached. In August 63, Satan was set free to begin the seven years of the apocalypse. Satan guided Gog and Magog, the Beast of Rome, Nero, and a cast of thousands of the rebellious to kill over three million Jews marked with death.

Each of the elect of God is at all times in the same place of God's knowledge, which is salvation. God wants the elect to be in Him honestly and humbly with forgiveness, peace, and love.

The following Bible verses about the resurrection are seen through the gospels of Matthew, Mark, Luke, and John with all their various views. The Holy Spirit provides the essential knowledge of God only to the elect.

❧ MARK 13:32 ❧

From August 63, that day of seven years, and until that hour of seven years ending August 70, no one knows, not the angels, nor the Son Jesus, only God the Father when Jesus would return. Jesus Himself was not given to know the beginning of that last seven years.

Matthew 24 speaks as a prophecy before Pentecost from June 14, 34, to begin the thousand years ending in August 63, which began the rapture, the first three years of the half hour of silence of Revelation 8:1 and the seven years of the apocalypse until August 2, 70.

❧ MATTHEW 24:3–5 ❧

Jesus sat on the Mount of Olives. The disciples asked Him, "What, Jesus, will be the sign of Your coming and the sign of the end of the old covenant age?" Jesus said, "Take heed that no religion or their gods and men deceive you elect. God will send false prophets in My name, saying, 'I am the Christ' and deceive even the elect."

God used the evil demons of Rome and the rebellious of Israel for the first three years during the half hour of silence of Revelation 8:1 to tactically gather all marked with death and their executioners into the trap, the pit, the prison— Jerusalem—in 66 to kill the Antichrist, John of Gischala of the Zealots, and John's nemesis, Simon of Gioras, with his twenty thousand Idumean demons as promised by Deuteronomy 28:15–68 with famine, pestilence, and the sword because of their unbelief (*The Jewish War*, book 2, chapters 13–21).

❧ MATTHEW 24:6 ❧

You will hear of wars and rumors of wars, but do not be troubled. These things (parable code for the temple) will be destroyed in 70 to begin the end time, the last forty-five days of the prophecy of Daniel 12:11–13 to end the old covenant age and the Jews marked with death.

❧ MATTHEW 24:7 ❧

The nations of Israel rose against the nations of Israel and the kingdoms of Israel against kingdoms of Israel during the seven years to end the seventh day of creation from August 63 with famines, pestilences, and the usual earthquakes.

❧ ACTS 11:28 ❧

Agabus was told by the Spirit that there would be a great famine, which happened during Claudius's reign.

During three years of famine in the time of Claudius, Queen Helena of Adiabene (in northern Iraq near Babylon) went to Jerusalem; she was a great blessing to the people of Jerusalem as a great famine oppressed them and many people died. Queen Helena, a proselyte to Judaism, purchased from Alexandria, Egypt, a great quantity of corn and from Cyprus brought cargos of dried figs. She distributed food to those in need. Her son Izates was informed of this famine, and he sent great sums of money to the principal men in Jerusalem in the fifth year, 51, the sixth year, 52, and the seventh year, 53 of Claudius's reign. Keep in mind that Claudius was succeeded by the Beast of Rome, Emperor Nero, in 54.

❧ MATTHEW 24:8 ❧

The day of Pentecost, June 14, 34, began the thousand years (twenty-nine years plus) of sorrow and tribulation and lasted until August AD 63.

≫ ISAIAH 65:12 ≪

"God numbered you, Israel, and marked you 666 with death in the religions of Judaism for the sword because of your unbelief. When I came in August 30 and called you Jews marked with death, you did not answer. When I spoke, you did not hear. Still in the fullness of the dispensation when I was calling you, you in your unbelief crucified Me."

Josephus chronicled the wonders, signs, and omens that followed the destruction of the temple. From Passover 62, Albinus, the governor of Israel, was the typical corrupt and evil Roman governor (*The Jewish Antiquities*, book 20, chapter 9, section 1). Albinus murdered James. A picture of the woe of Jesus the farmer is in *The Jewish War*, book 6, chapter 5, section 3.

Please forgive Josephus; God caused Josephus to write a brilliant work, but it is hard to read. God helped me get through it. Be assured that if you are among the elect, you are saved even if you cannot get your head around Josephus's book. God will cause the dummy in you to understand the last seven years of the old covenant age. The elect are blessed with life eternal and have no need to know any of the above chronicled by Josephus, whereas the dead cannot know.

≫ 2 CORINTHIANS 3:5–6 ≪

We are not sufficient in ourselves, but God alone is our sufficiency. The elect are made sufficient in this new covenant not by the letter or the Bible or the Law of Moses that kills; only by the Holy Spirit can there be eternal life in Jesus.

≫ LUKE 21:11 ≪

There will be in various places great earthquakes, famines, and pestilences with fearful sights, great signs, wonders, and omens from heaven.

The signs, wonders, and omens began at the time of Albinus, the Roman governor of Israel. A star resembling a sword stood over Jerusalem while a comet continued a whole year. At Pentecost, AD 62, great crowds came to the Feast of Unleavened Bread, and a great light shone around the altar of the temple appearing as bright as day and lasting a half hour. The scribes mouthed it a portent of the events to follow.

At the same festival, a cow was led to sacrifice in the temple of the high priests; the cow gave birth to a lamb (the Lamb Jesus) in the temple.

The eastern gate in the court of the temple was extremely heavy and required twenty men to open or shut it. Though the gate pivoted on a base of iron, it was fastened to one block of granite, one entire stone. The gate was seen by the sentries to open of its own accord about the sixth hour in the evening. The sentries that kept watch in the temple came running to the captain of the temple. They reported the gate opening. They went to close the gate and did so with great difficulty. The gate episode appeared to the people as a good sign, as if God had opened the gate of happiness. The scribes on learning saw the sign that the security of the temple had melted away and that their enemies and their desolations were coming.

A few days later, after the feast on May 21, a remarkable sign appeared. It was accounted as a parable to the wise. All Jerusalem saw the wonders. They saw what was to happen over the next seven and a half years; those marked with death died horrible deaths by the curses (Deuteronomy 28:15–68). They saw chariots and troops of soldiers in their armor surrounding the city among the clouds.

At that same feast at Pentecost, the priests were going by night into the inner court of the temple as was their custom to perform their sacred duties. They felt a quaking and heard a great noise, and after that, they heard a sound as of a great multitude saying, "Let us remove from here."

Came the Passover feast where it was the custom for everyone to make tabernacles to God in the temple. Jesus, the son of the farmer Ananus, mourned, "A voice from the east, a voice from the west, a voice from the four winds, a voice against Jerusalem, the holy house, against the bridegrooms and the brides and a voice against this the people Israel!"

This was Jesus's cry as he went about the city by day and by night in all the streets of Jerusalem. The city's elite were outraged at Jesus's calamitous cry. Jesus was arrested and whipped severely. Yet Jesus did not whine or snivel or say anything or in any way curse the man who had whipped him. Jesus went on about the city with the same dire words of woe.

He was then brought to Albinus and was whipped till his bones were laid bare. Yet Jesus did not beg or shed a tear; he simply kept saying, "Woe, woe to Jerusalem!" When Albinus asked him why he was saying that, Jesus did not respond; he continued his constant melancholy of woes. Albinus took Jesus to be a madman and dismissed him.

This Jesus did not go near any of the citizens during the apocalypse, nor was he seen by any though every day he uttered, "Woe, woe to Jerusalem!"

He continued his warning of woe for seven years and five months without growing hoarse or being tired until the very time that he saw his omen fulfilled by Titus's siege of Jerusalem. He cried out, "Woe, woe to the city again, the people and the temple!" Just as Jesus added the last "Woe, woe to and me also!" he was struck by a stone from a Roman war machine and was killed.

❧ MATTHEW 24:10–11 ❧

Jesus added, "Many will be offended, hate, and betray one another." God sent many false prophets to deceive even the elect. To understand the false prophets, read Revelation 13:11–18. There were many false prophets from the high priest down to the local camel groomer, and the situation is the same today. At various times, even the elect engage in stupid blabbing surely about what they were not given to know.

❧ MATTHEW 24:12 ❧

The injustices of the temple rulers and high priest and the ruling powers forced many to live in poverty in the mountain wilderness (ghettoes) and engage in brigandage, rapine, and plunder. The powerful of the dead religions of Judaism abounded in many, and through their injustices, they brought about the mountain hideouts of the lawless.

The illegals that come to our country most often have two things in common—a loving mother and a loving father. Loving parents run a tight love ship with righteousness, and the punishment of the unruly children proves life's essentials—education in forgiveness, peace, and love. My mom used to chastise me with a strap, but her hand was guided by the Holy Spirit.

It is incredible that some children brought up by the worst demon parents blossom as the most beautiful flowers of God. The only one absolute is that God is of the living. God alone is absolute. No man can know all of what God does and does what God wants. Poor or bad parents ought to expect a great blowback from the devils they create. Even children not raised in religions are predestined by God to eternal life, and they have no choice in the matter. The predestined stupid parents GGTBMF and end up in the lake of fire.

≈ MATTHEW 24:14 ≈

After the thousand years until August 63, when this gospel of the kingdom of heaven was preached throughout the world, Paul declared to all the nations, and Jesus began the seven years to end the seventh day of creation in 70 followed by the forty-five days of the end time (Daniel 12:11–13).

≈ ROMANS 1:8 ≈

"I, Paul, thank my God through Jesus Christ for you Jews of the ecclesia, God's chosen people, that your faith in Jesus is spoken of in the rest of the entire world."

≈ ROMANS 16:25–27 ≈

"God alone causes you Jews praised by God to live according to My gospel in the revelations of the mysteries of heaven on earth from the time the world began. However, in the first thirty-three years of this last forty years of this last generation, God has called the predestined elect from out of the Jews marked 666 with death that in these the latter days spoken of by Moses (Deuteronomy 32:29), you will have eternal life."

≈ COLOSSIANS 1:3–6 ≈

Giving thanks to God the Father of our Lord Jesus Christ, we disciples pray always for you elect Jews since we disciples have heard of your faith and love of Christ Jesus, the cause of your promised heaven and earth, which you elect Jews heard in the gospel. You bring forth fruit since you heard and knew the grace of God in truth.

❧ COLOSSIANS 1:23 ❧

Continue in the faith and be grounded in the gospel you elect have heard preached to every creature under heaven. Do not feel bad that you do not believe God's Word just as the gods of your religions are denied. God knows a repentant heart. Should you have a repentant heart, you are the elect foreordained to salvation.

❧ HEBREWS 4:1–16 ❧

Since the promise remains to enter His rest, we elect need not fear if we fall short. God has our back. The gospel was preached to the predestined dead, but they did not hear it. We elect believe and are promised rest. He said, "I swore in My wrath, 'They shall not enter My rest' (Psalm 94:11) although my works were finished at the foundation of the world." The elect entered God's rest, but the dead did not.

David said in Psalm 95:7–8, "Today, if you will hear His voice, do not harden your hearts as did Moses at the waters of Meribah" (Psalm 95:7–8). If Joshua had given them rest, why would God have spoken of another day? There remained a rest for God's chosen. At one's earthly demise, the elect of God have entered His rest having ceased from their works as did God.

Be diligent to enter that rest. The Word of God is alive and powerful and sharper than any two-edged sword; it pierces the soul, heart, spirit, and mind of those with God's spiritual DNA. He knows the intents of the heart. No man is hidden from His sight but naked to Him to whom he must give an account. Knowing that Jesus is in heaven, hold fast to your belief. Our High Priest sympathizes with our weaknesses and temptation and failures yet we are without sin and have eternal life.

What God had done at the foundation of the world was predestined; then, God rested. God loved the predestined when they were mere specks of God's Spirit.

❧ MATTHEW 11:12–13 ❧

Since the day of John the Baptist, the kingdom of heaven has suffered violence at the hands of the high priests.

John saw another Beast coming up out of the land, the false prophet with two horns like a lamb and who spoke like Satan. The false prophet exercised all the authority of Satan over the Beast of Rome and its image, Nero. He caused the land and those on it to worship the Beast of Rome, whose deadly wound was caused by Nero's suicide.

CHAPTER 12

The rapture is based on Revelation 8:1. The elect were sealed to life eternal (Revelation 7:1–4) from August 63 after Paul declared the gospel preached around the world. At the rapture, the elect were sealed: "The Lord with a shout descended from heaven and raised the dead in Christ" to be with the Lord eternally.

❧ 1 THESSALONIANS 4:16 ❧

The Lord descended from heaven with a shout of the archangel, and with the trumpet of God, the dead in Christ ascended first.

❧ 1 THESSALONIANS 4:17 ❧

The dead in Christ followed by the living went with the Lord in the air to always be with Him.

❧ REVELATION 5:8–12: THE RAPTURE ❧

Jesus took the scroll, and the four living creatures and the twenty-four elders fell down worshipping the Lamb with harps and golden bowls filled with incense and the prayers of the saints. A new song was sung by the saints: "You, Jesus, were slain and worthy to remove the seals from the scroll. Redeem us by Your blood, Jesus, from out of every people and nation, and make us a kingdom of God and priests who reign on earth."

John heard the voices of many angels at the throne, the living creatures, the elders, and ten thousand times ten thousand with a loud voice singing, "Worthy is the Lamb who was slain to receive the kingdom, power, wisdom, wealth, strength, honor, glory, and blessings!" At the rapture, Jesus came on clouds of wrath to kill over three million Jews marked with death.

✸ MATTHEW 13:30 ✸

"Let all men live until the harvest (August 63), and at the time of harvest, I will say to the reaper/angels at the falling away, 'Gather the tares (Jews marked 666 with death) and bind them in bundles to burn them.'" Jesus gathered the elect for eternal life.

✸ REVELATION 6:9–11 ✸

Jesus opened the fifth seal, and John saw under the altar the souls of the dead in Christ who had been slain for their testimony about the Word of God. They cried out, "How long, O Lord Jesus, holy and true, until You judge and avenge our blood on those who dwell in the land?" A white robe was given to the dead. Christ told them, "Rest a while longer until your fellow servants are in the bosom of Abraham until their redemption from out of Hades at the final judgment."

✸ REVELATION 20:4–5 ✸

John saw the thrones and judgment committed to them. John saw the dead in Christ who had been killed for their witness to the Word of God. The dead in Christ had not worshipped the Beast of Rome, Nero, and did not receive the mark 666 on their foreheads or on their hands. The dead in Christ reigned with the living elect in Christ from the resurrection to the end of the thousand years in August 63. The rest of the living from Jesus's resurrection reigned with Christ during the thousand years.

God chose us in Jesus before the foundation of the world that we be holy without blame in God's love. At God's will and pleasure, we elect are predestined sons at the adoption with Jesus Christ to the praise of the glory of God's grace when He called us elect to the beloved Jesus.

The dead in the world are also the gods and men of the religions in their carnal pursuit of gain. Today, those who defile God's Word through deception and greed are dead.

❧ REVELATION 7:1–4 ☙

In August 63, John saw four angels at the four corners of the land holding back the four winds (the four Roman legions from above the Euphrates River). Another angel from the east with the seal of the living God cried loudly to the four angels, "Do not harm the land, the sea, or the trees until the elect 144,000 are sealed on their foreheads."

❧ REVELATION 14:1–5 ☙

John saw in the prophecy the Lamb, Jesus, on Mount Zion, the New Jerusalem, with 144,000 having His Father's name written on their foreheads. John heard the voice from heaven as the voice of many waters and loud thunder and harps. They sang as a new song before the living creatures, but none could learn the song except the 144,000 redeemed. In the elects' mouths was found no deceit, and they were without fault before God.

❧ ROMANS 8:26–27 ☙

The Holy Spirit aids us elect in our weakness. We do not know what we pray, but the Holy Spirit makes intercession in our name, which we cannot know or hear. The Holy Spirit knowingly searches the elects' repentant hearts and minds and intercedes for them.

No one needs to suck up to God; He knows repentant hearts. No one can know God; it is only because God knows us and makes the elect known to him when God calls them so that we elect can begin to know God and not an errant delusion.

Our salvation is solely by the will of God. We have no say in the matter. When we are called by God to Jesus, the Holy Spirit has the complete power of God over our consciences to cause us to live in forgiveness, peace, and love.

Gay people who have come to God will tell you that their consciences were ravaged terribly. Does that mean we will always remain sinless? No one is without sin, but being the predestined elect of God, the gay man is redeemed as forgiven and is without sin. The Holy Spirit loves us, but He bludgeons the obstinate self-serving jackasses to bring them to forgiveness, peace, and love. Once the fool is called by God, the fool is doomed to life eternal with the mind of Jesus just as Paul the murderer was.

The dead cannot have the slightest hint or thought of God (Isaiah 6:9–10) because they are dead due to their unbelief. The dead cannot believe Paul's declaration because of their God-given delusion.

❧ REVELATION 20:5–8 ❧

The elect 144,000 were redeemed at the end of the thousand years at the adoption. Blessed and holy are they at their redemption. At their earthly demise, their second demise has no power because the elect continue to be priests of God, and they reigned with Jesus forever since the rapture.

❧ ROMANS 8:8–9 ❧

Those of the flesh cannot please God. You elect are not of the flesh. If anyone does not have the Holy Spirit, he is not of Christ or God.

CHAPTER 13

The rapture began the three years of silence. The Beast of Rome attacked Israel with the eventual target being Jerusalem. The three years of the half hour of silence of Revelation 8:1 began in the countryside by the Beast of Rome and the surrogates of the Beasts, the rebellious of Israel.

After Passover in 62, God used the two Roman governors Albinus and Florus to take advantage of the angry and the destitute in the outback of Israel who had escaped the injustices of the religious leaders. The priests were free to pursue their precious god of Gain. Gessius Florus's Roman soldiers protected the robber gangs in the countryside and took Florus's share of their booty to him from 63 until 66, when the rebellion brought the four winds from April AD 67—the four Roman legions (Revelation 7:1–4).

Here, you will see Daniel 7:25 with the time, times, and a half time of three and a half years that God changed to three years of the half hour of silence of Revelation 8:1 and the prophecy of Revelation 6:1–11 that was fulfilled by Nero and his surrogate, Florus (*The Jewish War*, book 2, chapters 13–19) and with the curses of Deuteronomy 28:15–68.

❧ REVELATION 8:1 ❧

From August 63, when Jesus opened the seventh seal, there was silence in heaven for about half an hour, the first three years of silence of Revelation 8:1 and Daniel 9:26, when God cut off Jesus from the Jews marked with death in the religions of Judaism because of their unbelief.

❧ MATTHEW 24:35–36 ❧

Jesus declared that heaven (the temple) and earth (the three million Jews marked with death) passed to eternal damnation, "But My Word will by no means pass away. But of that day (of seven years from August 63) of that hour (of seven years from August 63), no one knows, not the elect, not the Son Jesus, not the angels, but My Father only."

❧ 2 CORINTHIANS 3:14 ❧

The mind of the dead is veiled today in the reading of the Old Testament, but with the calling of the elect by God to Jesus, the veil is taken away.

The first three years of Jesus's coming was covered in *The Jewish War*, book 2, chapters 13–22. The Jews marked with death watched for the signs, but the signs escaped them by design until October 66, three years too late for those Jews predestined to the lake of fire.

❧ 2 CORINTHIANS 4:1–18 ❧

Paul declared that since we have the ministry of Jesus, we also have received mercy and we do not lose heart. The elect have renounced the hidden things of shame and do not walk in deception; they exhibit truth to every man's conscience in the sight of God. The gospel is veiled to the dead, who at their earthly demise will be damned for eternity.

Jesus, the Light, shines only on the elect; we are His bondservants. We have this treasure in the elect. We face trials and tribulations, but we are not crushed, perplexed, or in despair. We are persecuted but not destroyed.

The elect always carry the cross of persecution as did Jesus. Death was working in us elect as it was in Jesus, but we elect are eternal with Jesus. Since we are of the same spirit and with faith—"I believed and therefore I spoke" (Psalm 116:10)—we elect also believe and speak knowing that God, who raised the Lord Jesus, also raised us elect with Jesus at the resurrection.

God provides all things to the elect causing thanksgiving to abound to the glory of God. We elect cannot lose heart. Even though our fleshly bodies are perishing, the Holy Spirit in us, the elect, comes down as our daily bread from heaven. Our tribulation and affliction for a moment is working to guarantee life eternal in the glory of Jesus. We do not look at the things that are seen but at the things that are not seen, the righteousness of God. His gift of grace is our faith.

❧ DANIEL 7:21–24 ❧

Daniel was watching while Nero was warring against the elect of God and prevailing. Then, the Ancient of Days called and judged His elect. Rome was the fourth kingdom on earth after Greece, Persia, and Babylon. The fourth Beast devoured the whole earth and trampled it to pieces.

❧ DANIEL 7:25–27 ❧

Nero spoke against the Most High and persecuted the saints of the Most High intending to change the times and the law. Then, the elect were given into Nero's hand for a time, times, and half a time that God changed to three years of silence. Then on June 9, 68, the court destroyed Nero's dominion.

Revelation 6 is a prophecy of what had been happening before August 63 and continued but in the middle of the week, 2 September AD 66; see *The Jewish War*, book 2, chapter 17, section 2, lines 409–10 and Revelation 6:1–11. The specifics in every word came true in the horrible and violent curses of Deuteronomy 28:15–68 until 70.

❧ REVELATION 6:1–2 ❧

John saw Jesus open the first seal and heard one of the creatures command, "Come and see." John wrote, "I saw Jesus sitting a white horse with a gold crown with a bow going out to conquer to kill every Jew marked 666 with death in the religions of Judaism."

❧ *THE JEWISH WAR*, CHAPTER 13 ❧

Nero added four cities to Agrippa's kingdom, but the other parts of Judea were under Felix. The disturbances were caused by the Sicarii, the magicians, and the Egyptian false prophets. The Jews and Syrians had a conflict at Caesarea.

This chapter began the half hour of silence (Revelation 8:1) from August 63 that began the three years of silence (Daniel 7:25; Revelation 6:1–11) from the rapture, August 63.

❧ *THE JEWISH WAR*, CHAPTER 14 ❧

Festus succeeded Felix, who was succeeded by Albinus, who was succeeded by Florus, whose barbarity forced the Jews into rebellion and war.

❧ REVELATION 6:3–4 ❧

Jesus opened the second seal, and the second creature said, "Come see." He who sat on the fiery red horse was given a great sword and sent out to take peace from the land and kill all who were marked 666 with death over the coming seven years; he killed more than three million Jews marked with death.

The three years of silence occurred during Nero's reign and that of the Roman governor of Israel Gessius Florus. Both were clearly doing the work of God in the spirit of Satan to bring on the rebellion in every terrible detail. Nero, the Beast of Rome, moved all the dead Jews over the first three years of Israel to the pit, the trap, the prison of Jerusalem to be punished with the curses of Deuteronomy 28:15–68.

❧ *THE JEWISH WAR*, CHAPTER 15 ❧

Bernice's petition to Florus to spare the Jews was in vain after the seditious flame was quenched having been kindled by the evil Florus.

Read only chapter 16 if you need great pain. Josephus passed into an unending blabber about his version of history, so protect you mind.

❧ *THE JEWISH WAR*, CHAPTER 16 ❧

Cestius sent the Roman tribune Neopolitanus to see the condition of the Jews. Avoid Agrippa's blabber to the people of the Jews to divert them from their intentions of making war with the Romans. The elite establishment copied the Roman's love of gain.

✤ REVELATION 6:5–6 ✤

Jesus opened the third seal, and the third creature said, "Come and see." John wrote, "I heard him who sat a black horse with the scales of judgment saying, 'The results of judgment; a quart of wheat for a denarius and three quarts of barley a denarius; do not harm the oil and the wine.'"

The judgment of God was being imposed by the sword on the dead marked 666 (see Daniel 7:9–10). The Book of Life was opened, and the most horrible calamities began on the dead.

✤ *THE JEWISH WAR*, CHAPTER 18 ✤

God used Albinus and Florus to persecute the Jews who had escaped the religious leaders whom Rome protected. Florus's self-enrichment provoked the Jewish rebellion.

✤ REVELATION 6:7–8 ✤

"When Jesus opened the fourth seal, I heard the voice of the fourth living creature a flying eagle saying, 'Come and see.'" John saw a pale horse ridden by Death, who killed over a fourth—803,250—of the Jews marked with death from August 63 until October 66, when Jerusalem was surrounded by the Twelfth Roman Legion.

We have no reason to believe Josephus was called by God to Jesus. Atheists are unbelievers, but it is not about believing; it is about how God can cause even atheists to live in Him. Atheists are not all convicted because of what they think; God is the cause of what they do as doers, but most of all, God is the cause of the doers. Many of the dead, even ISIS kooks, perform God's work. Once upon a time, many Christians were the murderous kooks before the secular laws of 1648 and the Treaty of Westphalia end the embarrassment of the Reformation error from 1517.

❧ *THE JEWISH WAR*, CHAPTER 19 ❧

Cestius Gallus besieged Jerusalem but abruptly retreated to Antipatris nearer the coast having lost over five thousand soldiers to rebellious Jews and others who dogged them.

❧ *THE JEWISH WAR*, CHAPTER 20 ❧

Cestius sent ambassadors to Nero. The people of Damascus slew the Jews who lived with them. The Jews who had pursued Cestius returned to Jerusalem to prepare for its defense.

The Antichrist John of Gischala arrived in Jerusalem in October 67 to lead the Zealots. A short time later, Simon of Gioras, his nemesis, arrived with twenty thousand Idumeans to complete the hell on earth in the prison Jerusalem.

❧ *THE JEWISH WAR*, CHAPTER 21 ❧

General Josephus used stratagems against the plots by the Antichrist John of Gischala and recovered certain cities that had revolted against Him.

❧ *THE JEWISH WAR*, CHAPTER 22 ❧

The Jews made ready for war; Simon, the son of Gioras, was plundering.

When God renewed the covenant in the time of Moses, He pronounced a stern warning about the coming specific curses in Deuteronomy 28:15–68.

The dead did not know of Jesus or of His coming. Today, the dead of the religions still cannot know that Jesus came in August 63 and killed more than three million Jews marked with death because they had not been called by God to Jesus.

Nero was the biblical scourge promised in Daniel 7:1–4.

CHAPTER 14

REVELATION 6:12–17: THE EARTHQUAKE TO COME 2 OCTOBER AD 66

John saw Jesus open the sixth seal (Revelation 6:12–17), the great earthquake to come in October 66 with the promised curses of Deuteronomy 28:15–68 to come on the Jews marked with 666. The sun was to become black and the moon blood-red. The stars of heaven—the priestly system marked with death—were as overripe figs (Jews marked with death) that dropped as from trees from September 2, 66, when God as a mighty wind shook the fig tree, the promised earthquake.

The sky rolled away as did every mountain and island from out of its place. The Jews marked with death, kings, great men, rich men, commanders, mighty men, and every slave and freeman hiding in mountain caves were pleading to the mountains and rocks, "Fall on us! Hide us from the face of God and the wrath of the Lamb!" But who is able to stand against the wrath of the Lamb?

❧ DANIEL 9:26 ❧

From the Babylonian exile began the seven weeks or 49 years to rebuild Jerusalem, plus sixty-two weeks or 434 years for a total of sixty-nine weeks or 483 years when the Lord God by Revelation to Paul declared the gospel preached around the world began the last seven years to end the promised 490 years, 2 August AD 70.

⊱ DANIEL 9:27 ⊰

After the sixty-ninth week of seven years came August 63, when Jesus sealed the elect to eternal life at the adoption.

⊱ COLOSSIANS 1:5–6 ⊰

Paul declared, "Your hope in heaven that you have heard in the Word of the gospel truth has come to you also in all the world bringing forth fruit among you elect since the day you heard and knew the grace of God in truth."

The gospel had been preached according to Paul by August 63.

⊱ MATTHEW 24:14 ⊰

Jesus said, "When the gospel of the kingdom has been preached as a witness in all the nations of the world, the end will come."

On 2 October AD 66 came the abominations of the desolations pointed to the destruction of the Holy City and the desolate temple. Following that, the 144,000 became the bride of Christ.

Some wise Jews had the seventh day marked with a big *X* on their calendars just as some today have marked a big *X* on their calendar of the coming of Jesus Christ of the apocalypse to destroy the world as many of the religions preach. Though it happened over two thousand years ago, that scam is passed on and promoted by the dead of the various religions in this new covenant age.

The Lord made sure that some of the Jewish theologians and scholars knew of Daniel 9:26–27, but as you all know, the Jewish Bible is focused on the first five books, the Pentateuch; the rest of the Bible pointing to Jesus does not seem to ever be a topic of those stuck in Old Testament interest.

The mission of the Christian gods has always been the pursuit of wealth. The Old Testament prophecies point to the New Testament. In this new covenant, heretics cannot be killed, but keep in mind that more than a hundred thousand Anabaptists of the Reformation error were designated heretics and murdered by the good Christian Protestants.

Some had to know and perhaps even spread the Daniel 9:27 warning, but as usual, the religions of CNN—the Corny Newsy Nonsense—pass that on as truth. Christian religions are duped into believing men, not the Word of God. So surely, the great fear came upon some, but the rest of the herd listened for a day and continued to anticipate tomorrow's rumor.

Surely, many had such great fear as spoken in the prophecy or vision given by Jesus to fear if and when thirty days later an army would arrive at Jerusalem's walls. That became the most prescient and existential moment of their lives—their promised destiny in the lake of fire.

❧ LUKE 23:28–30 ❧

On the cross, Jesus said to the daughters of Jerusalem, "Do not weep for Me but for yourselves and your children. During the apocalypse, you will say, 'Blessed are the barren wombs that never bore and the breasts that never nursed!'"

❧ REVELATION 6:12–17 ❧

The dead said to the mountains, "Fall on us!" and to the hills, "Cover us!"

The global warming scare or scam was created by brilliant minds who twenty years earlier warned us of our days underwater. How are you faring underwater? Could you have believed you could breathe so comfortably underwater? Forgive them as Jesus warned; they cannot know what they cannot know because of God's delusions. God always awards the dead to know what they think they know and what they say and what they do.

❧ DANIEL 12:9–10 ❧

Jesus said, "Go, Daniel, for the words are sealed to the time of the end. The elect were purified and are doomed to eternal life in Jesus."

CHAPTER 15

The three years of silence following Revelation 8:1 ended 2 October AD 66. The days of vengeance began when John saw seven angels with trumpets before God. An angel with a golden censer stood by the golden throne of God with a large portion of incense offerings and the prayers of the elect. Smoke from the incense and the prayers of the elect ascended from the angel's hand before God. The angel with the censer filled it with fire from the altar and threw it to the earth causing thunder and lightning and confirming the promised earthquake prophecy of Revelation 6:12–17, the promised curses of Deuteronomy 28:15–68 in the coming the days of vengeance.

The seven angels with the trumpets were ready to sound. The first angel trumpeted; hail and fire mingled with blood was thrown on the land, and a third of the trees and all the grass burned up. That began the great tribulation.

For six hundred years, God had warned the Jews who had broken the covenant with Him that they would die the most horrible deaths by murder, famine, and cannibalism. If you continue to reject God, expect a version of hell on earth; God is creative and has no shortages of personal hells. Think booze, drugs, and thugs (Deuteronomy 28:15–68), the promised hell on all those who GGTBMF.

❧ REVELATION 16:16–18 ❧

The seventh angel poured out his bowl into the air, and a loud voice from the throne of God in the third heaven said, "It is done!"

The arrival of Gallus with the Twelfth Roman Legion was the sign that God had begun gathering the elect to Pella. God caused the elect to avoid the promised earthquake to come on Jerusalem at the sight of Revelation 6:12–17, the abomination of the desolation.

❧ PSALM 1:1–6 ❧

Blessed are the elect not in the counsel of the ungodly sinners in the seat of the scornful. The elects' light is in the Law of the Lord in whom the elect meditate day and night. God did plant the tree in the waters. He brings forth the elect as the fruit in season who prosper in whatever they do. The ungodly are dead and are like chaff blown away by the wind. The ungodly as the dead are not judged but once as sinners (born again) called to the congregations of the righteous. The Lord is the way of the righteous, but the ungodly are the perishing.

❧ ISAIAH 66:13 ❧

"As the mother comforts, I will comfort you elect and you shall be comforted in the New Jerusalem" (Revelation 21:1–4).

The earthquake continued as one of the curses of Deuteronomy 28:15–68. Revelation 8:1 was about the half hour of silence. Hell on earth was the curses of Deuteronomy 28:15–68 to continue with fire coming down from heaven to kill the dead.

❧ KINGS 17:1 ❧

Elijah of Gilead told Ahab, "This has been told me to know, by the Lord God of Israel there shall not be dew nor rain over the coming years, except in the future by My word."

⊱ 1 KINGS 18:1 ⊰

Three years later, the Word of the Lord came to Elijah saying, "Go, present yourself to Ahab, telling him, 'I will send rain on the earth.'"

Revelation 12 is God's judgment on those marked with death and those in the pursuit of their Roman god Caesar for GGTBMF.

⊱ REVELATION 12:1 ⊰

A great sign of a woman clothed with the sun and with the moon under her feet and on her (the nascent body of Jesus) head a garland of twelve stars (tribes) of Israel.

⊱ GENESIS 37:8–9 ⊰

Joseph's brothers asked, "Will you Joseph/Jesus reign having dominion over us?" Joseph's brothers hated him because of his dreams and words. Then Joseph dreamed another dream and told his envious brothers, "Look! I have dreamed another dream: the sun, the moon, and the eleven stars (less David/Joseph/Jacob Jesus of the tribe of Judea) bowed down to me." His father rebuked Joseph: "What dream have you dreamed? Are you telling us of this family that we bow down before you, Joseph/Jesus?"

⊱ REVELATION 12:2 ⊰

The nascent body of Christ with the child cried in labor and pain giving birth.

⊱ REVELATION 12:3 ⊰

The great Beast of Rome—the Roman governor of Syria at Antioch, Gallus, with the Twelfth Roman Legion with ten horns and a diadem on each of the seven heads—arrived in heaven at the walls of Jerusalem on 2 October 66.

❧ Revelation 12:4 ❧

The Beast of Rome's tail killed a third—795,217—of the stars of heaven and threw them to the earth. Satan stood before the woman who was ready to give birth to devour the nascent body of Christ as soon as He was born on October 2, 66.

❧ Isaiah 66:5–12 ❧

You who tremble hearing the Word of the Lord are blessed. Your brethren hate you; the Jews marked with death cast you out for My name's sake. Let the Lord be glorified that you elect see joy, but the dead will be ashamed. A voice from the temple said, "The Lord fully repays His enemies!"

Christ was born in pain. Who has heard or seen such a thing on the earth to give birth in one day or a nation born at once? When Zion, the holy mountain of Jerusalem, gave birth to the nascent body of Christ, the Lord God asked, "Should I bring to the time of your birth the nascent body of Christ and not cause the delivery? Shall I who cause the delivery stop the birth? Have joy, and be happy with her you who are the nascent body of Christ. Rejoice for joy with her and mourn for her that you elect feed and be satisfied with the comfort of her bosom, that you drink and be delighted in her abundance and glory."

The Lord said, "Behold, I will extend peace to the nascent body of Christ as a river and glory forever on the elect 144,000 called to her from out of the Gentiles: Buddhists, Jews, Muslins, Orthodox, the most holy Roman Catholics, Mormons, and Protestants as a flowing stream of doers. Then you elect will feed as when you are called by God and jiggled on her knees."

❧ Proverbs 26:5 ❧

Responding to a fool in his stupidity, the fool sees himself wise in his own eyes.

❧ Revelation 12:5–6 ❧

The Child was caught up to God (see Daniel 7:13–14). Jesus rules all nations with a rod of iron. God drew the elect to Pella and away from the Beast of Rome for 1,260 days God changed to four years until 2 August 70.

One can only imagine the visions given by Jesus to John the disciple regarding the seeming eschatological, apocalyptic end of times that Revelation pointed to.

❧ LUKE 10:17–18 ❧

During the ministry of Jesus, the seventy-two disciples returned to Jesus with joy saying, "Lord, even the demons are subject to us in Your name." Jesus replied, "I saw Satan fall from the third heaven as lightning to earth."

❧ REVELATION 12:9–17 ❧

Satan was thrown from the third heaven to earth and his bad angels with him. I, John, heard a loud voice saying, "Now salvation, strength and the kingdom of our God and the power of His Christ have come for Satan, who accused the brethren before God day and night. He was thrown from the third heaven to earth, and from the day of Pentecost, he was put into the abyss so he could not interfere with the gospel being preached during the thousand years while God was calling the elect 144,000 to Jesus. God's Word was their testimony, and they did not love their lives to death. O heavens, rejoice you elect who dwell in them, but woe to the dead inhabitants of the land and sea!"

In August 63, God took Satan from the abyss and put him over the Beast of Rome. Satan knew he had only seven years to persecute the nascent body of Christ while God was gathering the elect to Pella. Satan spewed water out of his mouth to drown the elect, but the elect survived. Satan was enraged with them for having kept God's Commandments.

❧ MATTHEW 24:19–22 ❧

Jesus said, "Woe to the pregnant and those nursing babies during the apocalypse. Pray that your flight not be in the winter of 67 or on the Sabbath. Unless those days are shortened to three years ending on October 2, 66, no flesh will be saved to flee to Pella."

But for the elects' sake, those days were shortened from three and a half years to three years, March 67 to 2 October 66.

All that God had promised came on the Jews marked with

death—demons, fear, pestilence, famine, murder, cannibalism and other calamities—because of their unbelief having GGTBMF.

❧ JOHN 8:6–8 ❧

A woman was brought before Jesus by the hypocrite priests to test and accuse, but Jesus stooped down and wrote with His finger on the ground as though not hearing the dead. Jesus said, "He who is without sin among you, throw the first stone at her."

❧ JEREMIAH 17:13 ❧

"O Lord, the only hope of Israel, all who forsake God are dead. The dead who reject Me are written in the earth as dead because they have forsaken the Lord, the fountain of living waters."

❧ REVELATION 12:1–3 ❧

The Twelfth Roman Legion's arrival was the great sign that appeared in heaven—a woman clothed with the sun and the moon under her feet and on her head a garland of twelve stars (the twelve tribes of Israel). The elect cried out in pain giving birth. A great dragon (the Beast of Rome) having seven heads and ten horns on his heads appeared in heaven on earth, Jerusalem, and slew a third (795,217) of the Jews marked with death.

In an overview of the three years of silence beginning with Revelation 8:1, Daniel 7:25, and Revelation 6:1–11 were the prophecies of the horrors of the first three years from August 63 found in *The Jewish War*, book 2, chapters 13–20. The Roman battle flags bore the image of Caesar. This chapter introduction begins with an overview of books three and four of *The Jewish War* that address the failure of Gallus and the Twelfth Legion, and later, Nero sent to Israel Vespasian with the Fifth, Tenth, Twelfth, and Fifteenth Legions to subdue all of Israel and destroy Jerusalem.

Vespasian arrived in Galilee circa April 67 to assure peace to those cities that remained in the Roman orbit and to attack the rebellious cities and destroy Jerusalem, but when Nero committed suicide on 9 June AD 68, the Beast of Rome died for eighteen months until Vespasian became emperor and sent his son, Titus, with four legions to destroy Jerusalem.

The following are the chapter headings.

Chapter 1. Vespasian Is Sent from Syria By Nero In Order To Make War With the Jews, beginning in Galilee.

Chapter 2. A Great Slaughter About Ascalon near the Mediterranean sea . Vespasian Comes and takes Ptolemais.

Chapter 3. A Description of Galilee, Samaria, And Judea.

Chapter 4. The Jews Commissioned General Josephus; who arrives at the city Sepphoris, but he was Repelled. Titus Comes With A Great Army To Ptolemais. Just one of the cities addressed to assure their loyalties.

Chapter 5. A Description of the Roman Armies And Roman Camps And of Other Particulars For Which the Romans Are Commended.

Chapter 6. Placidus Attempts To Take Jotapata And Is Beaten off, while Vespasian Marches Into Galilee.

Chapter 7. Vespasian, When He Had Taken the City of Gadaea Marched on to Jotapata. General Josephus was instrumental preparing the city for a Long Siege the City, but he was Betrayed By A Deserter, And Taken By Vespasian where Josephus was saved by God to live and write in depth about the Jewish war.

Chapter 8. How General Josephus Was Discovered By A Woman, who forced Josephus to give Himself Up To the Romans; And What Discourse He Had With His Own Men, When They Endeavored To stop Him; And (The Prophecy he delivered to Vespasian), When He Was Brought To Vespasian And After in What Manner Vespasian employed Him.

Chapter 9. How Joppa Was Taken, And Tiberias on the lake of Galilee and Taricheae of the Wormwood prophecy Chapter 10 and the city Taricheae was forced to surrender.

❧ DEUTERONOMY 29:18 ❧

Moses said, "There is no man or woman or family or tribe whose heart turns away today from the Lord our God can become a nation of Israel bearing a root of bitterness, wormwood."

✤ Revelation 7:1 ✤

John saw four angels standing at the four corners of the land holding back the four winds, the Fifth, Tenth, Twelfth, and Fifteenth Roman Legions led by Vespasian. He and Titus arrived at the mountainside city where the rebellious had taken over Taricheae.

✤ Revelation 8:8–13 ✤

The second angel sounded, and a third of the rebellious of Taricheae retreated to the Sea of Galilee, where they were slain. The third angel sounded, and a great burning star fell from heaven as a torch on a third of the rivers and springs. The name of the star was Wormwood; it caused many to die.

The fourth angel sounded, and a third of the sun was struck, a third of the moon, a third of the stars (the Jews marked with death) were killed, and a third of the day was darkened. I looked and heard an angel flying through the midst of heaven saying, "Woe, woe, woe to the inhabitants of the land."

✤ Revelation 16:1–15 ✤

John heard a loud voice from the temple to the seven angels say, "Go and pour out God's bowls of wrath on the earth." The first angel poured out his bowl upon the land, and foul and loathsome sores came upon the Jews marked with death.

The second angel poured out his bowl on the Sea of Galilee, Wormwood, on the blood of the dead so great that every living creature in the Sea of Galilee died.

The third angel poured out his bowl on the rivers and waters and on the springs becoming Wormwood. I heard the angel of the waters saying: "You are righteous, O Lord, Jesus who is and Jesus who was and Jesus who judges all these things. The Jews marked 666 have shed the blood of the elect and the prophets, and You, Lord, have given the dead blood to drink because they are dead."

One at the altar said, "Even so, Lord God almighty, Your judgments are righteous and true."

The fourth angel poured out his bowl on the sun; it had the power to scorch men with fire. Men who were scorched by the heat blasphemed the name of God, who had power over the plagues, but the dead did not repent or give God glory.

The fifth angel poured out his bowl on the throne of the Beast of Rome causing Nero to commit suicide on 9 June AD 68.

The sixth angel poured out his bowl on the Euphrates River, which dried up. Titus came with four Roman legions from Egypt eighteen months after the stand-down after Nero's suicide.

John saw the three unclean spirits, frogs, come out of Satan's mouth. The demons did great signs to the kings of the earth to gather the demons to battle in the trap, the pit, the prison of Jerusalem. Jesus, the sword, came as a thief. Blessed are the elect who watch and keep their garments white so as to not walk naked and all see their shame.

⁂ *THE JEWISH WAR*, BOOK 4 ⁂

Containing the Interval of About One Year. From the Siege of Gamala To the Coming of Titus To Besiege Jerusalem.

Chapter 1. The Siege And Taking of Gamala was a fortified city on a mountain finally taken by the Romans.

Chapter 2. The Surrender of the Small City of Gischala; While John the Antichrist Flies Away from It To Jerusalem. Details of "The Antichrist" John of Gischala how he escaped the city of Gischala causing the death of thousands and many sold into slavery.

Chapter 3. About "The Antichrist" John of Gischala escapes to Jerusalem and by deception gained power with the high priest and becoming the leader of the rebellious Zealots. How the Jews Raise Seditions One Against Another [In Jerusalem].

Chapter 4. The twenty thousand Idumeans asked for help by John of the Zealots, Came Immediately To Jerusalem; And When They Were Excluded Out of the City, They Lay All Night There. Jesus One of the High Priests Makes A Speech To Them; And the Idumean Makes A Reply To It.

Chapter 5. The Cruelty of the Idumeans When They had Gotten Into the Jerusalem During the Storm where shorty the Idumeans slaughtered many thousands of the city. And of the Zealots. Concerning the Slaughter of High Priest Ananus Jesus, And Zacharias; And How the Idumeans Retired in shame to Home.

Chapter 6. How the Zealots When They Were Freed from the Idumeans, Slew A Great Many More of the Citizens; How Vespasian Dissuaded the Romans When They Were Very Earnest and near To March Against the Jews from that time of the War.

Chapter 7. How The Antichrist John of Gischala Tyrannized the Rest; And What Mischiefs the Zealots who captured Masada with a great supply of arms. How Also Vespasian Took Gadara; And What Actions Were Performed By General Placidus.

Chapter 8. How Vespasian, Upon Hearing of Some Commotions In Gall, Made Haste To Finish the Jewish War. A Description of Jericho and the Great Plain; and the destruction of the people at the (Dead Sea) Lake Asphaltitis.

Chapter 9. That Vespasian, After He Had Taken Gadara Made Preparation For the Siege of Jerusalem; But Hearing of Nero's suicide He Changed His plans and stood down in Egypt. Concerning Simon of Gioras.

Chapter 10. How the Soldiers in Judea And Egypt, Proclaimed Vespasian Emperor; And How Vespasian Released Josephus from His Chains.

Chapter 11. That Upon the Conquest And Slaughter of # 9 Emperor Vitellius early December AD 69 Vespasian was Hastened to travel To Rome; But Titus His Son Returned To Jerusalem, arriving Passover 14, AD 70. From the Coming of Titus To Besiege Jerusalem, To the Great Extremity (Famine)To Which the Jews Were Reduced.

⊱ THE JEWISH WAR, BOOK 5, CHAPTER 1, SECTION 4 ⊰

There were three warring factions—Eleazar and Simon against the Antichrist John, who held the temple as his fortress. Those John plundered were the populace in his zeal against Simon of Gioras. This Simon had in his domain the upper city Jerusalem's grain supply. John of the three was in the middle, where John the Antichrist was in his temple fortress.

John was assaulted from below by Eleazar and from above by Simon of Gioras. Each section threw darts upon all who came against them. John opposed the attackers from the temple of God with his engines of war. At the lulls in the battles, free from Simon above him, John the Antichrist and his Zealots, though exhausted, got drunk, and one time while drunk, they went in great numbers against Simon and his Idumeans in the upper city attacking and burning the city's grain provisions against many years of siege.

The reverse was done by Simon when John retreated. Simon attacked the city controlled by John, and he destroyed the rest of the city's grain supplies laid up against many years of siege. Those grain supplies were reserved for times of siege, but the result of the sieges on the dead in the religions were promised by God (*The Jewish War*, book 5, chapter 1, section 4, lines 24–25).

❧ 1 JOHN 2:12–19 ❧

Because your (the elects') sins are forgiven you and for His name's sake, I write to you. Your fathers were predestined to know Him since the foundation of the world. I write to you because God has called you elect to overcome Satan. You elect were known by the Father from the foundation of the world.

Be strong in the Word, which causes you to overcome Satan. Love not the things and people of the world or their extortionist religions. Should any love the world or the religions of the world, it is because they are of the world and marked with death.

Lust is not of God, but the Father uses that dead as lure to the lust of the world. The passing away of the latter days is of the old covenant world along with its lust, but whomever God causes to be a doer will abide with Him forever.

This is the last hour (seven years), and you have heard that the Antichrist (John of Gischala) is coming along with other Antichrists. The Jews marked with death were cut off from Jesus; their names are in the Book of the Dead (see Daniel 9:26).

❧ REVELATION 3:5 ❧

"He who came at the end wore white garments, and I did not blot his name from the Book of Life but I confessed his name before My Father and His angels."

⪼ 1 JOHN 2:19–20 CONTINUED ⪻

"The Jews marked with death fell to the promised curses of Deuteronomy 28:15–68 and have eternal damnation. You, the ecclesia praised by God, have an anointing from the Holy One. You, the praised by God, know all things."

⪼ 1 JOHN 2:21 ⪻

"The reason I, John, have not written you Jews praised by God is not because you elect do not know the truth but because you know the truth. The Antichrists do not believe Jesus is the Son of God because God has veiled them. God cannot be fooled even by bright atheists and the gods of the extortionist Christian religions in pursuit of their god Lucre. God imparts His love to those He praises. By His love, we live in forgiveness, peace, and love."

⪼ 1 JOHN 2:22–29 ⪻

"He who denies Jesus is the Messiah is an Antichrist who also denies the Father. Whoever denies the Son is without the Father, but he who acknowledges the Son is the elect of God. Let that concept abide in you. God promised the elect life eternal.

"I have written to you elect concerning the dead in the pursuit of Mammon and their god Gain who deceive you. The anointing you and Jesus received from God abides in you, and none need teach you because your anointing teaches you all things. When Jesus appears, we are confident and not ashamed before God at Jesus's coming on the clouds in wrath at the apocalypse. If you know Jesus is righteous, you know that God loves everyone who practices righteousness."

To see up close the religions of Judaism's version of the Antichrist John of Gischala, see *A History of the Jewish People* edited by H. H. Ben-Sasson, 283–303. John of Gischala the Antichrist is portrayed as a Jewish hero. He was among the demons brought into Jerusalem; the people marked with death suffered most terribly during those last four years of the days of vengeance of the apocalypse. *The Jewish War* is a preview of the works of the evil scoundrel the Antichrist John of Gischala; see the index, "John of Levi" and notes 1–27 of the book of the life of Josephus Flavius, 42–44, which portrays the evils of the priests and of John of Gischala.

ﻬ THESSALONIANS 2:1–12 ﻬ

"You elect, do not be deceived by any means, for in the day of vengeance, John of Gischala, the lawless one, annulled the temple priesthood and reviled the temple with murders, a variety of sexual immorality, sexual perversions, and deviancies.

"John of Gischala exalted himself above all. The Antichrist John sits desolating the temple of God in Jerusalem showing himself as God. Don't you Thessalonians remember that when I was with you, I told you these things? You know what is restraining Jesus.

"In due time, the Antichrist John of Gischala will be revealed in Roman chains with ninety-seven thousand others after Jerusalem's fall. The mystery of the lawless Jews is already at work. Only Jesus, who restrains, will do so until the Antichrist John of Gischala is put in chains along with Simon of Gioras of the Idumeans and taken to Rome for the celebration when the temple is destroyed."

John of Gischala was the work of Satan through Nero with all signs, lies, and wonders, with all unrighteous delusion among those marked with death. Because of their unbelief, God sent those marked with death to eternal condemnation.

John of Gischala arrived in Jerusalem from the city of Gischala circa October 67; he was the Antichrist with a capital *A*. All who do not believe in Jesus were then as today lowercase antichrists.

The evil John of Gischala used six thousand men, women, and children to cover his escape to Jerusalem from the Romans, and the Romans killed many of them and sold many into slavery.

John of Gischala had arrived circa October 67 in Jerusalem and very soon allied himself with the high priest Ananus, but John wanted to rule Jerusalem. He became by stealth a member of the high priest's inner circle. Ananus began an effort to control the criminals and the rebellious who were murdering the people of the city. When John of Gischala discovered that Ananus was bringing together a force that could control the growing number of criminals, the seditious, the Sicarii, and the Zealots, he composed a message to the Idumeans to save Jerusalem from the devious high priest of their god Caesar. (See *The Jewish War*, book 4, chapter 3, sections 6–8).

The temple priestly system was annulled by John; he appointed a local yokel, Phannias, as the high priest and other criminals to the priestly positions flaunting the holy temple services for fun. They dressed in priestly garb and playacted bowing to Phannias in the temple as their way of GGTBMF. The Idumeans came.

⪼ Deuteronomy 29:14–19 ⪻

"This covenant and this oath are not with you alone but with those standing here today before the Lord our God as well with those not here today. We dwelled in Egypt, and we came through many nations. You of Israel saw their abominations, their idols of wood and stone and silver and gold, and there may not be among you a man, woman, family, or tribe whose heart turns away today from the Lord our God to serve other men and gods of their nations. There may not be among you a root bearing bitterness or wormwood; however, that it does not happen when the dead fool hears the words of this curse that the dead fool blesses himself in his heart saying, 'I shall have peace though I follow the dictates of my own heart' (God's delusion), his free will, such a fool, as though a drunkard could be included with the sober."

The high priest refused the entry of the Idumeans into Jerusalem on a night of continuous rain and thunder. Later, the captain of the city guard ordered the guards to go home. At night, John the Antichrist, then the leader of the Zealots, sent a team that sawed the gates of the city and allowed the Idumeans entry into the city. Over the following few days, the Idumeans killed over twenty thousand.

⪼ *THE JEWISH WAR*, BOOK 4, CHAPTER 5, ⪻
⪼ SECTION 6, LINES 345–46 ⪻

When the Idumeans discovered that they had been lied to by John of Gischala and the Zealots, they repented having killed so many of Jerusalem and departed the city.

THE JEWISH WAR, BOOK 4, CHAPTER 9, SECTIONS 5-7

Simon of Gioras played a large part in the defeat of the retreating Twelfth Roman Legion; John of the Zealots was very fearful of Simon's brutal and murderous ways and of war.

THE JEWISH WAR, BOOK 4, CHAPTER 9, SECTION 8

John of Gischala brought on himself heap big trouble fearing Simon of Gioras. John of Gischala sent a troop to seize Simon's wife and her many servants hoping to intimidate Simon, but Simon was not a gutless sissy as was John. Simon came to Jerusalem and killed or cut off the hands of any caught outside the walls of Jerusalem. Simon was a mean puppy. He wanted those who kidnapped his wife, period.

THE JEWISH WAR, BOOK 4, CHAPTER 9, SECTION 10, LINES 556-58

John relented and set free Simon's wife and servants. Simon returned to the Idumean nation and drove all before him. He gathered a great army and led it to Jerusalem's walls and again killed all he found outside the city. Ananus saw Simon as a greater terror to the people than John of Gischala or the Romans.

THE JEWISH WAR, BOOK 4, CHAPTER 9, SECTION 10, LINES 559-63

The Galileans made John the most powerful leader. John permitted his criminals all things they desired and plundered the people. He searched the houses of the rich, murdered the men, and did all that was immoral and abusive to the women.

All the booty they had taken by death and blood was devoured in feminine debauchery until they were satiated. In their temple perversions, they adorned their hair, put on women's garments, makeup, creams, rouges, perfumes, and ointments to appear very attractive to men. They had paint under their eyes to imitate wanton women. They went about the city as from a brothel with their slutty ways with faces of women. Their effeminate gait attracted unsuspecting men, whom they slew with swords they had hidden and then robbed.

❧ *THE JEWISH WAR*, BOOK 4, CHAPTER 9, ❧ ❧ SECTION 10, LINES 564–65 ❧

Simon of Gioras waited outside Jerusalem for all who fled John of Gischala or who were fleeing to the Romans. They were caught and dragged to the city gates so all could see the ruthless ways they were being killed.

❧ *THE JEWISH WAR*, BOOK 4, CHAPTER 9, ❧ ❧ SECTION 11, LINES 570–71 ❧

John of Gischala and the Zealot multitude overran the city fleeing to John's temple fortress where he prepared the Zealots to fight the Idumeans.

❧ *THE JEWISH WAR*, BOOK 4, CHAPTER 9, ❧ ❧ SECTION 11, LINES 566–70 ❧

Simon of Gioras of the Idumeans attracted many from the Zealots of John of Gischala in an attempt to destroy John. Out of envy of John's power and cruelty, Simon killed many of John's Zealots. Simon fell into a relation with the Izates of the king of Adiabene at the palace called Grapte just outside Jerusalem. Simon drove out the Zealots from the palace and gained John's plunder.

❧ *THE JEWISH WAR*, BOOK 4, CHAPTER 9, ❧ ❧ SECTION 11, LINES 572–76 ❧

The high priest, fearful of the Zealots setting the city on fire, assembled and took counsel. God turned their opinions to the worst advice to get free of John of Gischala; the high priests agreed to the tyrant Simon of Gioras. They sent the high priest, Matthias, to Simon to help the city. Many

Zealots in Jerusalem joined with Simon of Gioras hoping he would preserve their houses and wealth. He in a lordly way granted them his protection to deliver the city from the Zealots. The people and leaders were joyful and acclaimed Simon their savior, but when he moved in his army of twenty thousand Idumeans, he declared his authority over the city simpletons.

The tyrant Simon quickly gained power in the upper city and sent his son Eleazar to the lower city to attack John, who was holed up in the desolate temple fortress between them. John was attacked by Simon from the upper city and Eleazar from the lower city. All had engines of war. The attacks from above and below slew many of the temple priests and the pilgrims going about their daily sacred temple services.

❧ DEUTERONOMY 28:53–59 ❧

From the day of vengeance, the dead ate the flesh of their sons and daughters; the Lord your God has given you while you are in desperate straits by your enemy thugs and drugs. The very refined among you were hostile to their brothers, wives, and children, and he did not share the flesh of his children; he ate being destitute by the siege and enemies.

The woman among you so delicate that the sole of her foot never touched ground will refuse to share with her husband her sons and daughters and the placenta, and of her child, she secretly eats. "If you do not carefully observe this law in this book of Deuteronomy 28:15–68, fear the Lord your God, because the Lord will bring upon you and your descendants extraordinarily great and prolonged plagues of the sword, calamities, and famine."

❧ DANIEL 12:5–7 ❧

Daniel asked the Lord Jesus, "How long before the time of the end?" Jesus told him a time, times, and half a time; God changed that to four years.

❧ REVELATION 17:6 ❧

John saw the woman Jerusalem drunk with the blood of the elect and the murder of Philip, Stephen, and John, martyrs of Jesus. When John saw Jerusalem, he was amazed and marveled greatly.

❧ DANIEL 12:12 ❧

Blessed are the elect who endure the 1,335 days that God changed to 1,515 days ending the old covenant age on 15 September AD 70.

❧ REVELATION 9:1–7 ❧

The fifth angel trumpeted, and John saw Jesus come from the third heaven with the key to the abyss. Jesus opened the abyss and put Satan over Gog and Magog. John of Gischala became the leader of the Zealots, criminals, the seditious, the rebellious, the Sicarii, and John's nemesis, the twenty thousand Idumeans of Simon of Gioras all gathered by God in Jerusalem as the promised demons of the curses of Deuteronomy 28:15–68 with smoke from a great fire.

Scorpions and locusts were not to kill the Jews marked 666 but to torment them for five months until August 2, 70. In these days of vengeance, men wanted to die, but death eluded them. The dead desired an earthy demise, but death avoided them. The locusts battled as on horses with crowns of gold and faces of the men in hell in the prison Jerusalem.

❧ REVELATION 9:8–11 ❧

With women's hair, teeth of lions, iron breastplates, and the sound of wings, the four Roman legions came to battle. Their tails were with the sting of a scorpion and the power to hurt men five months from Passover in April 70 until 2 August AD 70. In Jerusalem, their king was the angel; in Hebrew, Abaddon, or in Greek, Apollyon of the abyss, the bottomless pit of Jerusalem.

Revelation 9 speaks directly to the conditions and straits brought on those suffering the famine because of the destroyed grains supply with the promised famine (Deuteronomy 28:15–68).

❧ EXODUS 4:9 ❧

God said to Moses, "If Pharaoh and the priests do not believe after these two signs or ignore you, you, Moses, take the Nile River water and pour it on the dry land." When Moses did, the Nile became blood.

⊱ REVELATION 11:1–7 ⊰

The angel gave John a measuring rod saying, "Go measure the temple, altar, and those worshipping there. Leave out the temple court. It has been given to the Beast of Rome by Satan to hold the criminals, the seditious, the rebellious, the Zealots, the Sicarii, the Idumeans, and foreigners trapped in the prison of Jerusalem under the sword for forty-two months that God changed to four years. Elijah and Moses prophesied in sackcloth for 1,260 days that God changed to four years; Moses and Elijah were the two olive trees by the lampstands before God. If any wanted to harm them, they were killed by fire proceeding from their mouths. Moses and Elijah have the power to shut heaven that no rain falls in the days of their prophecy; they had the power over the Nile to turn it to blood and to strike the earth with plagues."

When they finished their testimony, Satan came from out of the abyss to make war against those marked with death.

⊱ REVELATION 15:2–3 ⊰

John saw as a sea of the third heaven as glass mingled with fire, and those having victory over the Beast, his images and over his mark and over the number of his name standing on the sea of glass with the harps of God. They haunted the earth for Jews marked with death with the song of Moses and the song of the Lamb, saying, "Great and marvelous is Your work, Lord God almighty! Just and true the King of the saints!"

⊱ *THE JEWISH WAR*, BOOK 4, CHAPTER 9, SECTION 12 ⊰

Simon of Gioras got possession of Jerusalem in the third year of the war circa April 69; John of Gischala and his Zealots were confined to the temple and prohibited from coming out of the temple having lost their power in the city. Simon and his party had plundered John, and the Zealots were in despair of their deliverance. Simon made an assault on the temple with the assistance of the people while others stood on the cloisters and the battlements defending themselves from any assault. A considerable number of Simon's party fell, and many were wounded because the Zealots threw their darts easily from a superior place and seldom failed to hit their enemies.

The pilgrims in their zeal came from the ends of the earth to offer the prescribed sacrifices in the temple, but many were killed or injured by darts, rocks, and javelins. The priests and pilgrims whether Jew, Greek, Gentile, or barbarian fell at their sacrifices sprinkling the altar with their own blood. The men immersed in their own blood mingled with the dead bodies of strangers, countrymen, the profane, and the priests. The dead carcasses lay in lakes of blood in the temple.

❧ *THE JEWISH WAR*, BOOK 5, CHAPTER 1, ❧
❧ SECTION 1, LINE 2 ❧

The seditious tyrants in Jerusalem were divided into three parts, and two fought against John from each place.

The Jewish War, book 5, chapter 1, section 3, lines 16–18 are incomplete, and the following summary is incomplete. It speaks of the Jews who came from everywhere for Passover; they were searched at the temple for weapons. Many were slaughtered by the Zealots in the temple for their valuables.

❧ REVELATION 18:7–10 ❧

In the way Jerusalem glorified herself and lived luxuriously, she received torment and sorrow saying, "I am a queen and not a widow and cannot sorrow." Her plagues came with death, mourning, and famine. The Lord God judged her and burned her. The kings of the earth who committed fornication living luxuriously with her wept and lamented her passing when they saw her smoke burning from a distance; they said, "Alas, alas, that great city Babylon, that mighty city!"

Inside Jerusalem was hell on earth prior to Passover, April 14, 70. Life in the city became most cruel since the rebel leaders burned each other's grain supplies; that brought on a great famine in the city even before Jerusalem was surrounded by the four Roman legions.

CHAPTER 16

Revelation 9:12–21 is a scary overview of Jerusalem. Its grain supplies had been burned by the warring factions causing the people trapped there to endure a great famine even prior to the arrival of the four Roman legions.

❧ REVELATION 13:2–3 ❧

The Roman Beast John saw was like a leopard with the feet of a bear and the mouth of a lion. Satan gave him his power, throne, and authority. Then John saw one of his heads, Nero, dead by suicide; the Beast of Rome was wounded by civil war for eighteen months until the rise late December AD 69 of Emperor Vespasian; the Beast of Rome lived.

❧ REVELATION 13:4–10 ❧

They who had not been written in the Book of Life from the foundation of the world worshipped Satan, who gave authority to the Beast of Rome and worshipped the Beast of Rome asking, "Who is like the Beast? Who is able to make war with him?"

❧ REVELATION 9:12–16 ❧

Two more woes followed that John heard. "Release the four angels," the four Roman legions bound at the Euphrates River. After Nero's suicide, the attack on Jerusalem was put off until Vespasian's rule. The Romans killed a third—532,795—of the Jews marked with death because of their unbelief who were trapped in Jerusalem. The vision John saw was an army of two hundred million horsemen.

✎ REVELATION 9:17–21 ✎

John saw the horses and the demons John of Gischala, Eleazar, and Simon of Gioras along with the Romans, who had breastplates of fiery red, hyacinth blue, and yellow, and the horses' heads were as lions' heads. The fire, smoke, and brimstone that spewed from their mouths killed a third—532,795—of the Jews. Their power was of serpents. The predestined elect were not killed by those plagues because God had gathered them in Pella. Jesus was a servant to all, not a religious despot whose ring is kissed.

The elect of God had no reason to repent; they did not murder or engage in sorcery, sexual immorality, or thievery as did those marked with 666 with death.

Revelation 9:11–21 began from Passover in 70 and speaks of the last five months of the days of vengeance of all trapped in Jerusalem. One can only imagine the visions John saw as the eschatological apocalypse in the vernacular from August 2, 70.

Revelation 9:1–11 was the time before the four Roman legions arrived at Jerusalem beginning the days of vengeance on October 2, 66.

✎ EZEKIEL 38:14–17 ✎

Ezekiel prophesied to Gog, "You came against Israel as a cloud. It will be in the latter days I will bring you against my land; then they will know Me when I am hallowed. Because of you, Gog, they will know."

✎ EZEKIEL 38:17 ✎

Thus says the Lord God, "Are you Gog and Magog of whom I have spoken in former days by My servants the prophets of Israel, who prophesied for years in those the Days of Hezekiah that I would bring you, Gog and Magog, against the Assyrian king Sennacherib?"

❧ Ezekiel 38:18–23 ❧

"When Gog comes against the land of Israel," says the Lord God, "My fury will show on My face. My jealousy and wrath in the day of the promised seven years, the seventy weeks (Daniel 24), the earthquake promised (in Revelation 6:12–17) of the great tribulation on the land will make all the fish, birds, beasts, and creepies on the land and all men tremble at My presence. Jerusalem's steep walls were thrown down to the ground. I will call the sword against Gog and the people of the holy mountain Jerusalem. At the mountain (Jerusalem), every man's sword will be against other men bringing judgment with pestilence, famine, and bloodshed that rain on him, the troops, and many peoples with Gog and Magog on the holy mountain; flooding rains of hailstones, fire, and brimstone will come from the Beast of Rome's war machines. I will magnify and sanctify Myself. I will be known by the elect of God, and the nations will know that I am the Lord God."

❧ Deuteronomy 28:15–22 ❧

Moses addressed Israel, "If you do not obey the Lord's Commandments, curses will come down on you. Cursed will be your food supply and your empty kneading bowl. Cursed will be your land, cattle, and flocks. Cursed will be your going and coming. The Lord curses you in all you do because of your wickedness for GGTBMF."

The Lord brought the plagues to consume those marked 666 and gave them sicknesses, fevers, and inflammations until they perished.

❧ Deuteronomy 28:45 ❧

These curses have pursued and overtaken and destroyed you because you did not obey the commands of the Lord your God at the foundation of the world when you GGTBMF.

❧ DEUTERONOMY 28:48 ☙

Having served your Roman god Caesar; the Lord has sent against you hunger, thirst, nakedness, and every need; He has this yoke of iron around your neck until you are destroyed on 2 August 70.

❧ *THE JEWISH WAR*, BOOK 5, CHAPTER 3, SECTION 1 ☙

The war of the seditious in Jerusalem was revived on Passover, April 70. The temple governor, Eleazar, and his party opened the gates of the inmost court of the temple to admit those who were the people desirous of worshipping God.

Josephus assured us of the death of 1,100,000 besides the 97,000 captive Jews and rebellious.

❧ *THE JEWISH WAR*, BOOK 5, CHAPTER 11, ☙ ❧ SECTION 1, LINES 446–451 ☙

The banks around Jerusalem were greatly advanced with such great distress on Titus's legions. He had sent mounted soldiers to ambush all who left the city to gather food in the valley. Though many were indeed fighting men, most were very poor. Having families in the city, they were deterred from deserting. They would need to pay a great bribe to escape the seditious guards of the city.

The severity of the famine made them bold to not fear death by Romans; when they left the city, they concealed their weapons to defend themselves for fear of being punished thinking it was too late to beg the Romans for mercy. When captured by the Romans, they were whipped with every torment and torture before dying; they were crucified before the walls of the city.

Titus greatly pitied them. Over five hundred a day were caught and crucified on crosses. The reason Titus did not forbid the cruelty was that he hoped the Jews in the city might yield out of fear to avoid the same cruel treatment. The soldiers, out of their hatred for the Jews, nailed all they caught day after day, crucifying them on crosses so much so that trees for crosses became scarce within a twelve-mile radius.

Manneus, son of Lazarus, came to Titus telling him of the number of those carried out through that one gate—no fewer than 115,880 bodies between April and late August 70. Another ran to Titus telling that six hundred thousand dead were thrown over the walls of the city. Another told Titus that because of the Romans, the bodies had been laid in heaps in very large houses.

❧ REVELATION 6:5–6 ❧

Jesus opened the third seal, and the third creature said, "Come and see." John wrote, "I heard him who sat a black horse with the scales of judgment saying, 'The results of judgment; a quart of wheat for a denarius and three quarts of barley a denarius; do not harm the oil and the wine.'"

❧ *THE JEWISH WAR*, BOOK 5, CHAPTER 13, SECTION 7 ❧

A *medimnus* of wheat was sold for a talent, and herbs and edibles could not be gathered because the whole city was surrounded by the Romans. Many driven by terrible distress searched the common sewers and sorted cattle dung for grain to eat; they could only endure in the pursuit of whatever food they could come by while the seditious, rebellious criminals did not repent but suffered the same distress blinded by their coming fate in the lake of fire.

❧ *THE JEWISH WAR*, BOOK 6, CHAPTER 8, SECTION 2 ❧

The Roman garrisons resisted killing the deserters. Though a great number of them were slain, still many more were deserting Jerusalem. All were received by the Romans because they grew tired of killing the deserters and hoped to get bribes by sparing them. They sold the rest of the people and their wives and children at a very low price to the point that there were not any more buyers. Titus proclaimed that no deserter come alone; he set free about forty thousand men with wives and uneaten children.

In *The Jewish War*, book 5, chapter 6, section 3, lines 269–74, Josephus spoke as to the application of the stones of one talent thrown through the air from the Roman war machines and the people shouting, "Here comes the son or the sun or the promised Son of God Jesus Christ coming on the clouds of wrath from the Roman catapults."

❧ REVELATION 16:20–21 ❧

Islands fled away, and mountains were not found. A hail of rocks came from heaven from the Roman war machines and killed the blasphemous who cried, "Here comes the son" because the white stones from the catapults were seen and its hail was exceedingly great. The Romans later painted the stones black so as to not be seen in flight.

❧ ISAIAH 24:17–22 ❧

Fear you of the land (the pit of Jerusalem) and the snares (the Romans) outside the pit (Jerusalem). He who feared the noise of the pit was caught outside the city in the snares of the killers (the Romans) waiting on the dead. The windows on high of the third heaven were open as the foundations of the land were being destroyed.

The land was violently shaken. It reeled to and fro like a drunken, tottering tower because of the inequities of the Jews; Jerusalem fell forever. The Lord punished the exalted high priests and the kings of the land. The dead were gathered as prisoners in the pit (Jerusalem), and after four years, most all were killed by the sword, Jesus.

❧ ISAIAH 65:12 ❧

"I, God, numbered you Jews marked 666 with death because when I called you, you did not answer. You tried to take the kingdom for yourselves. When I spoke, you did not hear in the latter days in fullness of the dispensation. When I called you, you did evil before My eyes doing things in which I, God, did not delight."

Great sinners in the world, please do not be upset if and when God grabs you and makes you a fool for Christ with the mind of Jesus; you will be doomed to life eternal in Jesus. You will simply be overcome with the mind of Jesus, and God will have your back.

In this new covenant age, the dead will not believe you; they will mock you just as they mocked and nailed Jesus to the tree daily GGTBMF. The good presidents of the United States are always crucified as was Jesus, but they are rewarded with life eternal in Jesus.

This background is essential to understand the concocted dilemmas created by the gods of the religions of men. Keep in mind that just as Satan was always doing God's work, the gods of the religions of men though dead are doing God's work in their carnal pursuit for tithes, the wages of the dead.

❧ ECCLESIASTES 9:3–6 ❧

The evil under the sun is truly in the hearts of the evil dead with madness in their hearts. The elect called by God become the living, and there is even hope for a living dog or a lion marked with death. The dead cannot know that at their earthy demise, their reward is eternal life in the lake of fire. The dead's love is hatred and envy often demonstrated by their whining and sniveling, which is the sign of a perishing, self-serving jackass nevermore to share in life eternal under the sun.

Jesus the Christ and Presidents Lincoln, Reagan, and Trump carried their God-given crosses without any sniveling or whining. David was of the seed of Jesus Christ, but keep in mind that David was forgiven by God even though David raped Bathsheba, got her pregnant, and conspired with Joab to get Uriah killed in battle. God forgave David for all that. Let someone ask, What former president could come close to the villainy of David?

Do not judge. Judging is GGTBMF—not cool. What do the paid professional liars see when they look into the looking glass? The dead do not have the slightest hint of their state of deadness. All are born dead in Adams's free will, but when God calls the fools to eternal life, they repent their lives of folly, stupidity, and death and become fools for Christ with the mind of Jesus doomed to life eternal.

The farmer Jesus constantly circled Jerusalem crying "Woe! Woe to the people of Jerusalem" until he was killed by a rock thrown by a Roman catapult in late July 70 (see *The Jewish War*, book 6, chapter 5, section 3, lines 300–4) spoken of by Josephus seven years later at the destruction of Jerusalem witnessed in the prophecy presented to Josephus during the thousand years.

In *The Jewish War*, book 5, chapter 1, sections 3–4, read how God works to cause the dead to perish horribly, the hideousness of the rebellious leaders on each other, and the murders of the people in the city and the temple. The Jews could not know that their delusions were the narrative of their religions of the dead by many Old Testament prophecies.

❧ REVELATION 17:16–18 ❧

The ten horns on the Beast of Rome hated the harlot (Jerusalem), made her naked and desolate, caused her to eat her flesh, and burned her with fire. God had put it into Gog and Magog, a.k.a. the heart of the Beast of Rome, to fulfill God's purpose of destroying the great city of Jerusalem that reigned over the kings of the earth.

The same knowledge is rife and common, but the ignorant who rant on in stupidity are denied it ever so gently. Most of my closest associates know that I am the dumbest duck in the pond but only because I am so annoying and boring. That is my cross to bear. I admit I am an annoying dumbass.

Those who joyfully carry their God-given crosses are images of Jesus doomed to life eternal. God certainly uses the most ignorant but brilliant dead who pass on useless blabber, and still no matter how brilliant the mind, if dead, they cannot know they are dead because of their God-given states of mind, spirit, heart, and soul.

In the latter days, God used false prophets, priests, high priests, and the elders of Judaism marked 666 with their God-given delusions because of their unbelief just as today God uses the men of religions and those marked with death in their fleshly pursuit of their precious tithes. The dead gods once sold indulgences to escape hell for murder. Those who are stuck with God can only love the Samaritan living in God's forgiveness, peace, and love. Neighbors trod on with love will return love. Your neighbor is never the problem, puppy. It is you, puppy, who are the problem. God has provided you a cross to bear and with it judgment to come.

⚞ REVELATION 14:1–5 ⚟

John looked and Jesus, the Lamb on Mount Zion, with the 144,000 having His Father's name written on their foreheads. "I heard a voice from heaven and loud thunder with harpists playing. They sang a new song before the throne, before the elders and living creatures, and no one could learn that song except the 144,000. These were not defiled with women but were without sin. They followed the Lamb. These elect were the firstfruits to God and the Lamb, and in their mouths was no deceit. Without fault, they were before God's throne."

⚞ REVELATION 14:6–7 ⚟

John saw an angel saying that the everlasting gospel was preached (August 63) to all who dwelled on the earth to every nation, tribe, tongue, and people saying loudly, "Fear God and give glory to God for the hour" of seven years that began the apocalypse (August 63), God's judgment to kill more than three million Jews marked with death.

⚞ REVELATION 14:8–13 ⚟

The angel cried, "Jerusalem has fallen because of her inequities." A third angel said, "Anyone who worships the Beast of Rome and its images has received the mark 666 on his forehead or on his hand. The Beast of Rome has also drunk of the wine of God's wrath poured out in full strength into the cup of His indignation."

The Beast of Rome was tormented with fire and brimstone by the angels in the presence of the coming of the Lamb in wrath. The smoke of their torment ascended forever and ever, and the dead had no rest day or night. God causes the elect to keep the Commandments of God with faith in Jesus.

John heard a voice from heaven saying, "Write: 'Blessed are all the dead in Jesus Christ.' The elect rest from their labors, and the works of Jesus in them follows."

❧ REVELATION 14:14–16 ❧

John saw Jesus wearing a gold crown and holding a sharp sickle. From the temple, an angel cried to Jesus, "Thrust in Your sickle and reap (from August 63) the harvest. The elect figs on earth are ripe." Jesus thrust in His sickle, and the elect of God were reaped having been sealed in August 63, which began the seven years to end the seventh day of creation.

❧ REVELATION 14:14–20 ❧

Then another angel came on a cloud with a sharp sickle and said to the angel with the power with the sharp sickle from August 63, "Thrust in your sickle, and gather the vine of the earth (Jews marked with death) as overripe grapes." The angel did so and threw the vine into the great winepress, the great tribulation the wrath of God.

The winepress was trampled outside Jerusalem by the four Roman legions with 160 war machines causing the blood to come from out of the winepress (Jerusalem) up to the horses' bridles for 1,600 furlongs, 215 miles, the distance between San Diego and Santa Barbara, California.

❧ DANIEL 12:9–10 ❧

The Messiah said, "Daniel, the words are sealed till August 63 to end the seventh day of creation and the end time, the last forty-five days of Daniel 12:11–13." The elect 144,000 were purified, made white, and refined, but the wicked marked with death continued to do wickedly. The wicked could not understand, but the elect made wise by God's calling understood.

❧ HEBREWS 12:5–11 ❧

You have forgotten the exhortation that speaks to you as to sons, "My son, do not despise the chastening of the Lord, nor be discouraged when you are rebuked by Him. For whom the Lord loves, He chastens and scourges every son whom He calls" (Proverbs 3:11).

When God chastises you, He deals with you as His sons; what kind of a father does not chastise his sons? You without chastening are illegitimate and not sons of God. We of God pay respect to our fathers, who corrected us on earth because our spirits and life are subject to the hand of our Father God. At the hand of God; our fathers for a time chastened us, and we profited with salvation being called to His holiness. Presently, without chastening seems a joy, but because it is painful, after God's chastening comes the reward, which yields peaceable fruit of righteousness to the elect trained by it.

With the destruction of the temple and Jerusalem began the temple powers passing to the elect. The temples of God, the holiest of all, the elect remnant 144,000 bride of Christ were gathered by God in the wilderness at Pella for marriage to the Lamb of God.

✣ REVELATION 11:11–13 ✣

After the three and a half days, which God changed to four years, passed after the destruction of Jerusalem and the desolate temple at the hand of God, the breath of life from God entered Moses and Elijah, who stood, and great fear fell on all those in Hades marked 666 with death who saw Moses and Elijah and heard the voice of God from heaven saying, "Come up here."

They ascended to heaven in a cloud at the redemption at the final judgment, and those marked with death in Hades were condemned to eternal damnation.

The great earthquake was the days of vengeance of four years with the destruction of heaven on earth. The temple in Jerusalem was destroyed, and seven thousand people were killed by the Roman soldiers, but the rest of the yet living dead marked 666 were afraid and gave glory to the God of heaven from August 2, 70; that began the end time of the last forty-five days of Daniel 12:11–13 and the marriage of the Lamb, the redemption and the final judgment to end the old covenant people and the age.

There was not just one false prophet in the time of Christ; there was a variety of false prophets from the high priests down to the local camel groomer. At various times, our folly or stupidity is about things we cannot begin to know. Rumor and delusion are the sources of all knowledge to the stupid, but forgive them because they today are Christ haters who continue to hang the Christ on a tree daily yet cannot know what they know and do.

Those who joyfully carry their God-given crosses are imitations of

Jesus Christ, the flesh-and-blood images of Jesus doomed to life eternal with Jesus. God certainly uses the most ignorant and the brilliant dead. Forgive them for they know not what they do.

ⵁ 1 CORINTHIANS 3:16–17 ⵂ

Don't you know that you elect are the flesh-and-blood temples of God and that the Holy Spirit of God dwells in you? If anyone defiles the temples of God, God destroys them. The temples, the flesh-and-blood images of Jesus Christ, were sanctified.

The Spirit of life is eternal because the essentials of all human life are the same Spirit; in a wry sense, they have the same spiritual DNA of God along with Satan at the lake of fire and all with him. The living elect are the same spiritual image of God. The elect of God are the flesh-and-blood images of Jesus, the Firstfruit, with eternal life. The elect loved by God are the Spirit of God, and Jesus is their spiritual image of their hearts, souls, spirits, and minds, as said, the spiritual DNA of God. Though the dead have the same spirit, the dead who rejected God at the foundation of the world were noted in the big Book of the Dead that fill the big barns of the world.

There has always been an earthly demise even though spoken of as death as the most popular way expressed in the Bibles of the old covenant age from the foundation of the world. They were also known as the eternal dead or the eternal living. At one's earthly demise in the old covenant age, one's body decayed, but the spirit awaited in Hades for the coming of the Messiah and those called by God to Jesus from out of Hades to end the old covenant age on September 15, 70.

From the foundation of the world, all humanity has had the Spirit of God, but those who rejected God at the foundation of the world were cursed as dead forever. Those loved by God were called to life eternal in Jesus in the latter day in the fullness of the dispensation, when God was calling the elect to life eternal in Jesus in this new covenant age forever.

The Spirit of life is eternal because the essentials of all human life are the same Spirit of God. The dead are as Satan, but the elect are living spiritual images of God, flesh-and-blood images of Jesus Christ at their anointing with the Holy Spirit as was Jesus, the Firstfruit with eternal life as at Jesus's anointing by God at His baptism by John. The elect loved by God are the Spirit of God, and Jesus is our spiritual image of the heart, soul, mind, and spirit of God. The dead who rejected God at the foundation of the world live by their natural spirits lusting just below their shiny belt buckles.

There has always been an earthly demise even though spoken of as death as the most popular way expressed in the Bibles of the old covenant age from the foundation of the world at God's rest. All were predestined as the eternal dead or the eternal living. At one's earthly demise before the new covenant age, one's body decayed, but the spirits waited in Hades for the coming of the Messiah, Jesus, to end the old covenant age on September 15, 70.

From the foundation of the world, all humanity shared the Spirit of God, but those who rejected God were cursed as dead forever. Those loved by God were called and indwelled with the Holy Spirit, who through the parable code provides the knowledge of God, which is eternal life.

❧ 2 PETER 1:20 ❧

God's Word is denied any who have a different interpretation of it. Thirty-five thousand religions can never be of God simply because every religion has a different seminary narrative interpretation that separates it from all competition—other religions, sects, and churches down the street that are all in the business of competing with the others for Mammon; the tithe was annulled with the death of Jesus on the cross (Hebrews 9:8).

❧ 1 PETER 3:18–19 ❧

Christ suffered once for the sins of the just who were once unjust. Now, the elect are called by God to be crucified as Jesus while in the flesh making the elect alive with God's calling. While in the ground for three days, Jesus preached to the elect spirits in Hades and the prisons and put Satan in the abyss for the thousand years.

One of the last acts of Jesus was to destroy the temple and all the temple services, tithes, ordinances, sacraments, traditions, man-made temples, and commandments of men found in brick-and-mortar churchy temples by His death on the cross, which made the tabernacle biblically defunct. Temples, churches, chapels, and sanctuaries were used to collect tithes, which once supported the Levitical priesthood. In this new covenant age, the temple of God is the elect flesh-and-blood images of Jesus in fellowship with the people of God blessed by God.

Following are the actors of the great tribulation of the days of vengeance of the promised apocalypse with the promised curses of Deuteronomy 28:15–68 with every hideous terror, calamity, famine, and cannibalism by those God gathered as evil demons by the Beast of Rome and the Antichrist, John of Gischala of the Zealots, Eleazar, and Simon, the son of Gioras who in their desire to rule Jerusalem destroyed Jerusalem's grain supplies that had been in reserve for many years in the event of a siege. The arrival of General Titus and the four legions began the last five months of the Roman siege and the destruction of Jerusalem and the desolate temple. The temple powers passed to the elect 144,000 gathered by God from 2 October AD 66 to Pella at the end time, the last forty-five days of Daniel 12:11–13 to end the old covenant age.

Jesus was the sign of the temple powers to passing the elect in Pella at the temple's destruction. God had gathered the elect remnant 144,000 bride of Christ to Pella in the wilderness for the marriage with the Lamb of God followed by the redemption and the final judgment to end the old covenant age on September 15, 70.

❦ DANIEL 12:11–13 ❦

On September 2, 66, Jesus, in the name of Eleazar, the temple governor, brought an end to daily temple sacrifices and offerings to the Roman god Caesar. Thirty days later, at the wall of Jerusalem stood the Roman battle flags with the images of the Roman god Caesar. The blessed were the elect. The 30 days plus 1,440 days plus 45 days (of Daniel 12:11–13) God changed to 1,515 days to end the old covenant age on 15 September 70.

❦ MATTHEW 24:34 ❦

"I, Jesus, tell you elect now that this old covenant generation will by no means pass away till all these things (parable code for temple buildings) are completely burned."

At the temple's destruction, the temple powers (Jesus Christ) passed to the flesh-and-blood images of Jesus Christ. The elect 144,000 remnant bride of Christ married the Lamb of God. The sheep were redeemed on the right from out of Hades to life eternal in Jesus. The final judgment of the goats on the left from out of Hades sent them to the lake of fire forever. The new covenant age began September 15, 70.

❧ Hebrews 9:8–11 ❧

The Holy Spirit made it very clear that the way behind the veil to the holy of holies was the flesh-and-blood images of Jesus Christ. In the kingdom of heaven were the elect 144,000 brides of Christ gathered by God in Pella in the wilderness for the marriage with the Lamb of God. The marriage could not be consummated by God while the first desolate temple in Jerusalem was still standing. It was destroyed by August 2, 70.

God alone had provided the delusional BS seminary narrative to dead men then of the religions of the dead by Rome and today to the popes, priests, and pastors in this new covenant age in brick-and-mortar temples for the usual WPF wages of the dead. They have never given any regard to the conscience found only in the elect, those indwelled with the Holy Spirit, the predestined elect called by God through the indwelling Holy Spirit to life eternal in Jesus.

The coming of the High Priest, Jesus Christ, was the promise of the good things to come with the greater and more perfect elect flesh-and-blood images of Jesus Christ, temples of God, the holiest of all. The kingdom of heaven on earth was not made with human hands but only by God's calling the elect from the foundation of the world. All spirits had the same spiritual DNA of God as determined by God, and those spirits who rejected God at the foundation of the world were from then doomed to the lake of fire, and those God loved were doomed to eternal life in Jesus.

❧ Revelation 20:11–15 ❧

John saw a great white throne and God, who sat with his face on the earth (the Jews marked 666 with death). Heaven (the completely burned desolate temple in Jerusalem and the temple priests) had died. "I saw the dead, small and great, standing before God, and the books were opened (see Matthew 25:31–46) and the other book, the Book of Life."

The dead at the final judgment were judged according to their works and by the things written in the Book of the Dead. At the final judgment, Death, Hades, and the sea delivered up the dead, who were judged by their works. Then Death and Hades were thrown into the lake of fire, which was the second demise, not death.

Death and Hades do not now exist. The predestined dead at their earthly demise in this new covenant age experience their second demise in the lake of fire forever. Satan was a spirit of God, but he lives forever in the lake of fire because his name was not found written in the Book of Life.

Life is eternal because the spirit of men have the spiritual DNA of God. In this new covenant age, at one's earthly demise, the body decays, but the Spirit of life is eternal and death does not exist for the human heart, soul, mind, and spirit being in a sense the spiritual DNA of God. At their earthly demise, the elect continue in that Spirit of God, which is eternal; those who had rejected God at the foundation of the world were thrown into the lake of fire, their second demise from out of Hades forever at the final judgment prior to September 15, 70.

There can be no death because the hearts, souls, minds, and spirits of believers and nonbelievers had the spiritual DNA of God from the foundation of the world. They are eternal as foreordained as was Paul to eternal life though he could not know he had the Spirit of life eternal until he was called by God while on the Damascus Road, an illumination tour whereby Paul was indwelled by the Holy Spirit of God.

Paul, once dead in Adam's free will, was a member of a religion and a murderer of the Messiah's followers, the Jesus freaks dubbed Christians. There was no way Paul could know he was dead due to his God-given delusions on the dead Jewish religions as was foreordained.

The Spirit of life is eternal because the essentials of all human life are the same Spirit of God. The elect live as the spiritual images of Jesus at God's calling as the flesh-and-blood firstfruits who have eternal life. The elect loved by God are the Spirit of God, and Jesus is the spiritual image of our hearts, souls, minds, and spirits of God. Though the dead have the same natural spirit, having rejected God at the foundation of the world, their rejection was noted in the Book of the Dead.

There has always been an earthly demise even though spoken of as death as the most popular way expressed in the Bible of the old covenant age from the foundation of the world, but there were and are the eternal dead and the eternal living. At their earthly demise before the new covenant age, their bodies decayed, but their spirits waited in Hades for the coming Messiah Jesus to end the old covenant age on September 15, 70. Out of Hades, the predestined elect were redeemed to life eternal in Jesus. At the final judgment, the predestined dead, who had rejected God from the foundation of the world, experienced their second demise in the lake of fire with Satan forever.

From the foundation of the world, all humanity has had the Spirit of God, but those who rejected God were cursed as dead forever. Those loved by God were called in the latter days to life eternal in Jesus when they were indwelled with the Holy Spirit with the mind of Jesus and doomed to life eternal in Jesus.

There can be no argument with those who have always used the word *death* to define one's earthly demise, but spiritual death has always been in the spiritual sense misunderstood and misused. At the final judgment, the word *death* applies to animal creatures but not to human beings, who are the Spirit of God. Humanity has possessed the spirit, heart, mind, and soul of God from the foundation of the world until the redemption of the elect to life eternal. But at the final judgment, those who had rejected God from the foundation of the world were predestined to their second demise from out of Hades into the lake of fire with Satan forever.

Those in the pursuit of tithe-based incomed were initially provided sustenance in the Levitical priestly system, but not now of God since Jesus's death on the cross. The religions slowly became corrupt, and the Levitical priests were often denied the tithes; they starved and had to go to work to earn a living because the temple high priests and their Roman god Caesar kept the tithes for themselves. The temple priestly system found the Roman god Caesar to be their guarantee of their WPF.

Through their temple sacrifices, they were always in the pursuit of power through deception and greed along with their priestly injustices. They relied on their protector, the Beast of Rome and god, Caesar. Religions are never the servants of men; they are tyrants who must be served and their ring finger kissed by the duped. They are always in pursuit of power through a tithe-based income from their congregations.

In this new covenant age, all are born dead in the bondage of Adam and remain dead until they acquire room temperature, which then confirms their eternal damnation. The sheep on the right are also born dead, but

God calls the predestined elect sheep to Jesus with eternal life. As said, all are born dead in Adam's free will, but at God's calling, the elect have no choice but to pursue God with all their heart, soul, spirit, and mind of Jesus and be doomed to eternal life in Jesus.

God's elect are indwelled with the Holy Spirit and love God with all their heart, soul, mind, and spirit; the elect have no choice in being called by God with the mind of Jesus. The living and the dead have no choice being foreordained and predestined from the foundation of the world before then at God's rest; all were predestined so to speak and etched in the stone of God.

❧ MATTHEW 24:29–30 ❧

After the destruction of the desolate temple and Jerusalem, the powers of the heavens (temple) were shaken. The sign of the Son of Man in heaven passed into the flesh-and-blood images of Jesus, and then, the living tribes of the earth (the Jews marked with death) mourned, and they in Hades saw the Son of Man coming on the clouds of heaven with power and great glory for the redemption and the final judgment as promised to end the old covenant people and the age on September 15, 70.

Jesus said that the complete destruction of the desolate temple was the sign of the temple powers, Jesus, passing into the elect flesh-and-blood images of Jesus Christ, the temples of God, the holiest of all.

God gathered the elect remnant 144,000 to be the bride of Christ in Pella to consummate the marriage with Christ, the Lamb of God. All Israel yet alive marked with death on earth mourned, and those in Hades, all the three million plus Jews marked with death, were killed in the last seven years by Jesus having come on the clouds of wrath. The Son of Man as promised came on the clouds of heaven with power and great glory for the redemption of the sheep on the right to life eternal in Him and the final judgment of the goats on the left to the lake of fire forever.

❧ MATTHEW 25:31–46 ❧

At the final judgment, the Son of Man came in glory and the holy angels sat on the throne of glory. The living from the nations and those in Hades were gathered before the Shepherd, Jesus, who separated the predestined elect sheep from the predestined goats. He set the sheep on His right and the goats on His left. Jesus said to the sheep on the right, "Come, you elect sheep blessed by My Father from the foundation of the world. You sheep inherited the kingdom of heaven that was prepared for you. When I was hungry, you sheep gave Me food. When I was thirsty, you sheep gave Me drink. When I was a stranger, you sheep took Me in. When I was naked, you sheep clothed Me. When I was sick, you sheep visited Me. When I was in prison, you sheep came to Me."

Then the righteous sheep asked, "Lord, when did we sheep see You hungry and feed and give to you drink? When did we sheep see You as a stranger and take You in or naked and clothed You? When did we sheep see You sick or in prison and we came to You?" Jesus answered, "What you sheep did to the least of My brethren, you did to Me. Depart from Me into the eternal lake of fire first prepared for Satan and his angels. When I was hungry and thirsty, you goats gave Me nothing to eat or drink. When I was a stranger, you goats did not take Me in, and when I was naked, you goats did not clothe Me. When I was sick and in prison, you goats did not visit Me."

The goats asked Jesus, "Lord, when did we goats see You hungry, thirsty, a stranger, naked, sick, or in prison and did not minister to You?" Jesus replied, "Such as you goats did not do for least of them, you goats did not do to Me."

The goats passed on to the lake of fire with Satan, but the elect sheep went to eternal life in Jesus.

❧ REVELATION 18:1–22 ❧

John saw the angel Michael and the name of Jesus coming down from the third heaven and having great authority, and the earth was illuminated with his glory. Jesus said loudly, "Babylon/Jerusalem has fallen on August 2, 70. It is a dwelling place of demons, a prison for every foul and unclean spirit and the feast for the carrion birds! The nations of Israel have drank the wine of God's wrath of the harlot Jerusalem's fornication with the kings and merchants of the earth having become rich through the abundance of the harlot's luxury. Come out of Jerusalem, my people, lest you elect in her abominations receive the harlot's plagues."

Jerusalem's inequities reached the third heaven. God remembered the harlot's injustices saying, "Render to the harlot Jerusalem just as she has rendered to you elect. God has repaid the harlot Jerusalem's deeds deserving God's wrath mixed double for the harlot. Her self-serving works in greed glorified only herself living in luxury. Due to her works, in the same measure, give the harlot (the Jews marked with death) torment and sorrow as she has said in her heart, 'I, the harlot queen Jerusalem, am no widow and see no sorrow.'"

Her plagues came in one day, the seven years of the apocalypse—death, mourning, and famine. She will be utterly burned with fire for the Lord God has judged her. The kings of the earth having committed fornication with her and having lived luxuriously will weep and lament the harlot when they see her smoke rising from the burning of the harlot Jerusalem from far away and cry, "Alas, that great city Babylon/Jerusalem, the mighty city. In one hour, the promised seven years to end the seventh day of creation of the old covenant people, your judgment, Jerusalem, has come."

The merchants of the earth wept for Jerusalem's destruction because no one bought Jerusalem's merchandise—gold, silver, pearls and precious stones, fine linens of purple, silk, scarlet, and objects of citron wood, objects of ivory and objects of most precious wood, bronze, iron, and marble, cinnamon and incense, fragrant oils, frankincense, spikenard, wine, oil, and fine wheat flour, cattle and sheep, horses and chariots, and the bodies and the souls of men.

"The fruit of your souls marked 666 with death in the religions of Judaism and all things rich and splendid have not been found in you, Jerusalem. The merchants of those things became rich and stood from a far in fear weeping and wailing as she burned crying, 'Alas, alas, the great city harlot was clothed in fine linen, purple and scarlet adorned with gold and precious stones and pearls, but in one hour of the promised seven years, her great riches came to nothing.'"

Every shipmaster and sailor who traded across the sea stood at a distance crying as she burned and asked, "Who is this great harlot Jerusalem?" They threw up dust to come down on their heads and wept, wailed, and cried, "Alas, alas, the great harlot that bought and bribed the merchants with their ships that became rich with her wealth! In one hour of seven years of hell on earth, Jerusalem was made desolate. Rejoice over the death of the harlot Jerusalem. God has avenged the apostles and prophets and the predestined elect on her!"

A mighty angel threw a great millstone into the sea saying, "Thus with violence the great city Babylon/Jerusalem was thrown down August 2, 70; once heaven on earth, it will never be so again. The sounds of harpists, musicians, flutists, and trumpeters are not heard in her anymore. No craftsman of any craft was found in her, and the sound of a millstone has not been heard anymore. Your lamp light that was you, Jerusalem, as the bride of Christ, has not been of you since you, Jerusalem, were deceived by your sorcery, the great merchants and great men of the nations of the earth. In the harlot Jerusalem was found the blood of the murdered prophets, the Messiah, and the flesh-and-blood images of Jesus, the elect of God, heaven on earth."

❧ GALATIANS 5:18–26 ❧

You elect are led by the Holy Spirit, not by the defunct Law of Moses (Hebrew 7:14–20). The works of their flesh are evident in the pursuit of the usual WPF, adultery, fornication, uncleanness, lewdness, extortion, idolatry, sorcery, worldliness, hatred, contentions, jealousies, wrath, self-serving, and disputations and are lost to heresy, envy, murder, drunkenness, and revelries. Paul told you that you were dead from the foundation of the world. Beforehand, you elect were called by God to live forever, but those who practice such evils things are dead and cannot inherit the kingdom of God.

❧ REVELATION 19:1–21 ❧

"After these things (parable code for the destruction of the temple), I heard a loud voice of a great multitude in the third heaven saying, 'Alleluia! Salvation, glory, honor, and power to the Lord our God! True and righteous are His judgments because He has judged the great harlot Jerusalem, who corrupted the earth (the Jews marked with death) with her fornications. God has avenged her on the Jews marked 666 with death—three million plus Jews—because of their unbelief and their tribulations on the blood of His servants.'"

The servants cried, "Alleluia! The smoke of Jerusalem's destruction rose!" The twenty-four elders and the four living creatures worshipped

God sitting the throne saying, "Amen! Alleluia!" A voice from the throne came: "Praise God you elect servants and those who fear Him both small and great!"

"I heard the sound of many waters and mighty thundering from a great multitude saying, 'Alleluia! The Lord God omnipotent reigns! Rejoice and be glad giving Him glory for He has gathered the elect 144,000, the bride of Christ at Pella for the marriage with the Lamb of God has come in this last forty-five days of Daniel 12:11–13.'"

The predestined elect of God in faith, the bride of Christ, were arrayed in fine white linen, the symbol of God's righteousness. He said, "Write: blessed (happy) are the elect 144,000 bride of Christ called to the marriage with the Lamb!" The angel said, "These are the true words of God."

John fell to worship the angel. The angel said, "Holy cow, John! What are you doing? I'm your brethren, your fellow servant with the testimony of Jesus. Worship God! The testimony of Jesus is the spirit of prophecy."

Heaven opened, and Jesus, faithful and true, sat on the white horse. Righteous Jesus judged using Satan over Gog and Magog, the Beast of Rome, for seven years to end the seventh day of creation on August 2, 70. Jesus's eyes were a flame of fire, and he had many crowns on His head. His name was written so that no one knew except Himself. He was clothed with a robe dripping blood. Jesus is the Word of God. Clothed in clean white linen on white horses were the heavenly armies that followed Jesus. A sharp sword out of Jesus's mouth struck the nations of Israel and killed over three million Jews because of their unbelief. He ruled with a rod of iron. Jesus trod the winepress (Jerusalem) with the fierceness of the wrath of the almighty God. On Jesus's robe was written King of Kings and Lord of Lords.

John saw an angel standing in the sun crying with a loud voice calling the carrion birds to fly to feast on the cadavers. The birds having been gathered for the supper of the great God ate the flesh of Gog and Magog—the kings and those trapped in the prison of Jerusalem, the captains and mighty men and their horses and all who rode them and the flesh of all free and slave, small and great.

John saw the Beast of Rome and the kings of the earth and their armies gathered to make war against Jesus, who sat on the white (pale) horse, and Death followed against God's great army. The Beast of Rome was captured and with him the false prophet who wore the signs 666, Nero, who deceived those dead receiving the mark 666 of Nero and those who worshipped Nero's image. Nero, Satan, and the false prophet were thrown into the lake of fire burning with brimstone. The rest of the dead marked 666 were killed with the sword proceeding from the mouth of Jesus, who sat on the white (pale) horse of death, and all the eagles and carrions birds were filled with their flesh.

≈ REVELATION 11:13–19 ≈

In the great earthquake in that last hour, Jerusalem fell, but the prophecy of Isaiah (6:13) promised a tenth (at Pella) would live as the stump, the elect of God of the prophecy Isaiah lived in the new covenant age from September 15, 70.

At Jerusalem's earthquake, seven thousand people were killed, and yet the living feared and gave glory to the God in heaven. The second woe had passed, and the third woe had come. The seventh angel trumpeted on August 2, 70; there were loud voices in heaven saying, "The flesh-and-blood images of Jesus Christ have become the image of our Lord Jesus Christ, who reigns forever!"

In the third heaven, the twenty-four elders sitting before God on the throne fell on their faces and worshipped God saying, "We thank you, O Lord God almighty. The Messiah who was crucified has come as promised on the clouds of wrath to take power and reign. The nations of Israel were angry with those who destroyed the land, and the wrath of God has come on those marked 666 with death; they were to be judged from out of Hades at the final judgment. You elect remnant 144,000 and the prophets who feared God's name, small and great, were redeemed at the redemption."

At the temple's destruction, the third heaven was opened and the ark of His covenant was seen in His (the flesh-and-blood images of Jesus Christ) temple with lightning, noises, thunder, and an earthquake and great hail.

There are no religions of God. Those loved by God from the foundation of the world are the foreordained, the predestined elect, the ecclesia, the assembly of God, not a brick-and-mortar churchy abomination. The elect retained the same spiritual DNA of God. The same flesh-and-blood images of Jesus Christ are the only people in Communion with Jesus Christ because of God's calling. The elect are helpless. When dead fools are called by God, they become fools for Christ; with the mind of Jesus, they are doomed to eternal life.

❧ REVELATION 20:9–10 ❧

In August 63, God put Satan over Gog and Magog, a.k.a. the Beast of Rome, and fire came down from God out of heaven and devoured over three million Jews marked 666 with death during the following seven years to end the seventh day of creation or the seventy weeks of Daniel 9:24. On October 2, 66, Satan was sent upon the breadth of the land surrounding the camp (Jerusalem) of the Jews marked 666 with death in the days of vengeance on the religions of Judaism because of their unbelief. Satan was God's work to deceive the Jews marked 666 with death in the religions of Judaism, but at the final judgment, Nero, the false prophets, and those marked with death were thrown into the lake of fire and brimstone to be tormented day and night forever.

❧ *THE JEWISH WAR,* BOOK 6, CHAPTER 5, SECTION 3 ❧

From the beginning of the Jewish War, the farmer Jesus every day uttered, "Woe, woe to Jerusalem!" He was beaten and whipped without whining or sniveling; he did not curse those who beat him every day, and he had no good words even for those who fed him. Jesus continued day and night with his woes and was loudest at the festivals for seven years and five months until August 62, late in the siege, he gave out his woes upon the wall shouting, "Woe, woe to Jerusalem the people and the holy house!" until a stone from a Roman war machine killed him; Jesus gave up the ghost.

❧ *THE JEWISH WAR,* BOOK 6, CHAPTER 5, SECTION 2 ❧

The Roman Fronto slew all the seditious and the criminals accused by others, but the tallest, and the ringleaders, and the most handsome dudes were sent in chains to Rome for the gala celebration and their death. Those over seventeen years of age were sent in chains in ships to the Egyptian mines as promised (see Deuteronomy 28:68). Titus sent a portion of the warriors to the provinces and death in the local games. There in Jerusalem, eleven thousand died of starvation and all the old, sick, and injured were killed.

Titus was sent by God to Jerusalem to kill all who GGTBMF who at their earthy demise would confirm their arrival in Hades for the coming the final judgment. But Titus got a soft heart and set free forty thousand mothers, fathers, and uneaten children. Josephus assured us that the number of those who perished during the whole siege of five months was eleven hundred thousand, the greater number of whom were indeed of the same nation of Israel and the citizens of Jerusalem but not only the citizens, for all had come to the Feast of Unleavened Bread from other lands at Passover in 70 and were trapped in the prison Jerusalem and suddenly shut up by the four Roman legions. They were subject to great pestilential destruction and the promised famine that destroyed them.

The high priests who slaughtered the animal sacrifices for Passover allowed not less than ten to every sacrifice and as many as twenty in a company. The number of sacrifices was the 2,700,000 deemed holy. Those not counted were those with leprosy, those with gonorrhea, women who were having their monthly menstrual courses, others who were polluted and considered not lawful partakers at the sacrifice, and any foreigners who came to worship.

✽ DANIEL 9:24 ✻

The seventy weeks of the apocalypse (Daniel 9:24) began in August 63; it was a time for the elect and Jerusalem to finish their transgression and make an end of sins, to make conciliation for iniquity, to bring in everlasting righteousness, to seal up vision and prophecy, and to anoint the most holy, the elect 144,000 gathered by God at Pella as the flesh-and-blood images of Jesus Christ.

The following verses tell you what God did to finish the inequities by the elect, the ecclesia, His chosen people, the flesh-and-blood images of Jesus Christ to end the old covenant people and age on August 2, 70.

1. God ended the inequities of the elect 144,000 of God.
2. God reconciled the elect 144,000 of God called from out of the Jews marked 666 with death in the religions of Judaism to life eternal in Jesus.

3. God brought to the elect 144,000 of God the gift of everlasting righteousness (1 Corinthians 13:10). When Jesus, who is perfect, came on the clouds of wrath, all that facilitated the preaching of the gospel around the world—tongues, miracles, and special knowledge—was done away with.

4. God sealed the visions, tongues, and foreign languages that were given to the disciples to facilitate the gospel being preached during the thousand years until the gospel was preached around the world. God told Paul in August 63 that the gospel had been preached around the world. The prophecies and the miracles of men that facilitated the preaching of the gospel around the world to every scattered Jew ended.

5. God anointed the holiest of all.

✄ HEBREWS 9:8 ✄

The Holy Spirit has made very clear the way into the flesh-and-blood images of Jesus Christ, the temples of God, the holiest of all, the kingdom of heaven on earth. He gathered the elect at Pella but could not be manifest while the first tabernacle in the desolate temple of Jerusalem was still standing.

✄ 1 CORINTHIANS 13:8–10 ✄

Love never fails, but when Jesus, who is perfect, the holiest of all, came on the clouds of wrath in August 63, the prophecies failed, and the knowledge of foreign languages and tongues that had once facilitated the preaching of the gospel around the world failed. The special knowledge of God that unified the elect from out of the nations of Israel vanished. We know only in part of what it prophesied. Jesus, who is perfect, came on the clouds of wrath on all those who were not perfect, the dead in the religions of Judaism who waited in Hades.

The seventy weeks prophecy in Daniel 9:24 was of Jesus the Messiah coming on the clouds of wrath to end the seventh day of creation on August 2, 70, determined by God to end the seven years of the sword to kill the dead Jews marked 666 with death and to destroy the desolate temple by August 2, 70, with the promised curses of Deuteronomy 28:15–28 completing the destruction of the desolate temple and Jerusalem for having GGTBMF. (See Daniel 9:26.)

When Jesus died on the cross, the tithe, temple/churchy services, priesthood, sacraments, Lent, ordinances, traditions, religions, fish on Friday, the Commandments, and the Law of Moses and the laws of men were made obsolete at the reformation at Jesus's death on the cross and were all annulled (see Hebrew 7:14–22). Jesus's death made the elect perfect with the coming of Jesus, who is perfect.

❧ HEBREWS 7:14–22 ❧

Our Lord arose from Judah, the tribes of which Moses spoke nothing of. It is not in the likeness of Melchizedek such as the priest Jesus to come in the fleshly commandments of the Law of Moses, but Jesus came only with the power of an eternal life. God testified, "You, Jesus, are a priest forever of Melchizedek" (Psalm 100:4).

But at Jesus's death on the cross, the Law of Moses was annulled because it was not able to save anyone. The Law of Moses made no one perfect, but Jesus's death brought salvation to the elect God had called to Jesus. Jesus was a Priest with an oath, but the Levitical priests were without an oath. Jesus was with an oath by God, who said, "You, Jesus, are a priest forever in the order of Melchizedek" (Psalm 110:4). Only Jesus's death on the cross made the elect sinless. Jesus was perfect; He was the guarantee of our eternal life in this new covenant age starting September 15, 70.

❧ REVELATION 4:6 ❧

Before the throne in the third heaven appeared on a sea of glass as crystal around the throne and the four living creatures full of eyes in front and in back.

The holiest of all of Revelation 21:1–5, the flesh-and-blood images of Jesus, are pictured in detail below as told by God with the help of Genesis 101. For those God loves and for your edification, after August 2, 70, there was no more sea above the second heaven. It was once the crystal floor of the third heaven, but not since the destruction of the desolate temple on

August 2, 70, in Jerusalem. The elect of God live with the Spirit of God in the flesh-and-blood images of Jesus eternally.

✝ GENESIS 1:6–10 ✝

Then God said, "Let there be a firmament (the cosmos seen in the night sky) dividing the waters." God made the firmament (the cosmos seen in the night sky) that separated the waters of the first heaven earth from the firmament (the cosmos seen in the night sky) and from the waters above the firmament of the third heaven, and it was so. God also called the firmament seen in the night sky as the second heaven. The evening and the morning were the second day.

✝ REVELATION 21:1 ✝

John saw the new heaven and earth coming down from the third heaven to the first heaven as the flesh-and-blood images of Jesus Christ at the complete destruction of the desolate temple in Jerusalem, which had been completely burned by August 2, 70. With the first earth, the old covenant Jews marked 666 with death, more than three million passed away, and there was no more sea or third heaven not seen above the cosmos in the night sky. The sea was the glass-like floor of the third heaven as described in the following in Genesis; it is no more.

✝ GENESIS 1:9 ✝

Then God said, "Let the waters under the firmament the first heaven (earth) be gathered together into one place of the dry land on earth appear," and it was so.

✝ REVELATION 21:2 ✝

John saw the New Jerusalem, the Holy City coming down from the third heaven from God prepared as the bride of Christ adorned for her husband, Jesus, the Lamb of God.

❧ GENESIS 1:10 ☙

God called the dry land earth and gathered the waters of the first heaven, earth. He called the waters seas, and God saw that it was good.

❧ REVELATION 21:3 ☙

John heard a loud voice from heaven saying, "The tabernacle of God, the predestined elect 144,000 called by God to Jesus in Pella, those indwelled with the Holy Spirit, the flesh-and-blood images of Jesus Christ, the temples of God, the holiest of all in the kingdom of God, the elect remnant 144,000, the bride of Jesus God had gathered in Pella for the marriage of the Lamb of God, are blessed with eternal life."

    Genesis 101: for those God loves and for their edification, there is no more sea, ergo, no more third heaven; since the end of the old covenant age, the only heaven is the flesh-and-blood images of Jesus Christ forever.

❧ REVELATION 21:4 ☙

In the last forty-five days of Daniel 12:11–13, God wiped away every tear from their eyes and there was no more death of the elect of God, or sorrow, or crying. There was no more pain, for the former things (priests of man-made temples of the religions who crucified their Rock and Savior Jesus) have passed away.

❧ REVELATION 21:5 ☙

God, who sat on the throne, said, "Behold, I make all things new." He said to John, "Write, for these words are true and faithful."

❧ REVELATION 21:6–10 ☙

Jesus said, "It is done! I am the Alpha and the Omega, the Beginning and the End. I give the fountain waters of the elect with life freely. God causes the elect to inherit all things, and I, Jesus, will be the God of my elect as sons. The cowardly, the unbelieving, the abominable, the murderers, the sexually immoral, the extortionists, the sorcerers, the idolaters, and the liars will go to lake of fire with fire and brimstone; the dead will have their second demise in the lake of fire forever."

One of the seven angels who had the seven bowls filled with the seven last plagues came saying, "Come, John, I will show you the bride of Christ, the predestined elect remnant 144,000." John wrote, "In the Spirit, the angel carried me to the great mountain Zion showing me the great Holy City (spiritual), the New Jerusalem" having come down from the third heaven from God.

☙ REVELATION 21:22–27 ❧

John saw no temple, for the Lord God almighty, the Lamb, and the elect of God alone are the temples of God. The sun and the moon were not needed; the living temples of God were lit by the glory of God and the Light of the Lamb. The saved predestined elect 144,000, the temples of God, the elect of Israel, walked in the Light of the Lamb, and the elect are the kings of the earth who bring God their glory and honor. Its gates shall not be shut by day, and there is no night.

The Light of Jesus alone praises the elect with glory and honor. No such thing that defiles or causes abominations or lies can be, only the elect written in the Lamb's Book of Life after the complete destruction of the desolate temple in Jerusalem on August 2, 70, brought forth the prophecy in Revelation 7:13–17.

☙ REVELATION 7:13–17 ❧

John was asked, "Where did those in white robes come from?" John replied, "Sir, you know." The angel replied, "These are the elect who came out of the great tribulation. Their robes were washed and made white in the blood of the Lamb. They are before the throne of God day and night in His temple. He who sits the throne dwells among the elders. Never hunger or thirst anymore; neither the sun nor the heat strikes them anymore. For the Lamb on the throne will guide them to the fountains of living waters where God wipes away every tear."

That's what God had promised to come at the end time; the last forty-five days of Daniel 12:11–13 had come.

We are to have fellowship only with our elect brethren; we are not to cherish a brother who GGTBMF. Still, we are to treat those who GGTBMF as the dead in the world but not with persecution. Yes, in the world, even elect of God may serve the dead in the world in many ways to earn an income, but we are not to seek fellowship with the dead of the world after working hours. In the world, God expects us to work in an atmosphere of the world and even to bake a cake for homosexuals to serve at their weddings. The Pharisees no doubt dubbed the followers of the Messiah Jesus as Christian Jesus freaks, but remember that Jesus's daily walk was always with the dead sinners.

The temple could not pass away by any means until these things (parable code for the temple buildings, heaven on earth, being completely destroyed along with the priestly system) took place on August 2, 70, when they were burned by the temple priests and Roman soldiers.

❧ THE JEWISH WAR, BOOK 6, CHAPTER 5, ❧ SECTION 1, LINES 274–80 ❧

The people above were beaten back, and the whole city joined in the outcry. Many were worn out by the famine, and when they saw the temple on fire, they broke out in groans and cries. Their echo from the mountains surrounding the city blended with all the noise because the misery was great upon the hill of the burning temple. The spilled blood was greater than the fire at the great number slain, but the soldiers tramped over heaps of the dead. The multitude of the robbers ran from the inner court of the temple into the outer court, and the people fled into the cloister of that outer court.

Some priests were above the holy house with the spikes to keep away the birds. From there, they threw spikes at the Romans as if they were darts. The temple fire engulfed them while some escaped retiring to the wall eight cubits wide. They waited while a few went over to the Romans and some dove into the temple fire.

The soldiers came upon the cloisters of the temple; six thousand men, women, and children fled. Caesar had determined nothing about these people and had not given his commanders any orders, but the soldiers remained in a rage and began the fires in the cloisters, and many threw themselves into the cloisters on fire. None escaped with his life. A false prophet was proclaimed in the city the very day that God commanded them to get on the temple and receive signs of their deliverance. There were many false prophets induced by many tyrants to wait for deliverance from God, but they were kept from deserting.

REVELATION 3:20–21

Jesus said, "I stand at the door and knock, and the elect heard My voice and opened the door to dine with Me." God, who called the elect, has also caused the elect of God to overcome. Jesus added, "And the elect sit with Me, as I also had overcome the cross to sit with My Father on His throne."

LUKE 17:20–21

The Pharisees asked Jesus when the kingdom of God would come, and Jesus replied that the kingdom of God did not come with observation, "For the kingdom of God are the elect of God."

September 15, 70, began the new covenant age in which all are born dead in Adam's free will. At the elects' calling, they live only in God's will in liberty.

Jesus was laid in a manger because there was no room in the inn. It was after the winter wheat harvest in late July or early August when the shepherds were watching over their flocks allowed into the fields by night to glean the winter wheat. The angels came to the shepherds saying, "The glory of the Lord." The light made them greatly afraid. The angels said, "Do not be afraid. I bring you good tidings and joy to all people. This day, the Christ/Messiah, your Savior, was born as the seed of David."

However, only a few of the many of all the congregations are called to Jesus by God, and remember that the elect have no choice but to live as doers of the Word. That work Jesus alone does through the elect of God found in the Gentile congregations of Protestants, Christians, Roman Catholics, Mormons, Jews, Orthodox, Muslims, Buddhists, and all others. God is not partial. There can be no religions of God.

There has never been a purgatory except as a man-made tradition to extort money from the congregation who pay the deceivers, the most holy Roman Catholic popes, who get dead family members out of Purgatory and into heaven for a price. These are God-given delusions in the form of four-Pinocchio seminary narratives sermonized by the usual false prophets of the religions of men. There was never a Purgatory; there was once a Hades, but it was no longer since the final judgment. Hades was thrown into the lake of fire along with Death since the final judgment, September 15, 70, along with all those who lived in lifestyles that GGTBMF are doomed to the lake of fire with Satan forever.

Those praised by God are the elect of God having been called from out of bondage to life eternal in Jesus. Sorry, puppy, salvation has marked the elect from the foundation of the world, when their spirits clung to God or rejected Him. That clinging or rejection was noted in the Book of Life. Now in this new covenant age, your salvation has long ago been determined. It was not your choice; the dead have been determined from the foundation of the world when God rested. All have been predestined. Sorry, puppy, but you salvation is not your choice.

❧ DEUTERONOMY 31:29–30 ❧

Moses said, "I know that after my death, you, Israel, will become corrupted and turn away from the way that I have commanded, and evil will befall you in the latter days doing evil and provoking the Lord to anger through the work of your hands." Moses before the congregation spoke the Song of Moses to heaven and earth: "O heavens. O earth."

❧ ISAIAH 1:1–3 ❧

The vision of Isaiah, the son of Amoz, which he saw concerning Judah and Jerusalem in the days of Uzziah, Jotham, Ahaz, and Hezekiah, kings of Judah: "Hear ("O heavens, the temple priest") and hear ("O earth, the people of Israel"), the Lord has spoken: 'I have nourished the children who rebelled against Me; The ox knows its owner's crib, but Israel does not know and does not perceive.'"

REVELATION 22:1–13

John saw the angel pointing to the river of the pure, crystal-clear water of life coming from the throne of God and the Lamb. The Tree of Life was on both sides of the river of the new covenant era from September 15, 70, where each tree every month bears the twelve fruits that heal the nations without the curses and the elect in Jesus as heaven on earth with the Lamb of God serves the Lord God. The elect have God's name on their foreheads. There is no night or the need for lamps or the sun for the Lord God causes the elect to reign in the light of God forever and ever. The angel declared, "Faithful and true are these words."

The Lord God's prophets sent His angel to show His elect servants all things that must shortly take place before September 15, 70. Jesus said, "I am coming quickly! Blessed (happy) are the elect who keep the Word of the prophecy and of this book of Revelation."

John saw and fell to worship at the feet of the angel showing John those things. The angel said, "Holy cow, John! Don't bow to me. I am your fellow servant, your brethren, as are the prophets who kept the Word of this book. Worship only God. Do not seal the words of this prophecy of this book of Revelation because the end, the seven years of the apocalypse to end the seventh day of creation (August 2, 70) has come. Left are the unjust, and the filthy remain unjust and filthy while the righteous elect indwelled by the Holy Spirit remain righteous." Jesus said, "See, I am coming in wrath quickly to judge all by their work. I am the Alpha and the Omega, the Beginning and End, the First and the Last."

The Book of Life expired in the time of the final judgment in the last time of forty-five days of Daniel 12:11–13 ending September 15, 70. However, the Tree of Life is the reward of the predestined elect called by God to Jesus in the new covenant age from September 15, 70.

❧ Revelation 22:14–17 ❧

Blessed are the elect who live by the Word. They are awarded the Tree of Life in this new covenant age who through the New Jerusalem have come down from the third heaven, which has passed now with no more sea above. The world is of sorcerers, the sexually immoral, the murderers, the idolaters, and the extortionists who love and practice lies. Jesus sent His angel to testify to you elect these things; Jesus is the root and offspring of David. Jesus is the Bright Morning Star." The Holy Spirit of the elect remnant 144,000 bride of Christ says, "Come! Let the elect who thirst and are called by God drink the water of life freely."

❧ Revelation 22:18 ❧

John declared to all to hear the words of the prophecy of his book, "If anyone adds (a brick-and-mortar tithe exchange, churchy incorporated business in the place of the elect flesh-and-blood images of Jesus Christ), they are extortionist fraudsters whom God has doomed to the plagues written in this book of Revelation."

❧ 2 Corinthians 2:15–17 ❧

We elect called by God are the fragrance of Christ being saved. We are called from out of the Jews marked with death who are perishing. The dead marked with death have the aroma of death, and the elect called by God have the aroma of life in Jesus, which is eternal. We disciples are not the haters of God, who as the dead in their pursuit of WPF are peddling, selling, and profiting by the Word and earning the wages of the dead. The elect called by God are indwelled by the Holy Spirit. They speak the Word in the sight of God in Jesus Christ.

Most all Bibles use the abomination words *church* or *churches* instead of the word used by Willian Tyndale—*congregation*—the flesh-and-blood images of Jesus Christ still translated as "ecclesia" in the Latin Vulgate Bible.

Keep nearby a copy of the *Tyndale English Language New Testament Bible* for correct usage of the word *congregation*, not *church*. Keep handy

Young's Literal Translation Bible, which uses many of the variations of the flesh-and-blood images of Jesus Christ, the ecclesia, the assembly of God, not an incorporated brick-and-mortar tithe exchange business.

A brick-and-mortar man-made temple or church is an incorporated business in the pursuit of precious profit Mammon and big sister Greed in lifestyles that GGTBMF. God causes His elect to gather in fellowship with other as flesh-and-blood images of Jesus Christ in fellowship even in man-made incorporated temples or churches when they may or may not know. God is patient and forgiving.

Over one hundred times, the word *earth* is used in the place of the word *land* or *Israel* to enhance the BS seminary narrative that Jesus is coming back again in your future so you must give more money to help get the gospel preached around the world again. That is a God-given delusion that marks those of deception with death of the so-called religions of men. There are no religions of God.

☙ REVELATION 22:19 ❧

If anyone takes away the word *land* or *Israel* and replaces that with the word *earth* of this book of this prophecy, God will take away his part to come in the Tree of Life written in this book.

☙ REVELATION 22:20–21 ❧

Jesus testified, "I am coming quickly." Come, Lord Jesus! The grace of our Lord Jesus Christ always is with you elect of God, amen.

A few or many of your congregation are called and indwelled by the Holy Spirit of God; they have no choice because as the elect, they become alive and live as doers of God's work with life eternal in Jesus even if found in Gentile congregations of any religion or culture all over the world.

President Trump, Hannity, Rush, and Brett Kavanaugh carry their very large God-assigned crosses without any sniveling or whining. Charles Krauthammer also carried an enormous God-given cross, but he did not whine or snivel away his life. Good men of God are always given huge crosses to bear along with constant criticism, persecution, and judgment by the brilliant dead. The flesh-and-blood images of Jesus Christ are not of the religions of men. The elect are called by God and indwelled by the Holy Spirit of life. Their persecutors are perishing, and at their earthly demise as promised, they will receive life eternal in the lake of fire.

Presidents who are adored and praised openly are never among the living. God assigns His children to carry big crosses just as Jesus did. Most often, those loved by the world are dead. The judges and critics who are most obvious and most public on this mortal orb are doomed to the lake of fire forever.

❧ PSALM 1:1–6 ☙

He is blessed who does not walk in the counsel of the ungodly, or stand with sinners, or sit with the scornful. The elect delights in the Law of the Lord and meditates on it day and night. He is as a cottonwood tree by the river that brings forth fruit in season, whose leaves do not wither; he prospers in all he does. Not so of the ungodly, who are the chaff that the wind blows away. The ungodly sinners were the goats on the left at the final judgment and are not in communion with the righteous. The Lord knows the way of the righteous, but the way of the ungodly is perishing.

All the well-known brilliant people who GGTBMF are dead, and those who give the big middle finger to the flesh-and-blood images of Jesus are also dead. Their earthly demise will simply confirm that their eternal damnation will be in the lake of fire. God has made it very clear—the dead can never know they are dead, and God provides the dead's delusion that denies them eternal life in Jesus.

We can certainly also blame the government, but it is the ignorance of the whole democracy that continues to elect those who are bought and paid to shape our laws for the pleasure of the donors, who are always in the active pursuit of the death of democracies. Do not be angry with the dead Democrats; they are doing what the dead do, but when the Republicans are made comfortable with the crumbs that fall from their dead Democrat masters' table, look out—those who luxuriate in such crumbs are themselves negligible and perishing crumbs.

Most of what we are most comfortable to know is mere rumor, and too often, the source is a God-given delusion, stupidity. The world is dead because the world provides the rumors to those who live by God's delusion and lies; they are the source of the world's judgment. The dead now living cannot know who or what causes them to know or to think they know and act and do.

Satan, also with eternal life, manages the lake of fire forever. From the hand of God comes the essential rewards for unbelief and stupidity that reigns and brings down nations except for the elect of God. Killed or not killed, dead or alive, they are assured eternal life in Jesus.

❧ MATTHEW 12:31–32 ❧

Jesus said, "Every sin and blasphemy will be forgiven men, but the blasphemy to the Holy Spirit will not be forgiven men." At the foundation of the world when God created His spiritual DNA in the world, most of the spirits rejected the Holy Spirit of God and were noted as predestined to eternal damnation and those God loved were written in the Book of Life. Those who spoke against the Son of Man are forgiven by him, but whoever spoke at the foundations of the world against the Holy Spirit were written in the Book of the Dead both in this old covenant age and in the new covenant age to come September 15, 70.

❧ HEBREWS 4:3–6 ❧

We elect believe and are promised God's rest. He said, "I swore in My wrath, 'They who rejected Me cannot enter My rest' (Psalm 94:11) although My works were finished from the foundation of the world."

God spoke of His seventh day when He rested from all His works (Genesis 2:2): "Again, in these, the latter days, they who rejected Me at the foundations of world cannot enter My rest (Psalm 95:11). And it remains that those with the same spiritual DNA of God who rejected Me. Now you elect know why you elect are the flesh-and-blood images of Jesus Christ, the temples of God, the holiest of all, the kingdom of heaven on earth."

By Jesus Christ's visions, truth, and dialogue, George had no other way but to present this, my word.

In the same way, Jesus, in the name of George Sloan through the fool's mind, spirit, soul, and heart is merely God's workmanship, God's chosen elect from the foundation of the world to walk, talk, and write this parable code that Jesus daily has done through this fool, George.

✢ EPHESIANS 2:10 ✣

We elect are God's workmanship created in Christ Jesus at the foundations of the world to do the good works God has prepared in the elect of God (George) to walk in the works of God that Jesus Christ does through us.

✢ GENESIS 2:1–7 ✣

The host of heavens and the earth finished on the seventh day; God rested from all His work of creation. Then God sanctified the created heavens and the earth in the day of the Lord before any plant of the field was in the earth and before any herb of the field had grown, for the Lord God had not caused it to rain on the earth and no man to till the ground.

The Lord God is stuck with you whether you are the elect to life eternal with Jesus or the elect with Satan in the lake of fire forever.

CPSIA information can be obtained
at www.ICGtesting.com
Printed in the USA
BVHW031047220819
556529BV00006B/96/P